UNDERSTANDING MARX

A Reconstruction and Critique

of *Capital*

* * *

Robert Paul Wolff

PRINCETON UNIVERSITY PRESS
PRINCETON, NEW JERSEY

Copyright © 1984 by Princeton University Press
Published by Princeton University Press,
41 William Street,
Princeton, New Jersey 08540
In the United Kingdom:
Princeton University Press, Guildford, Surrey

All Rights Reserved

Library of Congress Cataloging in Publication Data
will be found on the last printed page of this book

ISBN 0-691-07678-2
ISBN 0-691-02231-3 (pbk.)

This book has been composed in Linotron Palatino and Cartier

Clothbound editions of Princeton University Press books
are printed on acid-free paper, and binding materials
are chosen for strength and durability.
Paperbacks, although satisfactory for personal collections, are not
usually suitable for library rebinding

Printed in the United States of America by
Princeton University Press
Princeton, New Jersey

UNDERSTANDING MARX

*

STUDIES IN MORAL, POLITICAL,
AND LEGAL PHILOSOPHY
* * *
General Editor: Marshall Cohen

For Toby and Patrick
in the hope that their world
will be better than ours

*

CONTENTS

✳

✳ CONTENTS ✳

PREFACE

✳

This book is, in a manner of speaking, a return to the traditions of my youth. My grandfather, Barnet Wolff, was a leader of the Socialist Party in New York City at the turn of the century, and one of the seven socialists who were elected to the New York Board of Aldermen in 1917. I grew up thinking of myself as a socialist, and as an adult came to define myself as a radical, but it was not until six years ago that I began to study Karl Marx's political economy seriously. Rereading volume one of *Capital* forced me to revise my unreflective view of Marx as merely a philosopher of the human condition, and to construe him instead as a theoretical economist before all else.

Fortunately for me, at the moment when I undertook to rethink Marx's political economy, I found myself teaching at the University of Massachusetts at Amherst, which has the finest faculty of radical and Marxian economists in the United States. Indeed, the entire university is virtually unique in this country as a center of serious radical thought. Senior faculty, junior faculty, graduate students, and undergraduates all have contributed to my study of Marx. Most valuable has been the opportunity to talk with, and learn from, a number of members of the Economics Department, including Samuel Bowles, Robert Costrell, William Gibson, Herbert Gintis, Stephen Resnick, and Richard Wolff. My acknowledgments to them in the footnotes do not begin to record my debt to them.

At an early stage in my study of Marx, I had the good fortune to attend a graduate seminar on classical, Marxian, and neoclassical value theory taught by John Eatwell of Cambridge University. It was his lectures, more than anything else, that pulled the subject together for me and gave it a shape. I doubt that Eatwell would agree with what I have to say, but I hope nevertheless that he will accept my thanks. I have benefited too from personal conversations and written exchanges with John Roemer, as well as from the important published work that has flowed from his pen in the past several years.

A special word of thanks must be offered to the undergraduates and graduates in Philosophy 594c, who listened to much of this book as lectures and offered their criticisms and comments. There cannot be many universities in this country at which one can find a class of students with so strong a command of Marx's writings, so serious an interest in theoretical issues of political economy, and so patient a willingness to engage with a teacher groping his way toward an understanding of *Capital*.

At a late stage in the preparation of the manuscript, two distinguished scholars, Gerald Cohen and Edward Nell, read the entire work for Princeton University Press. Both readers made valuable comments and criticisms, and Nell was especially insightful and sensitive in grasping the essence of my theoretical story and helping me to hold fast to its inner unity. My gratitude as well goes to Elizabeth Gretz and several other Princeton University Press copyeditors, whose work has contributed greatly to the readability of the text.

Finally, I wish to acknowledge my debt to my wife, Cynthia Griffin Wolff, and my colleague and closest friend, Robert John Ackermann, each of whom read an earlier draft of the manuscript and gave the highest proof of love and friendship by telling me honestly that it was no good! Much of whatever is valuable in the present work owes its clarity and coherence to their willingness to tell me the painful truth.

Belmont, Massachusetts
May, 1984

UNDERSTANDING MARX

*

Nolite perturbare circulos meos.

Valerius Maximus (8.7.7)

INTRODUCTION

*

Marx was born in 1818, 166 years ago.[1] He died sixty-five years later in 1883, just over one century ago. During his lifetime, he and Engels wrote enough books, articles, drafts, notes, letters, and sketches to fill forty large volumes in the East German edition of their works, and—what with the additional materials since uncovered—a projected fifty volumes in the complete English edition now under way. The heart and soul of Marx's lifework was a massive critical analysis of the political economy of bourgeois capitalism. If we restrict ourselves to the three volumes of *Capital*, the three parts of *Theories of Surplus Value*, the *Grundrisse*, and the *Contribution to the Critique of Political Economy*, we have, at a conservative estimate, five thousand pages of theoretical material. There is not, in the whole history of Western thought, a similar body of writings by a single author—not the three *Critiques* of Kant, not the works of Hegel, not even the *Summa* of Thomas Aquinas. The simplest sort of common sense demands that we estimate Marx's place in the intellectual history of our civilization on the basis of this mass of economic theory.

But a funny thing happened on the way to immortality. Marx published the first volume of *Capital* in 1867, a decade before the direction, terms, and methodology of economic theory were transformed by the triple revolution of Jevons, Menger, and Walras. The classical debates, initiated by the physiocrats, carried forward by Smith, brought to their highest theoretical development by Ricardo, and then vulgarized by Bailey, J. S. Mill, and the other post-Ricardians, gave way to the marginalist debates of the post-Walrasians. The central issues

---

[1] Portions of this introduction originally appeared in Wolff (1983).

of the classical school—the distribution of the social surplus and the conditions and causes of economic growth—were replaced by the marginalist concern with the static, ideologically safe question of the efficient allocation of scarce resources with alternative uses. After a brief period during which Marx was taken seriously as an economist by the Austrians, the concepts, methods, and theoretical problems of *Capital* simply faded from view, save in the writings of the religious Marxists, for whom *Capital* took the place of holy scriptures. Eventually, it became possible for the shallow and vulgar technicians of the neoclassical synthesis to dismiss Marx entirely as an economist, trivializing him, in Paul Samuelson's famous jibe, as a "minor post-Ricardian" and an "autodidact."[2]

For three-quarters of the century between his death and the present day, Marx's economic theories played no role in the literature of the mainstream of modern economic theory. The major development after the introduction of marginalism, namely Keynesian macroeconomics, grafted a sophisticated technique for divining the shadows on the wall of the cave onto the elegant but irrelevant micro-foundations of the original marginalism. The result was the bastard fusion now regularly taught in colleges and universities as the science of economics. Meanwhile, Marx became a world-historical figure of heroic proportions, the demigod of the Eurasian landmass, the darling of the New Left, the Promethean prophet of self-actualization—and, so far as anyone was seriously prepared to maintain—still the same old minor post-Ricardian and autodidact.

In the past quarter century, however, Marx has been rescued from the waxworks of Victorian curiosities, and has emerged at last as one of the most original, powerful, and relevant economists since Adam Smith. It is now possible for the first time actually to justify Marx's stature as a thinker coequal with Darwin, Freud, and Einstein, and to say in quite concrete,

---

[2] Samuelson (1957), p. 911. For the history of the classical, Marxian, and marginalist theoretical developments, see Dobb (1973).

particular ways how we can learn from him about the world in which we live.

From a purely formal standpoint, the key to the rehabilitation of Marx is the development, by Wassily Leontief, John von Neumann, Piero Sraffa, and a host of lesser theorists, of linear reproduction models of a capitalist economy.[3] These models, which make central the notion of an economy as a cyclical process of reproduction with a surplus, displace the marginalist notion of an economy as a network of bilateral trades in which actors maximize subjective satisfaction subject to scarcity constraints. The marginalist conception places concepts of efficiency and mutual satisfaction at the center of its analysis, thereby representing a capitalist economy as a fundamentally harmonious equilibrium. The classical and Marxian linear reproduction conception makes class conflict over the distribution of the social surplus the central problem of static analysis, and the conditions of balanced growth the central problem of dynamic analysis. This approach is thus better suited to understanding both advanced capitalist economies and the phenomena of growth and development in the Third World.

The classical economists and Marx had expressed their theories either in discursive form or else in quite elementary semiformal models. For a variety of reasons, Marx in particular failed to carry through the theoretical implications of his analytical premises, with the result that he arrived at incorrect or confused conclusions. Nevertheless, his formal intuitions were for the most part brilliant, and modern theorists have had relatively little difficulty recasting his arguments in acceptably rigorous forms. Indeed, Michio Morishima, one of the most important mathematical reinterpreters of Marx, offers the startling judgment that Marx "should in my opinion be ranked as high as Walras in the history of mathematical economics."[4]

---

[3] See Leontief (1941), (1951), Sraffa (1960), and von Neumann (1945).
[4] Morishima (1963), p. 1.

The mathematics is not difficult by the standards of the scientific and mathematical world. The principal tool is linear algebra, with the theory of partial differential equations playing a subordinate role. Nevertheless, the modern mathematical literature on Marx's economic theories is sufficiently forbidding and specialized in nature to put off many of the noneconomists who take a serious scholarly interest in Marx's critique of capitalism.

The principal aim of this book is to present an interpretation of the development of classical and Marxian political economy in a form that is accessible to readers unfamiliar with linear algebra. My goal is to articulate the central insights of the modern reinterpretation so that their philosophical and theoretical implications are clear, while keeping out of the body of the text all but the most elementary formal machinery. The device I have chosen is a series of little models of capitalist economies, in which two or three kinds of commodities are produced under capitalistic conditions of private ownership of the means of production, wage labor, and a free and competitive market. The fundamental ideas of Adam Smith, David Ricardo, and Karl Marx can be explicated, analyzed, and subjected to critique, I am convinced, without the more elaborate machinery that makes the modern economic literature on this subject so off-putting.

All that readers will be expected to know is the familiar technique for solving systems of two or three simultaneous equations—what is today taught as high school algebra. No calculus or linear algebra is used in the text. For readers who wish to pursue more formally the various statements made in the course of the exposition, rigorous proofs are provided in Appendix A. I have tried, without overburdening the text or notes, to indicate where in the literature one can find the first, or at least early, proofs of the formal propositions developed below.

Needless to say, my narration of the theoretical story of classical and Marxian political economy is what the French call "guilty." I have a particular view of what Marx was doing and to what extent he succeeded, and that view is inevitably controversial. Nevertheless, I hope that readers of many ideological persuasions will find their understanding of Marx deepened and made more precise, whether or not they end by agreeing with my interpretation.

THE CONCEPT

OF REPRODUCTION

1. The Concept of Reproduction in General

Human beings live by transforming nature to satisfy their needs. This act of transformation, or production, is repeated periodically in such a manner that the products or output of one period of production become the materials or input for the next period of production. In short, human beings live by a process of *reproduction*. There are three moments, or modes, of reproduction.

Material reproduction is the cyclical reproduction of the food, clothing, shelter, tools—and also the technical knowledge and craft skill—required for human life and for the continuation of the process of production. Classical political economy, arising as it did in the nations of Western Europe during a time when agricultural production predominated, organized its analysis of material reproduction around the annual cycle of Northern Hemisphere agriculture. For reasons of convenience, convention, and tradition, we shall follow that practice in this discussion. In the annual cycle of material reproduction, one year's output of grain, tools, raw materials, and so forth becomes the input into next year's production. The grain becomes seed as well as food. The wood becomes tools as well as chairs and tables.

Human reproduction is the day-by-day reconstitution of human powers and capacities by means of food, sleep, shelter, medical care, and so forth, and also the generational reproduction of the species through conception, birth, and child rearing. Here, as in all reproduction, the output of one cycle (the children) becomes the input of the next cycle (the parents).

Social or historical reproduction is the daily re-creation of society itself as a largely unintended collective human product. It is also the historical transmission and transformation of culture. This social reproduction is carried out in and through language, kinship and child-rearing practices, patterns and rituals of interpersonal interactions, religion, laws—and also, of course, through the reproduction of the social relationships of material production.

Material, human, and social reproduction constitute a single whole—they are three aspects of the same process. Nevertheless, they can be distinguished for purposes of analysis. Our primary focus throughout most of this book will be on the analysis of *material* reproduction, and on *human* reproduction insofar as it is construed as a sort of material reproduction. Classical political economy has a good deal to say about the relationship of human to material reproduction, as does Marx, and we shall have to explore that relationship at length.

2. A Preliminary Analysis of Material Reproduction

Consider an extremely simple, primarily agricultural economy in which there is only one kind or quality of labor and in which arable land is freely available. Assume that there are only two goods produced in this economy, namely corn and iron. Let the productive activities of the society be so differentiated that we can distinguish two sectors, in each of which only one good is produced. We shall call these the corn sector and the iron sector.[1]

---

[1] Or, for some shred of realism, the agricultural sector and the industrial sector. "Corn" is simply the generic term for the dominant grain grown in an area. No effort has been made at realism in the construction of this and other models. Corn and iron are treated as inputs into each other's production simply in order to illustrate the general idea that commodities serve as inputs into the production of other commodities.

Let us assume that at any moment in time, a single technique of production predominates in each sector. Abstracting from the actual technical processes of production and from the cultural, historical, social, religious, legal, and political context within which material production takes place, we may suppose that the two predominant processes of production can be analytically represented merely by the proportions in which the various inputs are combined to produce the several outputs. Assume, in fact, that the following proportionate relationships obtain.

Corn Sector: 100 units of labor, 2 units of corn, and 16 units of iron (in the form of tools used up, perhaps) combine to produce 49 units of corn.

Iron Sector: 90 units of labor, 9 units of corn, and 12 units of iron combine to produce 47 units of iron.

Labor, corn, and iron are measured in physical units—hours or weeks or years of labor, bushels or tons of corn, and pounds or tons of iron.[2]

Workers can labor only as long as they replenish their strength by eating and sleeping. Let us suppose that all workers have the same needs, and that under present conditions, each worker must consume two-tenths of a unit of corn and one-tenth of a unit of iron in order to be able to labor for one unit of time. Since a total of 190 units of labor is required in the corn and iron sectors, $(190 \times .2) = 38$ units of corn and $(190 \times .1) = 19$ units of iron are needed to reproduce the labor inputs. If we conceive of this economy as one in which, at the beginning of each annual cycle, the inputs for the entire year are laid out or distributed, then we can summarize the inputs

[2] The literature on the mathematical treatment of classical and Marxian political economy is, by and large, rather casual and unsystematic about the matter of units and dimensionality. A welcome exception is András Bródy, whose extended discussion of the subject is extremely illuminating. See Bródy (1970), pp. 95–100.

TABLE 1. System A

	Labor Input	Corn Input	Iron Input	Output
Labor		38	19	190
Corn Sector	100	2	16	49
Iron Sector	90	9	12	47
Total Input	190	49	47	

required by and the outputs obtained from our system by means of Table 1.

Inspection reveals that System A is just barely able to reproduce itself from year to year. A total of 190 units of labor, 49 units of corn, and 47 units of iron is required throughout the system, and exactly that much of each factor of production is produced. Since we have abstracted entirely, at this point, from any consideration of the institutional relationships in and through which production is carried on, we can, for analytical convenience, imagine that at the end of each year, the entire physical output—49 units of corn and 47 units of iron—is gathered together into one place and distributed all at once for the next cycle of production.

We are assuming that at any given time there is only one technique of production operative in the economy for each good produced. Consequently, if fewer than 49 units of corn or 47 units of iron are produced in a cycle, it is not open to the society to shift to a different technique of production, as represented by a different proportionate combination of inputs, in an effort to compensate for the shortfall. If there were a bumper crop of corn but a shortage of iron, for example, the society could not adopt a more corn-intensive technique of production (more seed, fewer tools) in order to get through the next cycle with fewer than 47 units of iron input.

Anything less than 190 units of labor, 49 units of corn, and 47 units of iron will result in a diminished scale of production. If the available techniques are permanently—not simply as a consequence of one bad harvest—incapable of reproducing themselves then the economy will contract progressively until it ceases to exist altogether.[3]

[3] It may not be immediately apparent that a permanent shortfall in the output of one of the sectors will result in the complete destruction of the economy, rather than in its contraction to a lower, but stable, level of activity. The following exercise will illustrate the underlying reasons for this fact. Suppose that the society is forced to mine a less rich lode of iron ore, with the consequence that 90 units of labor, 9 units of corn, and 12 units of iron can produce, in one year, only 36 units of iron. If we divide each set of figures through by the amount of the total output in that industry to obtain the quantities of inputs required *per unit output*, we find:

Corn Sector: 2.041 labor, .0408 corn, and .3265 iron yield 1 unit of corn.

Iron Sector: 2.5 labor, .25 corn, and .333 iron yield 1 unit of iron.

Labor: .2 corn and .1 iron yield 1 unit of labor.

Let us now, by construction, calculate *how much iron is required to produce one unit of iron.*

Step 1: 2.5 labor, .25 corn, and .333 iron yield 1 unit of iron.

Step 2: In order to produce 1 unit of iron, we must thus already have on hand 2.5 units of labor and .25 units of corn, in addition to the .333 units of iron. But this will have required, for its production, .51 labor, .0102 corn, and .0816 iron for the .25 corn, and .5 corn and .25 iron for the 2.5 labor. Thus, we will need (.333 + .0816 + .25) iron, which equals .665 iron.

Step 3: But we must also have on hand .51 more labor and (.0102 + .5) = .5102 more corn in order to produce the original .25 corn and 2.5 labor. This in turn requires 1.04 labor, .0208 corn, and 1.666 iron for the .5102 corn, and .102 corn and .051 iron for the .51 labor. So we need (.665 + .1666 + .051) = .8826 units of iron to produce one unit of iron.

Step 4: But we must also produce 1.04 units of labor and (.0208 + .102) = .1228 units of corn in order to produce the corn and labor needed to produce the corn and labor needed to produce the original unit of iron. And this in turn requires .2506 labor, .005 corn, and .0401 iron for the .1228 corn, and .208 corn and .104 iron for the 1.04 labor. So we need (.8826 + .0401 + .104) = 1.0267 units of iron to produce 1 unit of iron!

And now it is clear that we can never reproduce so much as a single unit of iron, because each unit of iron produced, under the conditions of production specified, consumes more than itself in the process of production. In the short run, we can of course operate the economy at a reduced level of activity while we run down our stocks of iron, but we must eventually reduce the level of activity again, and yet again, until in the end, the economy will run out of iron and be forced to shut down entirely. For a formal analysis of the necessary and sufficient conditions for an economy to be self-reproducing, see Appendix A, Section IV.

The economy we have just examined is an instance of a very simple class of economies which Marx calls simple reproduction without a surplus. As the name suggests, in such an economy enough, but only enough, of each output is produced to make possible a new cycle of production at the same level of activity. Several points need to be made about models of this sort, both those without a surplus and those which we shall be examining presently, in which a surplus is produced.

All models of this sort are what have been called *physical quantities* models. They are stated in terms of the physical quantities of inputs and outputs in each sector of the economy: hours of labor, tons of iron, bushels of corns, dozens of pairs of shoes, and so forth. As yet, we have introduced no method of valuing or pricing these inputs and outputs. Hence, we cannot yet speak of prices, of a money wage, or of a rate of profit. A great deal of theory is covertly contained in the decision to begin with the analysis of physical quantities, and although I shall try as we proceed to make the theoretical justification for this decision explicit, the reader is warned that the analytical framework articulated here is hardly innocent.

It should perhaps be observed that our model of simple reproduction without a surplus is *not* intended to correspond to any actual society or stage in history. Recent anthropological investigations have shown quite convincingly that so-called primitive societies are anything but bare subsistence economies in which the output of each cycle of production just covers the requirements for the next cycle with nothing left over. The model serves a purely analytical purpose.

Let us now suppose that improvements in the techniques of corn and iron production allow larger outputs to be achieved with the same inputs. (This is not the only form that technical innovation can take, of course, but it will serve for our purposes here.) Specifically, assume that the input-output relations of the dominant technique take the form of System B, shown in Table 2.

There now arises, at the end of each cycle of production, a physical surplus consisting of 251 units of corn and 43 units of iron. In order to complete our model in such a way as to allow

TABLE 2. System B

	Labor Input	Corn Input	Iron Input	Output
Labor		38	19	190
Corn Sector	100	2	16	300
Iron Sector	90	9	12	90
Total Input	190	49	47	

a contrast between "luxury" goods and goods required for reproduction, let us suppose that those persons (whoever they may be) who control the disposition of the surplus decide to use some portion of it to initiate the annual production of a luxury good, importing more workers for the purpose. In keeping with the mores and traditions of northern English Protestant capitalism, we shall imagine that the luxury good is of an edifying rather than of a sensual nature, suitable to the strong religious bent of a Manchester businessman— namely, theology books. Assuming that 20 units of labor, when combined with 1 unit of corn, 2 units of iron, and 2 theology books already in existence, suffice to produce 40 new works of theology (passing over in silence the subtle and philosophically profound distinction between composing new theology and reprinting old!), we are now ready to set out the input-output relations of the economic system whose characteristics shall occupy us throughout the first part of this book. The system, with a surplus in this case of 246 units of corn, 39 units of iron, and 38 theology books, is shown in Table 3.

Immediately, three questions are thrust upon us by the emergence of a physical surplus, and all of classical political economy can be looked upon as an attempt to provide theoretically sound answers to them. The questions are:

Who Gets the Surplus?

In System C, 246 units of corn, 39 units of iron, and 38 theology books are produced each year over and above what is

TABLE 3. System C

	Labor Input	Corn Input	Iron Input	Books Input	Output
Labor		42	21	0	210
Corn Sector	100	2	16	0	300
Iron Sector	90	9	12	0	90
Books Sector	20	1	2	2	40
Total Input	210	54	51	2	

required to *reproduce* the material inputs of the economy for another cycle. To whom does this physical surplus go? Who owns it, assuming that the society has instituted a system of property rights? Or, more generally, who *appropriates* the surplus?

How Do the Surplus-Getters Get the Surplus?

What institutional arrangements, what planned or unplanned interactions, what system, if any, brings it about that the physical surplus gets distributed as it does among the several segments or classes of society? It is to answer these questions that Smith introduces, and Ricardo develops, the concept of the competitive market, with the associated theories of prices, wages, rents, and profits.

What Do the Surplus-Getters Do with the Surplus Once They Get It?

Once the physical surplus has been distributed and appropriated, what is done with it? Do those who appropriate some portion of the surplus simply waste it, allowing it to rot or rust? Do they consume it for their personal enjoyment, or perhaps use it to support servants who wait upon them? Or do they use it to *expand* the scale of production, so that gross output increases in the next cycle of production? Here we find the classical theories of growth and stagnation and the Marxian theory of economic crises.

Let us now examine the classical economists' answers to these three fundamental questions, beginning with Adam Smith's introduction of the central analytical concept of *natural price*.

T W O
* * *

ADAM SMITH AND THE CONCEPT
OF NATURAL PRICE

In *An Inquiry into the Nature and Causes of the Wealth of Nations,*
Adam Smith poses three questions, the answers to which serve
to constitute or found the discipline of political economy.
What, he asks, is the real nature of economic wealth—of the
wealth of nations? In what way, and by what institutional
processes, is wealth distributed among the several classes of
society? And what are the causes of an increase in national
wealth, which is to say, of economic growth? His first answer,
in effect, establishes the physical quantities approach as fundamental. His second answer specifies both *who* gets the physical surplus and *how* they get it. And his third answer tells us
what is done with the surplus.

To the first question Smith replies, in contradistinction to
the mercantilists, that the real wealth of a nation consists in
the "necessaries and conveniencies of life which it annually
consumes," not in the gold and silver hoarded within its
boundaries.[1]

His answer to the third question, in brief, is that the progressive division of labor and the reinvestment of the annual
surplus in an expansion of the scale of production will, together, bring about an increase in real, as opposed to merely
nominal or monetary, wealth.

[1] Smith (1937), opening sentence of Introduction.

17

It is in his attempt to answer the second question that Smith makes his boldest and most important theoretical advance. The institutional arrangement through which the wealth of a nation is distributed to its several classes is the *market*, according to Smith, and with his introduction of the concept of *natural price* he lays the theoretical foundation for all of the political economy and economic theory that has followed.

Smith takes up and adapts to his purpose the ancient and very powerful thesis of the rationality of being—an idea which had for two millennia served as the basis for philosophical and theological accounts of the ontological structure of nature and of the relationship of human beings to God and to being in general.

The central idea is familiar enough and by Smith's day had become a commonplace. The universe has been created or organized by a divine being according to a rational plan, which is embodied in nature in the form of certain universal laws or structures. The human mind has been created by this same divine artificer, and has had implanted within it a spark of the divine reason. To know being is to grasp the rational structure that the creator has imposed upon it. Our minds are adequate to the task of apprehending the objective rational order of being precisely because our reason is an imitation of the creative reason which has constituted the objective order. So nature is rational and the mind's power of reason is adequate to the task of apprehending nature's rational structure, its laws.[2]

Smith now advances a powerful thesis, extending this traditional concept of nature. Society, Smith in effect asserts, is a *second nature*. Despite its conventional origins, it too has an order governed by laws, and hence it can also become the object of rational investigation. Indeed, left to itself, society will function regularly and in a law-governed manner. As he argues in his earlier *Theory of Moral Sentiments*, in a passage devoted to a criticism of Hobbes and others, "human society,

---

[2] As the term was once used, "nature" *meant* the rational structure or form of some being. Hence, to say of a thing that it had a nature was to say that it had a cognizable rational structure. Where we speak of the order of nature, earlier philosophers would simply have spoken of nature as that order.

when we contemplate it in a certain abstract and philosophical light, appears like a great, an immense machine, whose regular and harmonious movements produce a thousand agreeable effects."[3]

Inasmuch as human society is not the intentional product of a purposeful and rational creator, it is not immediately clear on what grounds we can attribute to it a rational structure whose formal characteristics can become the object of our scientific investigations. In order to get over this difficulty, Smith joins to the ancient doctrine of the rationality of being a more modern notion: the public benefits of private self-interest. In effect, he seeks to *deduce* the order of society from the interactions of countless persons whose actions can be comprehended, anticipated, and calculated precisely because they are grounded in rationally comprehensible self-interest. In place of the mind's capacity to grasp God's plan, Smith invokes the mind's capacity to grasp the rationally self-interested plans of other human beings. The rational order of society is thus the unintended consequence of the actions of privately rational agents.

Since there is no overarching goal, no telos toward which individual actions are oriented, it is essential both to the objective rationality of society and to the subjective rationality of our cognition of society that each individual agent act in a self-interested, and hence calculable, fashion. Acts of beneficence or charity, or acts done from habit or custom, because they spring from the non-rational portions of the soul, will be inherently unpredictable and incalculable.[4] Smith recognizes this fact in one of the best known of the many quotable passages in *The Wealth of Nations*: "It is not from the benevolence of the butcher, the brewer, or the baker, that we expect our dinner, but from their regard to their own interest. We address ourselves, not to their humanity but to their self-love,

---

[3] Smith (1897), Part 7, chap. 1.

[4] As John Stuart Mill acknowledged three-quarters of a century later, the intrusion of habit and custom into the market undermines the possibility of the theoretical calculations on which classical political economy rests. See Mill (1897), Bk. 2, chap. 4, "Of Competition and Custom."

and never talk to them of our own necessities but of their advantages."[5]

We arrive thus at the concept of the market as a *system* of individual interactions which naturally and unintendedly combine in stable patterns, regulated by rational laws. According to Smith, the key to an understanding of the market, and thereby of society, is the concept of economic exchange, which he traces, with characteristic eighteenth-century wit and superficiality, to a "certain propensity in human nature . . . to truck, barter, and exchange one thing for another."[6] Announcing his intention to investigate "the rules which men naturally observe in exchanging [goods] either for money or for one another," he introduces the distinction between value in use and value in exchange which was to be taken up by Ricardo, by Marx, and indeed by virtually all economists up to the present day. The passage is worth quoting in full:

> The word VALUE, it is to be observed, has two different meanings, and sometimes expresses the utility of some particular object, and sometimes the power of purchasing other goods which the possession of that object conveys. The one may be called "value in use," the other "value in exchange." The things which have the greatest value in use have frequently little or no value in exchange; and on the contrary, those which have the greatest value in exchange have frequently little or no value in use. Nothing is more useful than water: but it will purchase scarce anything; scarce anything can be had in exchange for it. A diamond, on the contrary, has scarce any value in use; but a very great quantity of other goods may frequently be had in exchange for it.
>
> In order to investigate the principles which regulate the exchangeable value of commodities, I shall endeavour to shew,
>
> First, what is the real measure of this exchangeable value; or wherein consists the real price of commodities.

[5] Smith (1937), Bk. 1, chap. 2.
[6] Ibid.

Secondly, what are the different parts of which this real price is composed or made up.

And, lastly, what are the different circumstances which sometimes raise some or all of these different parts of price above, and sometimes sink them below their natural or ordinary rate; or, what are the causes which sometimes hinder the market price, that is, the actual price of commodities, from coinciding exactly with what may be called their natural price.[7]

Smith now undertakes, by a series of logical and conceptual maneuvers, to define a new object of investigation, namely *natural price*. He also advances a theory of natural price—more precisely, a theory of the factors which regulate or determine natural price. But as we shall see, his attempts at a theory are almost entirely unsuccessful.

Since much of this book is devoted to the efforts of Smith, Ricardo, and Marx to arrive at a satisfactory theory of natural price, it might be useful to ask at the outset why such a theory is so important to a critical understanding of capitalist economy and society. Briefly, the answer is this: the central social and economic issue in any society is how the annual surplus shall be divided up, and what shall be done with it once it has been divided. The question of distribution is important in its own right, and important as well through its implications for questions of economic growth, political domination, and cultural hegemony.

In a capitalist society, the social product is distributed to the several classes in the form of wages, rents, profits, and interest. Some of what is distributed is required for the reproduction of the economy and society at the existing level of output and activity. The rest is surplus, and may be wasted, consumed unproductively, or invested to expand the scope and level of production. As we shall soon have occasion to note, what are actually distributed are quanta of value in the form of money, not (by and large) physical stocks of corn, iron, or theology

[7] Ibid., Bk. 1, chap. 4.

books. In order to determine how much money is allotted to workers as wages, to landlords as rents, to entrepreneurs as profits, to financiers as interest, and so forth, and in order as well to determine what that money will buy, we must have a *theory* of the factors influencing and determining prices, wages, rents, profits, and interest. Such a theory is precisely a theory of price, or, in the language current when Smith wrote, a *theory of value.*

In the unfolding of the argument in *The Wealth of Nations*, Smith advances his theory first, and only then presents an explicit definition of natural, as opposed to market, price. But we shall reverse the order of our analysis, for the concept of natural price is actually Smith's major theoretical contribution to the discipline of political economy.

> There is in every society or neighbourhood an ordinary or average rate both of wages and profit in every different employment of labour and stock. This rate is naturally regulated, as I shall show hereafter, partly by the general circumstances of the society, their riches or poverty, their advancing, stationary, or declining condition; and partly by the particular nature of each employment.
>
> There is likewise in every society or neighbourhood an ordinary or average rate of rent, which is regulated too, as I shall show hereafter, partly by the general circumstances of the society or neighbourhood in which the land is situated, and partly by the natural or improved fertility of the land.
>
> These ordinary or average rates may be called the natural rates of wages, profit, and rent, at the time and place in which they commonly prevail.
>
> When the price of any commodity is neither more nor less than what is sufficient to pay the rent of the land, the wages of the labour, and the profits of the stock employed in raising, preparing, and bringing it to market, according to their natural rates, the commodity is then sold for what may be called its natural price.[8]

[8] Ibid., Bk. 1, chap. 7.

As introduced here, the concept of natural price does not rise much above the level of the most naive observation of surface phenomena. Practical men of affairs become aware, as they conduct their business, that a certain wage, rent, or rate of return is customary in a particular locale. Without asking *why*, they come to expect that they shall have to pay those rates, and like the occupants of Plato's cave, they may even become adept at predicting fluctuations in the shadows on the wall. In the most elementary attempt at theory, Smith identifies the natural price of a commodity with the sum of the amounts which the entrepreneur must lay out in order to produce the good plus the profit which he himself is to reap.

Now, however, Smith rapidly advances his analysis with a series of arguments which carry him well beyond mere observation to genuine theory. First of all, he justifies his inclusion of the natural profit as a component of the natural price of the commodity by an appeal to the workings of material self-interest in a free, competitive market:

> The commodity is then sold [i.e., when its price exactly covers the natural wage, natural rent, and natural profit] precisely for what it is worth, or for what it really costs the person who brings it to market; for though in common language what is called the prime cost of any commodity does not comprehend the profit of the person who is to sell it again, yet if he sells it at a price which does not allow him the ordinary rate of profit in his neighbourhood, he is evidently a loser by the trade; *since by employing his stock in some other way he might have made that profit.*[9]

---

[9] Ibid. Emphasis added. Note that in Smith's formulation of the natural price of a commodity there is no allowance for the cost of the non-labor inputs, such as seed, fertilizer, tools, and so forth. Smith ought to say that the price at which the entrepreneur sells his commodity suffices to pay the rent of the land, the wages of the labor, *the price of the non-labor inputs*, and the profit on his stock (some of which he has advanced for wages, some as rent for land, some for tools, etc.), all at their natural rates. This flaw in Smith's analysis corrects itself when he moves to a discussion of social aggregate outlays for wages, rents, and profits, for the cost of intermediate goods

As Smith makes clear in the next paragraph, the argument turns essentially on a number of assumptions concerning the workings of a competitive market. Each entrepreneur is presumed to be engaged in a rationally self-interested pursuit of profit, in an economy which permits him to "change his trade as often as he pleases."[10] With good, if not perfect, information, entrepreneurs will quickly learn of opportunities for greater profit in other lines of production, and unhindered by law or custom, will move their capital freely to follow the fluctuations of the rate of return.

"The actual price at which any commodity is commonly sold," Smith now says, "is called its market price."[11] Market price is regulated by the relative strength of supply and demand. As these fluctuate widely, so will market price. Entrepreneurs, eager for greater profit, respond to the cues of market price by moving their capital hither and yon, fleeing from sectors of production in which an excess supply has driven market price below natural price, and moving toward sectors where an excess of "effectual demand" has driven up market price and produced a temporary superprofit for the shrewd or fortunate capitalists engaged in that line of production.

Smith now advances his analysis by the introduction of a powerful metaphor: "The natural price, therefore," he says, "is,

---

drops out of the aggregates. Marx, in his discussion of Smith in part one of *Theories of Surplus Value* remarks in passing that Smith's omission of the cost of the means of production is an "oversight" (Marx 1963, p. 90). Marx then launches into an extended attempt to ascertain "who [it is] that labours in order to replace the equivalent of the constant capital already expended in production" (ibid., pp. 107–151; see p. 108 for quote). The answer, of course, is that the workers do, as part of their *necessary* labor, for if, as Marx generally assumes, capitalist consumption is effectively zero, then all final demand, leaving aside what goes to expand production, is for wage goods, and the replacement of the constant capital employed in the production of these wage goods is traceable ultimately to the *necessary* labor performed by the workers. See Appendix A, Section V.5.

[10] Smith (1937), Bk. 1, chap. 7.
[11] Ibid.

as it were, the central price, to which the prices of all commodities are continually gravitating."[12]

Although Smith makes very little of the image of natural prices as centers of gravity, it is worth exploring for a bit, because a number of deep and powerful theoretical assumptions are encapsulated within it. The use of the term *natural* is clearly intended to suggest an objective law-governed system, a "nature" analogous to physical nature, with a rational structure apprehendable by human reason. To characterize natural prices as centers of gravity is to impute to them some causal efficacy, or at least to claim that they could correctly be understood as having causal efficacy in a theoretical model designed to articulate the underlying structure of the market. They are clearly not to be thought of merely as statistical averages or unexplained regularities, but are to be construed rather as centers of force ineluctably drawing market prices to them. As bodies of a system in equilibrium, when displaced from their positions, tend to move back to their equilibrium locations, so prices, displaced momentarily by fluctuations in supply or demand from their natural levels, will tend to move back to their equilibrium positions. What is more, natural prices, like physical centers of gravity, form a system of interacting forces. As the movement of one mass anywhere in Newtonian space affects all other masses, so a change in one natural price will produce alterations in all other natural prices, which changes will then return to affect the original natural price. Smith himself does not draw out the implications of his metaphor, but they are implicit in it, and eventually become explicit in the theory of David Ricardo.

By characterizing natural prices as centers of gravity, Smith encourages us to conceive of them as objectively real determinants of the economic system. Once we have accepted the distinction between natural price and market price, we must inevitably ask: What are the determinants of natural price? In short, Smith sets for himself and for all subsequent political

[12] Ibid.

economists the task of formulating a satisfactory *theory of natural price.*

Smith does not yet have a coherent notion of an economy in *equilibrium,* but the elements of such a notion are present in his distinction between natural and market price and in his account of the mechanism by which deviations of market from natural price, brought about by fluctuations in effective demand, are corrected through the self-interested responses of rational consumers and entrepreneurs.[13]

[13] There is a rather interesting methodological difference between Smith's procedure and that adopted by Newton, reflection on which brings to the fore a deep difference between theories of physical nature and theories of society. Newton puts forward gravitation as the universal force which unites a multiplicity of masses into a physical system, but he deliberately and pointedly makes no attempt to explain how gravitation operates. In the General Scholium written for the second edition of the *Principia,* Newton directly addressed the possibility of explaining the phenomenon of gravitational attraction. "Hitherto," he wrote, "I have not been able to discover the cause of those properties of gravity from phenomena, and I frame no hypotheses; for whatever is not deduced from the phenomena is to be called a hypothesis, and hypotheses, whether metaphysical or physical, whether of occult qualities or mechanical, have no place in experimental philosophy. In this philosophy particular propositions are inferred from the phenomena and afterward rendered general by induction. Thus it was that the impenetrability, the mobility, and the impulsive force of bodies, and the laws of motion and of gravitation, were discovered. And to us it is enough that gravity does really exist and act according to the laws which we have explained, and abundantly serves to account for all the motions of the celestial bodies and of our sea" (Newton 1953, p. 45). When David Hume undertook, in *A Treatise of Human Nature,* to elaborate a science of man equal to the science of nature achieved by Bacon, Newton, and the other natural philosophers of the preceding century, he embraced the experimental method, and foreswore speculations about inner causes. "And tho' we must endeavour to render all our principles as universal as possible, by tracing up our experiments to the utmost, and explaining all effects from the simplest and fewest causes, 'tis still certain we cannot go beyond experience; and any hypothesis, that pretends to discover the ultimate original qualities of human nature, ought at first to be rejected as presumptuous and chimerical" (Hume 1888, *Introduction*). In keeping with this Newtonian resolve, Hume advanced his principle of the association of ideas (modeled, of course, on gravitation) without any explanation of the inner causes of its working. Nevertheless, when Hume came actually to develop his theory of the mind's association of ideas, he was forced to appeal to a variety of hypotheses about the propensities, dispositions, and inner capacities of the knowing mind. In the field of moral science, it seems, mere contingent regularities did not suffice to ground a satisfactory

Smith grounds his attempt at a theory of natural price in some elementary assumptions about the subjective tastes and preferences of individuals. First of all, he takes it for granted that laboring is unpleasant and painful—something one would engage in only from force of necessity. "Equal quantities of labour, at all times and places," Smith asserts without argument, "[are] of equal value to the labourer. In his ordinary state of health, strength, and spirits; in the ordinary degree of his skill and dexterity, he must always lay down the same portion of his ease, his liberty, and his happiness."[14]

There are powerful theoretical motives for this attempt by Smith to locate something in the economic world whose worth is everywhere and always the same, motives that prompted Ricardo, half a century later, to search for an "invariable standard of value." The problem is this: the *price* of a commodity expresses how much of that commodity one will give in the market for other commodities, or, what is the same thing, how much of other commodities one can obtain with the given commodity. The price of a commodity is actually a *relation* between it and other commodities. A relation, or ratio, changes when either of its terms changes (or, save in special cases, when

---

theory. Smith, like Hume, is unable to rest with empirically established regularity. His theory of natural price, unlike Newton's theory of gravitation, is founded on a hypothesis about the inner causes or determinants of natural price, namely the hypothesis of universal rationally self-interested calculation of profitability. Without this behavioral assumption, or others equally capable of legitimating a priori deductions of economic behavior, Smith would be unable to justify his introduction of the concept of natural price.

[14] Smith (1937), Bk. 1, chap. 5. In the first edition of *The Wealth of Nations*, Smith actually wrote that "Equal quantities of labour must at all times and places be of equal value to the labourer," thereby making the equality a matter of necessity, not merely of fact. It is difficult to see what could serve as an argument for such a claim. Indeed, the claim is implausible, unless it is reduced to triviality by stipulating that differences in subjective evaluation be always interpreted as grounded in differences in intensity or quality of labor, rather than in changes in the subject's preferences. As the text makes clear, these are not matters about which Smith thought deeply or systematically.

both terms change). If a bushel of corn will buy more cloth today than it bought yesterday, that may be because something has happened to make corn worth more, or it may equally be because something has happened to make cloth worth less. From the mere fact of the change in their relative value, nothing can be concluded concerning the causes of the change.[15]

[15] The remarks of this paragraph are actually rather more controversial than they may appear. Ricardo (and Marx) held that relative, or exchangeable, value is grounded in absolute value—that eight bushels of corn exchange for ten yards of linen because eight bushels of corn contain ten times as much absolute value as one yard of linen. A number of critics of Ricardo—most notably Samuel Bailey—rejected completely the notion of absolute value, arguing that only the notion of relative or exchangeable value could be given a coherent meaning. From this, Bailey concluded that Ricardo's search for an invariable standard of value was a mistake. For a useful discussion of this point, with a defense of Ricardo, see Dobb (1973), chap. 4. See also Marx's extended discussion of Bailey in part three of *Theories of Surplus Value*, chap. 20.3d. There are really three distinct positions one might hold on this matter, not two. In the first place, one might argue that the *value* of a commodity is an objective property, about which something quantitative can be said quite independently of the relations of the commodity to all other commodities. One would then *explain* the long-term, or equilibrium, ratios in which it exchanged with other commodities by appeal to the relation between the absolute or objective values of itself and the commodities with which it was exchanging, the implicit assumption being made that rationally self-interested agents would refuse to accept, in trade, less value than they were yielding up. This does in fact seem to be the notion that Ricardo and Marx have in mind, and it *is* open to Bailey's criticism. Secondly, one could hold that the ratios in which commodities exchange are, in long-run equilibrium, determined by some objective characteristic of the commodities, such as the quantity of labor required to produce them. From this, it would follow that an alteration in the exchange ratio between two commodities must be the result of some (possibly unobserved) change in the objective characteristic of one, the other, or both. This too seems to be what Ricardo had in mind, and this position is *not* vulnerable to Bailey's criticism. Finally, one might, in modern fashion, seek to explain exchange ratios by appeal to the subjective evaluations of buyers, and one might further claim that judgments of relative value are simple, unanalyzable evaluations which must be taken as the unquestioned starting point of any theory of price. On this view, changes in exchange ratios would be "explained" by changes in the subjective comparative evaluations of consumers, which subjective changes would themselves be utterly inexplicable within the confines of the theory. Such a view, which, I take it, has close affinities to the modern theory of consumer demand, really would completely undermine the Ricardian position, and all of classical economics with it, but it is so incompatible with the theoretical orientation of the classical school that it can hardly be construed as a criticism of one particular tenet of that school.

Smith was persuaded, as was Ricardo, that a satisfactory theory of natural price should be able to tell us which of two commodities has changed in value when the rate of exchange between them alters. To Smith, this could only mean finding some one special commodity whose value, being constant, would serve as a standard against which all other commodities could be measured, and in terms of which we could chart the fluctuations in the value of those other commodities.

To an earlier age, the precious metals, gold and silver, might have seemed natural candidates for the role of invariant standard, but Smith was quite conscious of the fact that the influx of precious metals from the New World in the sixteenth and seventeenth centuries had depressed their price dramatically. So he hit upon labor as a commodity whose value to its owners was ever constant: "Labour alone, therefore, never varying in its own value, is alone the ultimate and real standard by which the value of all commodities can at all times and places be estimated and compared. It is their real price; money is their nominal price only."[16]

If labor never varies in its value, what then determines the value of other commodities? Smith actually advances *three* different answers to this question, two of which at least he somewhat confusedly considers equivalent to one another. His first answer, on which Ricardo erected his own theory, is that *goods exchange in the market in proportion to the quantities of labor required to produce them.* Although Smith considered this explanation to be correct only in a primitive state of society, and therefore devoted scarcely a page to it, it is in fact the theoretically most promising of his three attempts, and will repay close analysis. Here is the explanation in its entirety, in one of the best-known passages in the text:

> In that early and rude state of society which precedes both the accumulation of stock and the appropriation of land, the proportion between the quantities of labour necessary for acquiring different objects seems to be the only

[16] Smith (1937), Bk. 1, chap. 5.

circumstance which can afford any rule for exchanging them for one another. If among a nation of hunters, for example, it usually costs twice the labour to kill a beaver which it does to kill a deer, one beaver should naturally exchange for or be worth two deer. It is natural that what is usually the produce of two days or two hours labour, should be worth double of what is usually the produce of one day's or one hour's labour.[17]

What we have here, in the graceful and ingenuous style characteristic of Smith's exposition, is a theorem in the theory of rational choice. The logic of the proof is clear enough, but a world of presuppositions, abstractions, and simplifications are hidden within it. We are to imagine a state of affairs in which hunters are capable, on average, of catching a beaver in twice the time required to catch a deer. Smith does not say so, but the argument demands that they hunt with their bare hands, for the use of weapons comes under the heading of "the accumulation of stock" and introduces theoretical difficulties which were to remain unsolved until the publication of Ricardo's *Principles*. Under the circumstances, let us posit one day's barehand hunting per beaver, and two days' per deer. It is essential to the argument that all hunters be equally skilled at hunting either beaver or deer, and that there be no economies of scale or efficiencies from specialization and the division of labor.

Now we are to imagine two hunters, Diana and Orion, encountering one another in a clearing in the forest after two weeks' hunting, Diana bearing ten deer and Orion five beaver (assuming a five-day work week). Let us suppose that each has declining marginal utility for beaver and deer, and hence wishes to trade a portion of his or her catch for a portion of the other's catch. In what proportions will they be willing to trade, assuming that each is self-interestedly rational?

To begin with, each views the labor of hunting as painful and tedious, a cost rather than a benefit, even in the idyllic conditions here posited. Hence neither will work a day longer

[17] Ibid., Bk. 1, chap. 6.

than necessary. Furthermore, each is quite capable of catching a beaver in two days of averagely stressful labor or a deer in one day of equally stressful labor.

With these premises, we can now deduce what the shape will be of each hunter's bargaining space. Suppose that Diana offers to trade one of her deer for one of Orion's beaver. After some reflection, Orion will refuse, for he will reason thus: If I make this trade, I will be in possession of four beaver and one deer, for which I will have expended ten days' labor. (Smith assumes that there are no transaction costs, and that the bargaining process, being neither a joy nor a labor, does not figure in the calculation.) But if what I want is four beaver and one deer, I can have them for only nine days' labor—eight hunting beaver, and a ninth hunting deer. I can then spend the tenth day resting, and as I prefer four beaver, one deer, and a day's rest to four beaver, one deer, and no rest, clearly this trade is not in my interest. To be sure, I have already expended ten days' effort, and that is therefore a sunk cost. But in future—which is to say, in long-run equilibrium—I would do better to do all my hunting myself rather than concentrate on beaver and trade for deer.

So Orion rejects Diana's offer and proposes instead that she give him three deer for one beaver. By an analogous process of reasoning, Diana concludes that such a trade will not be in her self-interest, and she rejects the proposal.

After some time, "by the higgling and bargaining of the market, according to that sort of rough equality which, though not exact, is sufficient for carrying on the business of common life," Diana comes to see that two deer are the most it is rational for her to part with for one beaver, and Orion in turn comes to see that two deer are the least he will accept for one of his beaver.[18] Since their bargaining spaces intersect at a single point, the two consummate a deal at precisely that point, and so it comes to pass that the going exchange rate for deer and beaver is two deer for one beaver.

[18] Ibid., Bk. 1, chap. 5.

I have gone on at such length about so simple an example not merely because it is the archetype of all such examples in economic theory, but also because contained within this classic pastoral tale, either explicitly or implicitly, are many of the theoretical assumptions that play so large a role in the more sophisticated theories of Ricardo and Marx. We can name, among the principal assumptions: the total instrumental rationality of the agents, the disutility of labor, the social achievement of a degree of standardization and homogenization of laboring activity sufficient to allow us to say precisely how long it takes to catch "a" beaver or "a" deer (as opposed to this beaver or that deer). Also present, but quite unnoticed by Smith, is the crucially important assumption of the standardization of the *product*—the beaver and the deer—so that either, by a process of selective breeding, all beaver have come to be of equal size and usefulness and all deer the same, or else some way has been found to index the multidimensional variations among beaver and deer so that one can calculate the standard time required to catch the standard beaver or deer.

Equally important is the willingness of Diana and Orion to adopt purely functional attitudes toward their hunting activity. Neither imbues the hunt with a religious, mythic, aesthetic, or familial significance that would interfere with the cost/benefit calculations out of which arises the natural price of two beaver for one deer. *Non olet*, as Marx reminds us.[19]

In addition to the theory that commodities exchange in proportion to the amount of labor required to *produce* them—a theory which came to be known as the "labor embodied" standard—Smith also argues that commodities exchange in proportion to the amount of labor which they can, in effect, *command*—what came to be known as the "labor commanded" theory of price. Smith argues thus:

[19] Marx (1967a), p. 110. It is said of the Emperor Vespasian that he sent his son to collect the taxes from the public urinals. The son, repelled by a chore which he considered beneath him, flung the money disgustedly at his father's feet. *Non olet*, his father replied equanimously, "It stinketh not," thereby showing that whereas his son exhibited the non-rational finickiness of the aristocrat, he possessed the true entrepreneurial temperament.

Every man is rich or poor according to the degree in which he can afford to enjoy the necessaries, conveniencies, and amusements of human life. But after the division of labour has once thoroughly taken place, it is but a very small part of these with which a man's own labour can supply him. The far greater part of them he must derive from the labour of other people, and he must be rich or poor according to the quantity of that labour which he can command, or which he can afford to purchase. The value of any commodity, therefore, to the person who possesses it, and who means not to use or consume it himself, but to exchange it for other commodities, is equal to the quantity of labour which it enables him to purchase or command. Labour, therefore, is the real measure of the exchangeable value of all commodities.[20]

It is not immediately clear how we are to interpret these and other similar remarks by Smith. Perhaps the most natural interpretation is simply to construe Smith as claiming that commodities will exchange in proportion to the quantities of labor which each will buy. If a bushel of corn will exchange in the market for half a day's labor (which is to say that I can hire a worker for half a day for a wage of one bushel of corn), and if a yard of cloth will exchange in the market for a full day's labor, then two bushels of corn, Smith might be saying, will exchange for one yard of cloth. For:

$$1 \text{ bu. corn} = 1/2 \text{ day's labor}$$

and

$$1 \text{ yd. cloth} = 1 \text{ day's labor}$$

imply that

$$(1 \text{ bu. corn})/(1 \text{ yd. cloth}) = (1/2 \text{ day's labor})/(1 \text{ day's labor})$$

$$= 1/2$$

---

[20] Smith (1937), Bk. 1, chap. 5.

or

$$2 \text{ bu. corn} = 1 \text{ yd. cloth.}$$

But this claim, although true, is trivial. It amounts to nothing more than the assertion that a consistent, complete price system exists. So although many of Smith's assertions appear to reduce to the claim that commodities will exchange in proportion to the quantity of labor they can purchase in the market, we must search for a more interesting interpretation of the text if we are to rescue Smith from triviality.

According to a second interpretation, for which a good deal of textual evidence can be cited, a commodity can be said to command a quantity of labor in the sense of commanding or purchasing or exchanging for another commodity into whose production a certain quantity of labor has gone. Thus, if it takes ten hours of labor, one way or another, to produce one yard of cloth, and if two bushels of corn will purchase a yard of cloth, then one bushel of corn might be said to "command" five hours of labor. As Smith says: "The power which that possession [of a fortune] immediately and directly conveys to him [who possesses it], is the power of purchasing; a certain command over all the labour, or over all the produce of labour which is then in the market. His fortune is greater or less, precisely in proportion to the extent of this power, or to the quantity either of other men's labour, or, *what is the same thing*, of the produce of other men's labour, which it enables him to purchase or command."[21]

Smith does not distinguish this labor-commanded theory of price from the labor-embodied theory that holds in the "early and rude state" and on occasion he seems to identify the two. Ricardo was exceedingly critical of Smith for this confusion (as Ricardo saw it), and indeed it is not difficult to see that in general the two theories are quite distinct.[22] Suppose that

[21] Ibid. Emphasis added.
[22] See Ricardo (1951–73), vol. 1, chap. 1, pp. 13ff. See also Dobb (1973), pp. 49–50, especially note to p. 49.

under current conditions of agricultural production, it takes one hour of labor to produce one bushel of corn. Then a bushel of corn *embodies* one hour of labor. Suppose as well that an agricultural laborer's wage for an eight-hour day is four bushels of corn. Then one bushel of corn *commands* two hours of labor. A rise or fall in the wage, unaccompanied by an alteration in the technology of corn production, or alternatively a change in the technique of corn production unaccompanied by a change in the wage, will cause one of these two quantities (labor commanded or labor embodied) to vary while the other remains unchanged, thus decisively proving that they are distinct.[23]

As soon as we leave the early and rude state and enter a society in which the appropriation of land and the accumulation of stock have taken place, the simple beaver/deer explanation of exchange ratios ceases to apply. To see why this is so, let us imagine that while Diana and Orion have been out hunting, Demeter has been raising grain on her ten-acre plot of land. Before she begins her planting, she must spend 100 days felling trees, pulling stumps (also, for the sake of theoretical simplicity, with her bare hands), and generally preparing the field. Another 100 days of planting, weeding, and reaping produces, at the end of the year, a total harvest of 800 bushels of corn. The question now arises in what proportions will Demeter, Diana, and Orion exchange their corn, deer, and beaver with one another? The terms of trade between Diana and Orion have not altered—two deer for one beaver. But when they attempt to enter into stable patterns of exchange with Demeter, many troublesome problems crop up. Demeter has spent 200 days raising 800 bushels of grain, which is to say she has spent a day's labor for each four bushels she has grown. She therefore proposes to exchange four bushels of grain for one deer, or

---

[23] Later on, we shall see that labor embodied equals labor commanded precisely when the profit rate in the society is zero, and since this corresponds to the "early and rude state" that precedes the "accumulation of stock," Adam Smith, in some sense, had his finger on a valid theorem, although he was unable to articulate it correctly.

eight bushels for one beaver. At first sight, this might appear a reasonable proposal, but neither Diana nor Orion is likely to accept it, for in fact it is heavily biased in Demeter's favor.

The point, of course, is that once her field has been cleared by the 100 days' labor, it is fit for cultivation for many seasons, not for one season only. We can imagine Orion reasoning to himself thus: I now hunt 200 days each year for an annual catch of 100 beaver. If I want 80 bushels of grain, I can obtain it by spending 10 days clearing an acre of forest and 10 more days cultivating the soil. The 20 days lost to beaver hunting will diminish my annual catch by 10 beaver, so it might seem equally reasonable for me to hunt the year round and exchange with Demeter 10 of my beaver for 80 bushels of her grain, at a ratio of 1 beaver to 8 bushels. But the following year, I shall still want 80 bushels of grain and 90 beaver (or else I shall be able, if that is what I have, to trade without trouble). In that time period, since my acre will already be cleared, I will have to work only 190 days total—180 to catch 90 beaver and 10 on the cleared land to raise 80 bushels of grain. It follows that I can do better by hunting and farming than by hunting and trading with Demeter. So I will reject her offer.

The same reasoning leads Diana to refuse Demeter's proposed terms of trade.

If we could specify how long the field will remain cleared—over how many cycles of production—we might be able to come up with a proposal that would win the agreement of Diana, Orion, and Demeter. But now we realize that there are other factors to be taken account of, even in this simplest and most fanciful of examples. Diana's bow takes some time to fashion (assuming that she has moved beyond bare-hand hunting), and it lasts for more than one season. So too does Demeter's hoe. And the wood from which the bow and the hoe are made is of a special sort, carefully gathered at an earlier time and aged before being worked. In addition, Diana and Orion cannot so easily shift to agriculture, for the best land has already been spoken for by farmers who will demand a price for its use.

In short, we have come face to face with that "appropriation of land and accumulation of stock" which Smith correctly identified as the reason why goods fail to exchange in proportion to the labor time directly required for their production. Smith himself offers a rather curious and superficial explanation for this failure:

> As soon as stock has accumulated in the hands of particular persons, some of them will naturally employ it in setting to work industrious people . . . in order to make a profit by the sale of their work. . . . [the employer] could have no interest to employ [the workmen], unless he expected from the sale of their work something more than what was sufficient to replace his stock to him; and he could have no interest to employ a great stock rather than a small one, unless his profits were to bear some proportion to the extent of his stock.

And, a bit later on in the same chapter:

> As soon as the land of any country has all become private property, the landlords, like all other men, love to reap where they never sowed, and demand a rent even for its natural produce.[24]

But these "explanations," although charming, are not really explanations at all. Smith tells us that the prudent entrepreneur is *unwilling* to venture his capital without a return, and that the greedy, feckless landlord seeks to use his monopoly of the land to get something for nothing. But Smith has not explained what determines how great a return the entrepreneur can reasonably expect, and he has therefore not told us what effect the profits of stock will have on the rate at which commodities exchange with one another. (Strictly speaking, he has also not explained why the entrepreneur can rationally expect any return at all on his investment, but that is an objection first raised by Marx, and we shall have to postpone consideration of it for a bit.)

[24] Smith (1937), Bk. 1, chap. 6.

At this point, Smith offers what some readers of *The Wealth of Nations* have taken to be a theory of price, namely the so-called adding-up theory. As Smith says, "when the price of any commodity is neither more nor less than what is sufficient to pay the rent of the land, the wages of the labour, and the profits of the stock employed in raising, preparing, and bringing it to market, according to their natural rates, the commodity is then sold for what may be called its natural price." [25] But this is not a *theory* of natural price. It is, as we have seen, merely a *definition* of the term "natural price."

In fact, Smith has no theory of the determination of natural price. Hence, he has no theory of wages, rents, and profits, and so no theory as well of the distribution of the social product among the several great classes of society. Nevertheless, Smith has successfully identified the object of investigation of political economy, namely the market, and he has formulated the central analytical concept, natural price. It remained for David Ricardo, forty-one years later, to advance the first coherent, fully worked-out theory of natural price.

[25] Ibid., Bk. 1, chap. 7.

DAVID RICARDO AND
THE LABOR THEORY
OF NATURAL PRICE

1. THE *Essay on Profits*

David Ricardo's first attempt at a theory of wages, rents, and profits is his 1815 "Essay on the Influence of a low Price of Corn on the Profits of Stock, shewing the Inexpediency of restrictions on Importation: with Remarks on Mr. Malthus' Two Last Publications." The central idea, which Ricardo deploys with great effectiveness, is that the agricultural sector is, in effect, a miniature one-commodity economy. Workers eat corn as their wage, they plant corn as the sole capital input, and they harvest corn as the output. Since all inputs and outputs are measured in corn, the rate of profit in the corn sector is a pure number determined as the ratio of two physical quantities: net output and aggregate inputs. The sole determinant of the profit rate (leaving rent to one side for the moment) is the difficulty or facility of producing corn. No fluctuation in relative prices throughout the rest of the economy can affect the profit rate in the corn sector. And inasmuch as competition, combined with the free flow of capital and labor from sector to sector, guarantees a uniform rate of return in the economy as a whole, it follows that the economy-wide profit rate is entirely determined by the physical conditions of production in the corn sector.[1]

The workings of an economy of this sort are rather peculiar and counterintuitive. If at any particular moment the rate of return in corn is higher than in the rest of the economy, then capital will be drawn to the corn sector. Output will rise and the price will drop, which is to say that corn will buy less of other commodities. However, the profit rate in the corn industry will be unaffected by these changes in the relative price of corn, for the corn industry uses only corn as an input, and hence its profit rate is determined solely by the ratio of physical output to physical input. Thus movements of capital will affect the relative prices in the economy—the price of corn relative to other commodities, and even, indirectly, the prices of other commodities relative to one another. But throughout these adjustments, the long-run, or equilibrium, rate of return will remain unchanged, for that will always be a ratio of output to input determined entirely by the technical conditions of production in the corn industry. As Ricardo puts it:

> Profits then depend on the price, or rather on the value of food. Every thing which gives facility to the production of food, however scarce, or however abundant commodities may become, will raise the rate of profits, whilst on the contrary, every thing which shall augment the cost of production without augmenting the quantity of food, will, under every circumstance, lower the general rate of

[1] Let O be the output in the corn sector in bushels, L the total labor input, W the wage per unit of labor in bushels, C the capital input in bushels of seed corn, and π the rate of profit. Finally, let p_c equal the price of corn.

$$(LWp_c + Cp_c)(1 + \pi) = Op_c \qquad \text{(i)}$$

$$(LW + C)(1 + \pi) = O \qquad \text{(ii)}$$

$$\pi = (O - LW - C)/(LW + C). \qquad \text{(iii)}$$

All the terms on the right-hand side of (iii) are quantities of bushels of corn. This interpretation of the *Essay on Profits* is due to Sraffa (cf. Ricardo 1951–73), vol. 1, pp. xxx–xxxiii). For a recent exchange concerning Sraffa's reading with references to the literature, see Hollender (1983) and P. Garegnani (1983).

profits. The facility of obtaining food is beneficial in two ways to the owners of capital, it at the same time raises profits and increases the amount of consumable commodities. The facility in obtaining all other things, only increases the amount of commodities.[2]

Ingenious as this argument is, it will not withstand close scrutiny, as Malthus among others was quick to point out. The problem is that agriculture cannot plausibly be construed as a self-contained one-commodity economy. Agricultural production requires tools and equipment as well as seed corn. Hence, the rate of return in agriculture ought to be affected by the facility or difficulty of mining and refining iron ore, of felling, dressing, and shaping timber, and so forth. Furthermore, agricultural laborers cannot with any measure of accuracy be represented as consuming nothing but grain. Clearly, the purchasing power of their money wages will be affected by the prices—and hence by the conditions of production—of cloth, tea, and housing as well as of bread.

So it is not possible, after all, to take a shortcut to a theory of profits by separating out of the economy as a whole a fragment—the corn sector—whose structure is so simple as to evade all the troublesome problems of analysis and whose autonomously determined rate of return will, by the effects of competition, rule the economy as a whole.

Furthermore, the argument of the *Essay on Profits*, although certainly apposite to the then ongoing debate about the desirability of import duties on corn, leaves quite unsettled the larger issue of the determination of prices in general. It therefore allows for no full-scale analysis of natural prices, wages,

---

[2] Ricardo (1951–73), vol. 4, p. 26. By "giving facility to the production of food," Ricardo means either reducing the amount of some input required in agriculture for a given output, through a technical improvement, say, or increasing the output obtainable from given inputs. In terms of the notation of the previous footnote, $\pi = O/(LW + C) - 1$. Obviously, a decrease in L or C, and also an increase in O, will have the effect of raising π. Although Ricardo does not at this point call attention to the fact, it is clearly the case that with O, L, and C constant, π varies inversely with the real wage, W. In his *Principles*, this relation of the wage to the profit rate, suitably generalized, becomes a central theme of Ricardo's mature political economy.

rents, and profits in a competitive economy. Two years later, Ricardo provided such an analysis in his major work, the *Principles of Political Economy and Taxation* of 1817.

2. The theory of the *Principles*

The theoretical problem bequeathed by Adam Smith forty-one years earlier was how to analyze the determination of prices, and thereby of rents, wages, and profits, in that developed state of the economy which results from the "appropriation of land and the accumulation of stock." In analytical terms, this meant producing a satisfactory theoretical treatment of *rents* and of *capital stock* (which is to say capital other than outlays for wages). In addition, Ricardo needed to put forward a theory of the determination of the wage, for although he had made some remarks on the subject in the *Essay on Profits*, he did not yet have a coherent explanation for the magnitude and movement of wages.[3]

To handle the problem of rent, Ricardo adopted the analysis that had been developed by his contemporaries West, Torrens, and Malthus.[4] We shall examine it presently. Ricardo assimilated the determination of the wage to the general problem of price determination by means of Malthus's theory of the pressure of population on the food supply. That too we shall examine shortly. We are left, then, with the core analytical problem: how to take account of the role played in production, and thereby in the determination of natural price, by the accumulation of stock, in the form of cleared fields, buildings, tools, factories, raw materials, machinery, and so forth.

---

[3] In the *Essay on Profits*, Ricardo remarks at one point in the argument, "If, then, the price of labour falls, *which it must do when the price of corn is lowered....*" (1951–73, vol. 4, pp. 35–36; emphasis added). But this does not explain why the real wage of the laborer (i.e., the amount of corn purchasable with the money wage) does not simply rise as corn grows cheaper!

[4] Ricardo had already espoused this theory in the *Essay on Profits*. Despite Ricardo's unambiguous acknowledgment of his intellectual debt to Malthus and the others, history has awarded him the credit for this ingenious theory, which has come to be known as the Ricardian theory of rent.

Ricardo's solution is to extend the principle which Smith invokes for the simple case of the "early and rude state." The title of section three of the first chapter ("Of Value") of Ricardo's *Principles* reads:

> Not only the labour applied immediately to commodities affects their value, but the labour also which is bestowed on the implements, tools, and buildings, with which such labour is assisted.

Commenting on Smith's beaver/deer example, Ricardo observes that even in so simple a case, some capital will be necessary in the form of weapons.

> Suppose the weapon necessary to kill the beaver, was constructed with much more labour than that necessary to kill the deer, on account of the greater difficulty of approaching near to the former animal, and the consequent necessity of its being more true to its mark: one beaver, [Ricardo reasons] would naturally be of more value than two deer, and precisely for this reason, that more labour would, on the whole, be necessary to its destruction. Or suppose that the same quantity of labour was necessary to make both weapons, but that they were of very unequal durability; of the durable implement only a small portion of its value would be transferred to the commodity, a much greater portion of the value of the less durable implement would be realized in the commodity which it contributed to produce.[5]

The phrase, "only a small portion of its value would be transferred to the commodity," introduces us to the central concept on which both the Ricardian and the Marxian theories of natural price are based. Ricardo speaks most often of the labor "bestowed" upon a commodity, meaning by this not only the labor *directly* employed in fashioning the commodity,

[5] Ricardo (1951–73), vol. 1, p. 23.

but also the labor *indirectly* required, for example to produce the raw materials and tools which are used in making the commodity, or the labor which is expended in bringing those raw materials and tools to the place of manufacture, or the labor employed in building the ships which bear the raw materials and tools to the place of manufacture, and so on.

It has become common practice to speak of the labor directly or indirectly required for the production of a commodity as labor "embodied" in the commodity, and this locution ineluctably draws us into thinking of a commodity as a container in which labor has been stored up. Ricardo encourages this way of thinking by speaking of a "portion of the value" of a tool being "transferred" to the commodity which is produced with its assistance. We are clearly invited, by this language, to suppose that as a tool or implement wears out over the course of its useful life, the value stored within it—which is to say, the labor bestowed upon it in the past—is slowly shifted over to the commodities produced with its aid, until finally, at the moment when the tool ceases to be useful, its store of embodied labor, or value, is exhausted.

Thus construed, the notion of "embodied labour" is clearly crackbrained—the rankest sort of bad metaphysics. However, the concept of a quantity of labor directly or indirectly required for the production of a commodity is, under certain assumptions, perfectly coherent and meaningful, and quite susceptible to precise calculation.

At issue here more generally is what accountants and economists call the problem of *imputation*. When a factor of production is employed in the production of a number of units of some commodity, the question arises of how to impute or attribute or credit the cost of that factor to the several units of output for the purpose of determining how much each unit has cost to produce. One brief example will illustrate some of the complexities of the subject.

Suppose Diana is uncertain how much of the cost of her bow to impute or attribute to each of the deer she kills, in order to determine what price to charge for them. Clearly she must impute *something*, for otherwise she will be failing to take account of the labor it cost her to acquire the bow, over and above the labor she expended directly in the hunt. Were she to forego the imputation, she would find, when the bow finally wore out, that she had failed to accumulate a sinking fund for the replacement of the used-up implement. She can simply divide the original cost of the bow by the average number of deer killable with one bow, and then impute the resulting fraction to the price of each deer. Or, she can take account of the fact that a bow requires some breaking-in before it is maximally functional, and so charge a larger fraction of the cost to those deer killed during the subefficient breaking-in period. Or, she can take into consideration the appearance in the weapons market of new, more efficient bows, and impute to each deer only as much as it *would* cost her per deer were she using one of the more efficient bows (thus explicitly acknowledging the sound accounting principle that it is the cost of replacement at current prices and levels of technology that governs the imputation of costs). Indeed, should she have an armamentarium of bows of various ages, dating from different periods in, and price structures of, the weapons market, she could impute her costs using the first in first out (FIFO) method, or alternatively the last in first out (LIFO) method, and so forth.

Let us return to the simple corn/iron/theology books model, System C, which we imagined to arise as the consequence of the emergence of a physical surplus in the production of corn and iron. The structure of System C, it will be recalled, is as shown in Table 3.

TABLE 3. System C

	Labor Input	Corn Input	Iron Input	Books Input	Output
Labor		42	21	0	210
Corn Sector	100	2	16	0	300
Iron Sector	90	9	12	0	90
Books Sector	20	1	2	2	40
Total Input	210	54	51	2	

According to Ricardo, the value (i.e., the natural price) of these commodities is affected (i.e., determined, or at least primarily determined) by the amount of labor indirectly as well as directly bestowed upon them. This means that as between two commodities, say corn and iron, their prices will stand in the same ratio to one another as do the amounts of labor directly and indirectly required for their production.

Leaving to one side for the moment the very important qualification "or at least primarily determined," what we have here is a *theory* of the determination of natural price. The theory states that *the natural price of a commodity is proportional to the quantity of labor directly and indirectly required for its production.*

How can we ascertain whether this theory is confirmed by System C? Clearly, we must find some way to calculate the quantities of labor directly and indirectly required for the production of each of the three commodities produced by the system—corn, iron, and theology books. Then we must find some independent way to calculate the *natural prices* of these same commodities—which is to say, the prices that prevail when the supply and demand for each commodity are in balance, and a uniform rate of profit is therefore returned on the value of capital invested throughout the system. Finally, we must form the ratios of labor required to natural price for each commodity and see whether they are indeed equal to one another.

Before we can determine the correctness of Ricardo's thesis, we must find some way to make it precise. To this end, let us adopt a series of notational conventions, of the sort customarily used by mathematicians and economists. First of all, we shall define a number of variables standing for the prices of the commodities produced in System C. Specifically, let p_c stand for the natural or equilibrium price of corn, let p_i stand for the natural price of iron, and let p_b stand for the natural price of books ("p" for "price"). Then, let us define variables standing for the quantity of labor directly or indirectly required for the production of single units of corn, iron, and books. Following what has become a tradition in the literature on this subject, we shall use the Greek letter lambda to stand for this quantity. Thus, λ_c, λ_i, and λ_b shall stand for the quantities of labor directly and indirectly bestowed upon, or required in the production of, one unit of corn, iron, and books respectively.

With this notation in place, we can now restate Ricardo's thesis in the form of an algebraic equation. When Ricardo says that commodities exchange in proportion to the quantities of labor directly or indirectly bestowed upon them in production, he is, in effect,[6] asserting:

$$(\lambda_c/p_c) = (\lambda_i/p_i) = (\lambda_b/p_b). \tag{1}$$

If we wish to determine whether (1) is true for the commodities in System C, we must find some way to calculate the values of the price variables p_c, p_i, and p_b, and the "labor value" variables (as they are usually called), λ_c, λ_i, λ_b. Then we can substitute those values into (1) and see whether the equality holds.

Let us begin by attempting to determine how much labor is required in System C, directly and indirectly, to produce 1 unit of corn. In short, let us try to calculate the value of λ_c. The information available to us is the data on inputs and outputs summarized in Table 3. This tells us that 100 units of labor are employed directly in the production of 300 units of corn. Consequently, 1 unit of corn requires 1/3 unit of "direct labor." Thus, λ_c, the quantity of labor required directly or indirectly for the production of 1 unit of corn, must be at least 1/3. We can express this by the incomplete expression.

$$\lambda_c = 1/3 +$$

indicating that more labor than the 1/3 unit of direct labor may be required.

---

[6] Ricardo himself never carried out calculations of this sort, nor did Marx or any of the other economists of the classical period. The analysis that follows is a modern reconstruction of the theories of Ricardo and Marx.

But Table 3 also tells us that 2 units of corn are required in order for the 300 units of corn to be produced as output, and 16 units of iron as well. It follows that the production of a single unit of corn requires 1/150 of a unit of corn and 4/75 of a unit of iron.

Now 1/150 of a unit of corn will require for *its* production (1/150)(1/3) units of labor directly applied, so the original unit of corn manifestly requires an additional 1/450 of a unit of corn *indirectly* for its production. The 4/75 of a unit of iron will require in turn $(4/75)(1) = 4/75$ of a unit of labor for its production, for as the input/output proportions in the iron industry show, it takes 1 unit of labor directly applied to produce 1 unit of iron. We see therefore that we must add some labor *indirectly required* to the 1/3 unit of labor directly required for the production of a unit of corn. In short:

$$\lambda_c = 1/3 + 1/450 + 4/75 +$$

Thus far, we have a total of 7/18 of a unit of labor *directly and indirectly* required to produce 1 unit of corn. But we are not done, for of course the 1/150 of a unit of corn required to produce the original unit of corn itself requires corn and iron for its production, as do the 4/75 of a unit of iron, and these in turn require some labor for *their* production, and so on. Quite obviously, we have here an unending series of quantities of labor more and more indirectly required for the production of the original unit of corn, in addition to the 1/3 of a unit of labor directly required. What are we to do?

As it happens, this series "converges," as mathematicians say. That is, it gets closer and closer to some finite amount, the more terms we add. And there *are* ways to figure out what that finite amount is—what the "limit" is of the infinite sum. But we need not carry out any such summation in order to arrive at the total amount of labor directly and indirectly required for the production of a single unit of corn in System C. Instead, we may make use of a mode of calculation that derives from the input/output analysis of the Russian-American economist Wassily Leontief, and which has now become universally accepted as the correct analytic reconstruction of Ricardo's notion of a quantity of labor "bestowed" upon a commodity.[7]

The central idea of the modern method of "required labor" calculations is simply that the total quantity of labor embodied in a certain physical magnitude of output exactly equals the quantity of labor directly bestowed upon it in the course of production plus the quantity of labor indirectly bestowed upon it by way of the non-labor inputs which are used up in the production process. Continuing to use λ_c, λ_i, and λ_b to stand for the quantities of labor directly and indirectly required for the production of one unit of corn, iron, and books respectively, we are now able to translate the conditions of production defined in System C into a series of equations.

The input/output data for the corn industry specify that 100 units of labor are directly required, together with 2 units of corn and 16 units of iron, in order to produce 300 units of corn as output. The 100 units of labor contribute 100 units of embodied labor to the output, obviously. Each unit of corn input embodies λ_c units of labor, according to the convention we have adopted (we don't yet know how much labor that *is*, of course—finding that out is the point of this exercise). Therefore, the 2 units of corn used as input must contribute $2\lambda_c$ units of labor to the end product. Similarly, the 16 units of iron must contribute $16\lambda_i$ units of labor. The output, which consists of 300 units of corn, must embody $300\lambda_c$ units of labor. So, putting this all together, we can translate the conditions of production in the corn sector into the following "labor value equation":

$$100 + 2\lambda_c + 16\lambda_i + 0\lambda_b = 300\lambda_c. \qquad (2)$$

By exactly the same process of reasoning, we can translate the conditions of production in the iron and books industries

[7] Leontief's original analysis can be found in Leontief (1937) and later in Leontief (1941). Leontief's ideas were taken up and applied to the analysis of Ricardo and Marx by Kenneth May (1949–50), and then by Burgess Cameron (1952). By 1961, the modern analysis of the subject had reached an advanced stage of sophistication in Morishima and Seton (1961). A widely quoted treatment of the subject is Alfredo Medio in Hunt and Schwartz (1972).

into two more labor value equations, namely:

$$90 + 9\lambda_c + 12\lambda_i + 0\lambda_b = 90\lambda_i \qquad (3)$$

and

$$20 + \lambda_c + 2\lambda_i + 2\lambda_b = 40\lambda_b. \qquad (4)$$

Equation (2) asserts that 100 units of labor directly bestowed on 300 units of corn output plus 2 times the amount of labor "embodied in" a unit of corn (and hence "transferred" to the output in the production of which it is totally used up) plus 16 times the amount of labor "embodied in" a unit of iron equals 300 times the amount of labor bestowed on, and thereby "embodied in" a single unit of produced corn. And similarly for equations (3) and (4).

Assuming that these equations correctly capture Ricardo's intuitive notion of labor bestowed on the output of a process of production, we can now proceed with little difficulty to ascertain how much labor is required directly or indirectly for the production of a single unit of corn, iron, or books. All we must do is find the values of the variables λ_c, λ_i, and λ_b. Now, equations (2) through (4) constitute a system of three independent linear equations in three unknowns. There is precisely one set of values of the variables that satisfies all three equations. Elementary algebra permits us to solve the system of equations. As the reader can check, by substituting back into the equations to see whether they balance, the values of the variables that solve the equations are:

$$\lambda_c = .4$$
$$\lambda_i = 1.2$$
$$\lambda_b = .6$$

What this means in economic terms is that .4 units of labor (measured in hours, weeks, years, or whatever) are required, *directly and indirectly*, to produce 1 unit of corn in System C, and that 1.2 units and .6 units of labor respectively are required directly and indirectly to produce single units of iron and books. These quantities are customarily referred to as the "labor values" of corn, iron, and books in System C.

We are thus in a position to determine how much labor is required to produce corn, iron, and theology books, despite the fact that inputs other than labor are employed in the production process.

A closer look at equations (2) through (4) reveals that although they do indeed form a system of three independent linear equations in three unknowns, equations (2) and (3) actually form a subsystem of two independent linear equations in two unknowns. Theology books enter into the production only of themselves. They play no role in the production of corn and iron, although corn and iron do play a role in their production. The values of the variables λ_c and λ_i are thus entirely determined by equations (2) and (3). No change in equation (4) can affect the values of those variables. This corresponds to the economic fact that the labor values of corn and iron are entirely determined by the combined conditions of production in the corn and iron sectors. A change in the conditions of production of either corn or iron could be expected to have an effect on the labor values of corn, iron, and theology books, but a change in the conditions of production of theology books will affect only the labor value of the theology books themselves.

It is a good deal more difficult to determine the natural prices of corn, iron, and books in System C. To calculate the labor values, we required only the input/output physical data contained in Table 3. Hence our results are valid for any economy employing the technology summarized in the table. But before we can calculate the natural prices that would rule in a system having the physical proportions of System C, we must introduce a number of assumptions concerning the knowledge available to economic agents, the rules or principles that guide their choices, and the institutional and legal setting within which they act economically.

Modern economists are more explicitly self-conscious about their behavioral and institutional presuppositions than were Smith, Ricardo, and the other classical theorists. Nevertheless, with the benefits of hindsight, we can reconstruct a number of basic background assumptions implicit in their arguments.

The first assumption on which Smith and Ricardo build their theories of distribution and growth is that the economic actors in a capitalist system—the workers, landlords, entrepreneurs, and consumers—have perfect knowledge, or at least tend to acquire perfect knowledge, concerning the characteristics of commodities, market prices, wage and profit rates, opportunities for increased return, and so forth. Producers are assumed to know what the ruling technique of production is, what prices are being charged for labor and raw materials, what prices they can expect to sell their output for, and what rental they will be charged for agricultural land. They are also assumed to know, or at least to learn pretty quickly, when one of their number starts to make an unusually high return on an investment.

The point of these assumptions, which are theoretical simplifications rather than realistic descriptions, is to factor out of the picture any of the complications that result from industrial secrets, imperfect or uneven distribution of market information, duplicity, etc. We can think of these assumptions, and others to be discussed, as playing the same role in the classical theory of the market as is played by the assumptions of point masses or frictionless surfaces in Newtonian mechanics.

The second assumption is that everyone in the system is motivated by self-interest defined in a narrowly economic sense. Workers seek the highest wage, regardless of where it is offered or in what line of work, and they exhibit very little hesitation about leaving one job and moving to another. Capitalists seek the highest rate of return on their capital, regardless of whether it is derived from the manufacture of luxury cars or the collection of garbage. Consumers seek the lowest price, unhampered by loyalty to one vendor rather than another.

Finally, we assume a system of private property, in which each actor is free to make legally binding contracts for the sale of goods and services, *including labor services*, without constraints on the terms of those contracts save that they be legally voluntary.

A number of useful conclusions follow from these assumptions. First of all, as a consequence of the behavior of consumers and producers, a single economy-wide set of prices for commodities will come to prevail. If corn is being sold for less in one shop than in another, consumers will know about it (the knowledge assumption), and they will hurry over to buy the cheaper corn (behavior assumption). Capitalists who have been charging a higher price will lower their price in order to avoid losing all their sales (behavior assumption), and no government agency or local ordinance will stop them from doing so (institutional assumption).

In a similar manner, a single economy-wide wage will rule, because workers will know whether an employer is offering more than the going wage (knowledge assumption), will look for jobs wherever higher wages are being offered (behavior assumption), and will be free to make the best wage bargain they can (institutional assumption).

Most important (and most complicated) of all, capitalists will tend to earn the same rate of return on their invested capital, for they will learn about any industry in which higher returns are being earned (knowledge assumption), they will shift their capital as soon as they can to that industry (behavior assumption), they will be unconstrained by law or custom in the reinvestment of their capital (institutional assumption), the additional output they contribute to the market will drive down the market price (knowledge, behavior, and institutional assumptions), and as a consequence the rate of return will tend to approximate the economy-wide rate.

On the basis of these assumptions, we can translate the input/output data of Table 3 into a number of new equations expressing the relation between the price a capitalist must pay for his labor and materials, the profit markup he puts on his costs, and the price at which he sells his output in the market.

Since there is a single price for each commodity, we can assume that each capitalist, no matter in what line of production, pays the same amount for a unit of corn, iron, or books, and that this is also the price at which he sells a unit of each.

As in equation (1), we will let p_c stand for the price of corn, p_i for the price of iron, and p_b for the price of books. In addition, we can let w stand for the wage, for our assumptions imply that all workers earn the same amount per unit of time that they work.

Finally, since all capitalists earn the same rate of return, we can define the Greek letter π as the uniform rate of return on the value of invested capital.

With these five variables: the three prices, the wage, and the profit rate, symbolized by p_c, p_i, p_b, w, and π, we can now translate the data of Table 3 into equations expressing the relation between a capitalist's costs, his profit markup, and the price at which he sells his output. In the corn industry, for example, the capitalists as a group pay $100w$ for their labor, $2p_c$ for their corn inputs, and $16p_i$ for their iron inputs. They put a $(1 + \pi)$ markup on their costs, in order to net a rate of return of π, and all of this must equal $300p_c$, which is what they sell their output for. In short:

$$(100w + 2p_c + 16p_i + 0p_b)(1 + \pi) = 300p_c. \qquad (5)$$

By the same process, we can arrive at price equations for the iron and books industry, namely:

$$(90w + 9p_c + 12p_i + 0p_b)(1 + \pi) = 90p_i \qquad (6)$$

and

$$(20w + \ p_c + \ 2p_i + 2p_b)(1 + \pi) = 40p_b. \qquad (7)$$

Equations (5) through (7) form a system of three equations in *five* unknowns. Consequently, there cannot possibly be a single set of values of the variables that uniquely satisfies all three equations. Instead, there is an infinite number of such sets of values. In order to make the system determinate, we must somehow introduce more information, and thereby reduce the number of variables.

A first step (standard in the analysis of models of this sort) is to appeal to the fact that we do not really need three price variables. A system of prices is usually expressed in terms of one commodity, which is chosen as the unit of money in the system. For example, a pound of silver may be chosen as the unit of money, or "numeraire," and all other prices may then be expressed as multiples or fractions of pounds sterling. Or an ounce of gold may be selected as the unit of money. Or, in System C, a unit of corn may serve. When this is done, the "price" of a unit of the commodity functioning as money is arbitrarily set equal to 1. (This is mathematically the equivalent of dividing all of the other prices by the price of the money-commodity.)

Suppose that we choose corn as numeraire in System C and set its price equal to 1, thereby making all the other prices "corn prices," or prices expressed in units of corn. If we now substitute into equations (5) through (7) the new information, $p_c = 1$, we have:

$$(100w + 2 + 16p_i)(1 + \pi) = 300, \qquad (5')$$

$$(90w + 9 + 12p_i)(1 + \pi) = 90p_i, \qquad (6')$$

and

$$(20w + 1 + 2p_i + 2p_b)(1 + \pi) = 40p_b. \qquad (7')$$

This is a system of three equations in four unknowns: the relative prices of iron and theology books, the money wage in units of corn, and the profit rate (which is a pure number, or percentage, and hence is unaffected by choice of units). This is better, but our system still has one degree of freedom (one more variable than equations), and hence does not have a unique solution. What new information can we add to this model to advance our analysis?

Modern theorists recognize two economically meaningful ways to analyze this system. The first is to close the system by specifying the wage exogenously (i.e., from outside the system), which has the effect of reducing the system to three equations in three unknowns. Once we have added this new information about the wage, the remaining variables do in fact become determinate.[8] The second way is to reduce the

[8] See Appendix A, Section IV for a formal treatment of the necessary and sufficient conditions for the price equations to have economically meaningful solutions.

system to a single equation in two unknowns, the wage and the profit rate, and then to study the relationship between them.

Ricardo's original idea was rather deeper than either of these. He was convinced that prices were determined solely by the technical conditions of production, whereas the wage and the profit rate—the distributional variables—were determined by an ongoing struggle between the laboring class and the entrepreneurial class. The implication of this idea was that a system of equations like (5') through (7') should be soluble for the relative prices without specifying the wage or the profit rate. In fact, System C has deliberately been constructed to exemplify Ricardo's conjecture, as the following algebraic manipulations demonstrate:

$$(100w + 2 + 16p_i)(1 + \pi) = 300. \tag{5'}$$

$$(90w + 9 + 12p_i)(1 + \pi) = 90p_i. \tag{6'}$$

From (5')

$$1 + \pi = 300/(100w + 2 + 16p_i).$$

Substituting in (6')

$$90p_i = 10(30w + 3 + 4p_i)/(100w + 2 + 16p_i)$$

or

$$100wp_i + 2p_i + 16p_i^2 = 300w + 30 + 40p_i.$$

$$16p_i^2 + (100w - 38)p_i - (300w + 30) = 0$$

We can solve this equation, using the quadratic formula. Since the unknown quantity is a price, negative values of the variable have no economic meaning.

$$p_i = \{-(100w - 38) \pm [(100w - 38)^2 + (4)(16) \\ (300w + 30)]^{1/2}\}/32$$

$$p_i = \{-(100w - 38) \pm [(100w + 58)^2]^{1/2}\}/32$$

$$p_i = (-100w + 38 + 100w + 58)/32$$

$$p_i = 96/32$$

$$p_i = 3.$$

Thus, the wage drops out of the computation, showing thereby that relative prices are determined by the technical conditions of production, independently of the distributional variables.[9]

Finally, we are in a position to determine whether Ricardo's theory of natural price holds in System C. According to Ricardo, as we have interpreted him, natural prices are proportional to labor values, which is to say:

$$\lambda_c/p_c = \lambda_i/p_i = \lambda_b/p_b. \tag{1}$$

Substituting the values we have obtained for these six variables we have:

$$1/.4 = 3/1.2 = 1.5/.6,$$

which is true. So, in System C, Ricardo's labor theory of natural price, as we may call it, holds. What we have done, let me repeat, is to use the input/output technical data summarized in Table 3 to determine the labor values of the commodities produced in System C. Then we have used the same data, together with a number of powerful knowledge, behavioral, and institutional assumptions to determine the relative prices of the commodities. And finally, we have used the values and prices thus arrived at to test Ricardo's theory of price in System C.

[9] The price of theology books, p_b, can be determined once the price of iron is known. Thus:

from (7'),

$$(20w + 7 + 2p_b)(1 + \pi) = 40p_b;$$

from (6'),

$$(1 + \pi) = 300/(100w + 2 + 16p_i);$$

therefore

$$(1 + \pi) = 6/(2w + 1);$$

thus

$$(20w + 7 + 2p_b)[6/(2w + 1)] = 40p_b.$$

Simplifying

$$120w + 42 = (80w + 28)p_b;$$

$$p_b = 3/2.$$

If we substitute the values of p_c and p_i back into (5'), we can, by a few manipulations, arrive at the expression,

$$1 + \pi = 6/(2w + 1),$$

which exhibits the relationship between the wage and the profit rate. As w rises, $(2w + 1)$ rises, and hence $6/(2w + 1)$ falls. Therefore π falls. And conversely. We can immediately conclude that the distributional variables, π and w, are inversely related. This relationship, to which Ricardo attached great importance, is very difficult to observe when the interactions of prices, wages, and profit rates are analyzed verbally. In algebraic form, however, it is immediately manifest. It is the formal reflection of the necessary conflict of interest between the capitalist and laboring classes.

The central purpose of a theory of natural price, it will be recalled, is to assist us in analyzing the distribution of the physical surplus of commodities generated by the productive activities of the economy. In our original discussion of System C, we treated the food, clothing, and shelter consumed by the workers as part of the inputs required to keep the economy going. Modern economists tend to treat wages as a share of the surplus (speaking, in modern terminology, of the "net national product" as being "gross of wages"). But we shall continue to treat worker consumption as part of the physical requirements of the system, for that is how it was understood by Ricardo and Marx.

In order to study the allocation of the physical surplus, therefore, we must first specify how much corn, iron, and theology books are required in each cycle of production to reproduce the working class. The workers, of course, receive their wages in the form of money, and then buy their food, clothing, and shelter in the market at going prices. But if we are to determine the size and composition of the *physical* surplus, we must make some assumptions about precisely how they spend their wages.

Ricardo, and Marx after him, argued that workers by and large received wages adequate only for subsistence living, and that as a class they spent their money in pretty much the same way, for plain food, plain clothing, and simple lodging. They also assumed that as a class workers do not save. Since we have broken the economy of System C into only three sectors—corn (or food), iron (or non-agricultural necessities and capital goods), and theology books (somewhat facetiously construed as luxury items)—we may, following Ricardo and Marx, suppose that each worker spends his or her money wage for the same quantity of food, clothing, and shelter (corn and iron) with nothing left over for luxuries (theology books).[10] Since we are making no particular effort at historical realism in the analysis of System C, we may simply assume that workers receive a money wage of .5 per unit of labor (where the wage is measured in terms of the numeraire, corn), and that they all spend their wage on .2 units of corn (costing .2) and .1 units of iron (costing .3). The actual market basket of commodities, (.2 corn, .1 iron), purchased with the money wage is called by economists the *real wage*. Thus, we are assuming that in System C, the real wage is .2 units of corn and .1 units of iron per unit of labor delivered by the workers to the capitalists.

As we saw earlier, in System C the relationship between the money wage and the profit rate is given by the equation

$$(1 + \pi) = 6/(2w + 1).$$

It follows that with a money wage of .5/unit of labor, the profit rate, π, is 200 percent. (No attempt has been made to achieve historical realism!) Since we have assumed that (.2 corn, .1 iron)/unit of labor is a subsistence wage, it follows that the entire physical surplus is appropriated by the capitalists. To determine the size of the physical surplus, we must subtract the physical inputs, including those required by the

[10] At some relatively high level of aggregation, this assumption is not unrealistic for the world Marx and Ricardo were confronting. It may be that even workers on the margin of subsistence exhibit some measure of variation in the precise pattern of their expenditures, but if we group all spartan, non-luxurious foodstuffs together as "corn" and abstract from minor variations in the particular details of housing and clothing, it is likely that virtually all workers will spend their wage on the same basket of commodities.

workers as food, clothing, and shelter, from the gross outputs of corn, iron, and theology books. The result is a physical surplus of 246 units of corn, 39 units of iron, and 38 theology books.

At the natural prices prevailing in the system, this surplus has a value, in corn-money units, of:

$$(246 \times 1) + (39 \times 3) + (38 \times 1.5) = 420.$$

The total profit earned in all sectors can be ascertained by multiplying the price of all inputs by the profit markup. As Table 3 shows, a total of 210 units of labor, 12 units of corn, 30 units of iron, and 2 units of books are consumed as inputs throughout the system. Hence, the total profit appropriated by all capitalists, with the prices we have calculated and a profit rate of 200 percent is:

$$(210w + 12p_c + 30p_i + 2p_b) \times \pi = 420.$$

As expected, the profit appropriated by the capitalists just suffices to purchase the physical surplus remaining after the inputs for the next cycle have been deducted.[11]

With this analysis before us, it is now possible to give a preliminary account of Ricardo's answer to the three questions posed by the emergence of a physical surplus in an economy periodically reproducing itself. Who gets the surplus? The

---

[11] The question arises whether the *composition* of the physical surplus, not merely the value, will match the demand of the capitalists who go into the market to spend their profits. In the short run, of course, all manner of mismatches may occur, but in the long run one wishes to know whether the physical composition of the surplus will come to match capitalist demand (assuming, needless to say, that capitalist demand is itself stable). There are three possibilities for capitalist expenditure of profits: (1) the capitalists spend their entire profit on consumer goods, (2) the capitalists spend some of their profits on consumer goods and the rest on capital goods for the purpose of expanding output (the surplus and the money profit are both net of capital replacement, remember) or, finally, (3) the capitalists invest their entire profit in expanded output. Although it is not obvious, in fact, in all three cases, there is a set of activity levels for the several industries that just suffices to guarantee the correct mix of output, no matter how capitalists choose to combine expansion with luxury consumption. See Appendix A, Section V.1 for a formal proof.

capitalists, or entrepreneurs get the surplus. (We have not yet introduced Ricardo's villain, the landlord). How does the surplus-getter get the surplus? That is not quite so clear. The entrepreneur buys inputs, including labor, combines them, and sells the output at a profit. The simple answer, therefore, is that the capitalist class appropriates the physical surplus by making a money profit and then using it to buy the physical surplus. But it is not yet clear, as Marx was quite dramatically to point out, how it comes about that the capitalists make a profit. Finally, Ricardo, following Smith, argues that capitalists use their share of the physical surplus to expand the scope of production, thereby generating economic growth. Landlords, on the other hand, spend whatever money they can get on luxuries, drawing a portion of the physical surplus away from production and restricting economic growth.

Ricardo's theory of natural price works in System C. Does it work in every economy engaged in reproducing itself cyclically in the manner of System C? As a test of the theory, let us suppose that a more efficient technique has been discovered by the farmers in System C for producing corn. Previously, 100 units of labor were required to be combined with 2 units of corn and 16 units of iron to produce 300 units of corn. Henceforward, the same capital stock can produce the same output when combined with only 50 units of labor. (Once again, I stress that technological realism plays no role in this discussion.) The result, which we shall label System D, is as given in Table 4, assuming that subsistence remains unchanged.[12]

In order to calculate the labor values of corn, iron, and books in System D, we must form new labor value equations, for the conditions of production in the corn sector have now changed.

---

[12] For convenience, I have assumed that the labor force contracts sufficiently to maintain the same levels of output of corn, iron, and books. This corresponds, more or less, to Marx's picture of the situation. Ricardo, on the other hand, would expect that first the market price of corn would drop, leading to a secular growth in the labor force and an increased demand for corn coupled with a decline in the market price of labor to its natural level. Eventually, the economy would stabilize at a higher level of output.

TABLE 4. SYSTEM D

	Labor Input	Corn Input	Iron Input	Books Input	Output
Labor		32	16	0	160
Corn Sector	50	2	16	0	300
Iron Sector	90	9	12	0	90
Books Sector	20	1	2	2	40
Total Input	160	44	46	2	

Following the procedure by which we formulated equations (2) through (4), we obtain:

$$50 + 2\lambda_c + 16\lambda_i + 0\lambda_b = 300\lambda_c, \qquad (2')$$

$$90 + 9\lambda_c + 12\lambda_i + 0\lambda_b = 90\lambda_i, \qquad (3')$$

and

$$20 + \lambda_c + 2\lambda_i + 2\lambda_b = 40\lambda_b. \qquad (4')$$

When we solve equations (2′) through (4′) in order to obtain the labor values of corn, iron, and theology books in System D, using the same algebraic manipulations that gave us the labor values in System C, we find that:

$$\lambda_c \cong .2312$$

$$\lambda_i \cong 1.1811$$

$$\lambda_b \cong .5946$$

The change in the technology of corn production has altered not only the labor value of corn, but the labor value as well of iron and books. In each case, the new value is lower than the old one. A moment's reflection will show why this is so. The "labor value" of corn is simply the quantity of labor directly or indirectly required to produce a unit of corn. If a new technique of corn production is introduced which lowers the quantity of some commodity required as input, then clearly less labor will be required for the production of the corn output, because part of the labor required is precisely the labor embodied in the inputs. But with less labor required for the production of the same output of corn, the labor embodied in each unit of corn output will be smaller. Now, corn is required as an input into the iron and books industries. Hence, in those industries as well, less labor will be required indirectly for the same output, and so the labor value of iron and books will fall as well. In this way, a change in the conditions (or "facility") of production in one industry radiates throughout the entire economy.

To calculate the relative prices in System D, we must form new price equations, reflecting the altered conditions of production in the corn industry. Following the same procedure as before, with corn chosen as "money" or numeraire, we have:

$$(50w + 2 + 16p_i)(1 + \pi) = 300, \qquad (5^*)$$

$$(90w + 9 + 12p_i)(1 + \pi) = 90p_i, \qquad (6^*)$$

and

$$(20w + 1 + 2p_i + 2p_b)(1 + \pi) = 40p_b. \qquad (7^*)$$

When we attempt to calculate the relative prices and the profit rate in System D, we encounter a disturbing problem. In manipulating equations (5^*) through (7^*), we find that the wage, w, does *not* drop out of the calculation. In fact, the prices and the profit rate do not become determinate until we specify the wage. Following the same procedure used above, we will fix the real wage at .2 units of corn and .1 units of iron. If we substitute into our equations the expression $w = .2p_c + .1p_i$, and solve for the values of the variables, we obtain:

$$p_c = 1$$

$$p_i \cong 3.869$$

$$p_b \cong 1.962$$

$$w \cong .5869$$

$$\pi \cong 2.217$$

We can check to see whether Ricardo's theory of natural price holds for System D, as it did for System C, by substituting the labor values and prices just obtained into equation (1). When we do, we find that:

$$(p_c/\lambda_c) \cong 4.325$$

$$(p_i/\lambda_i) \cong 3.276$$

$$(p_b/\lambda_b) \cong 3.3$$

$$(w/\lambda_w) \cong 3.572$$

So it turns out that in System D, the natural prices are *not* at all proportional to the labor values. Ricardo's labor theory of natural price is wrong. This is not just a fluke. In fact, quite the opposite is the case. In order to make System C conform to Ricardo's theory, it was necessary to select the input/output figures very carefully. In most linear reproduction models of the sort we have been examining, relative prices are not particularly proportional to labor values at all.

Modern analysis has made it possible to determine exactly where Ricardo's theory goes wrong. Presently, we shall state the necessary and sufficient conditions for the labor theory of natural price to hold, and we shall see that an understanding of those conditions is essential for a proper interpretation of volume one of *Capital*. We shall also see that the impossibility of establishing the prices in System D independently of the wage and the profit rate is, formally speaking, merely a different manifestation of the same structural feature that makes the prices diverge from their corresponding labor values. For the moment, however, let us follow Ricardo's own thinking in this matter, for he knew full well that prices are not always proportional to labor values, and he even saw essentially *why* they are not.

As we have seen, in the heading of section three of the chapter on value in *Principles*, Ricardo announces the theory that the natural prices of commodities are determined by the labor indirectly as well as directly bestowed on them in the process of their production. Immediately following section three, Ricardo acknowledges the existence of other factors that affect natural price. The headings of sections four and five tell the story:

SECTION IV

The principle that the quantity of labour bestowed on the production of commodities regulates their relative value, considerably modified by the employment of machinery and other fixed and durable capital.

SECTION V

The principle that value does not vary with the rise or fall of wages, modified also by the unequal durability of capital, and by the unequal rapidity with which it is returned to its employer.

Ricardo states the point exactly correctly when he says: "If men employed no machinery in production but labour only, and were all the same length of time before they brought their commodities to market, the exchangeable value of their goods would be precisely in proportion to the quantity of labour employed."[13]

The problem, to put the point abstractly, is that the production of commodities requires time in addition to nature and human labor. In the calculation of the labor values—the quantities of labor directly and indirectly required for production—no account is taken of the time that must elapse between the moment when the bestowing of labor commences and the moment when the commodity appears on the market, available for sale. But in the rational calculations of prudent entrepreneurs, time plays a central role. A rate of return on capital invested is a percentage increment per period of time elapsed. If the ruling profit rate is 10 percent, the prudent capitalist will seek to earn 10 percent per annum on the value of capital invested, which is 21 percent in two years, 33.1 percent in three years, and so forth. Those commodities produced in a

[13] Ricardo (1951–73), vol. 1, p. 32.

TABLE 5. System E

	Labor Input	Corn Input	Iron Input	Output
Labor		3	3	6
Corn Sector	2	12	4	20
Iron Sector	4	1	1	10

more "roundabout" manner, to use Böhm-Bawerk's felicitous phrase, must sell at prices that deviate more significantly from their labor values in order for their producers to earn the society-wide rate of profit.

To see exactly how the varying roundaboutnesses affect relative prices, consider the detailed example in Table 5, constructed from the analysis of a simple corn/iron model, where the real wage is .5 units of corn and .5 units of iron per unit of labor. In this economy, $\lambda_c = .5$, and $\lambda_i = .5$. Thus, the labor theory of natural price predicts that corn and iron will exchange on a par in the market. But if we set $p_c = 1$, we find that $p_i = .6$, not 1. The money wage $w = .8$, and the profit rate $\pi = .25$, or 25 percent. Iron and corn each require for their production 1/2 unit of labor, directly and indirectly, per unit, but when they are brought to market, they exchange in the proportion 5:3, not at par. What causes this divergence?

Our analysis of the problem will be made easier if we rewrite Table 5 to exhibit the amounts of labor, corn, and iron inputs needed for the production of *single* units of corn or iron output. This can be accomplished simply by dividing the corn sector figures through by 20 and the iron sector figures through by 10. The result is given in Table 6.

A unit of corn requires only .1 unit of labor *directly* bestowed on its production, whereas a unit of iron requires .4 units of direct labor. The remaining .4 units of labor embodied in the unit of corn derive from the non-labor inputs, and are transmitted in production to the corn. Now, this .4 units of labor can be thought of as having been expended in earlier cycles of production. If we label the present production period P, then

TABLE 6. Unit Input Requirements for System E

	Labor Input	Corn Input	Iron Input	Output
Labor		.5	.5	1
Corn Sector	.1	.6	.2	1
Iron Sector	.4	.1	.1	1

the .6 units of corn and .2 units of iron which are required now (in P) for the production of a unit of corn were themselves produced in the just previous period $P - 1$. These bits of corn and iron themselves required direct labor inputs for their production in the previous time period. They also required, in their turn, corn and iron inputs, which, in an even earlier time period, required labor, and corn and iron, and so on.

To see explicitly how the compounding of the profit rate distorts prices away from labor values, let us first trace back through several periods the direct labor inputs that have led up to the production of a single unit of corn and of iron. Then let us calculate the current *prices* of those labor inputs, keeping in mind that their price has been progressively augmented, from period to period, by successive compounded applications of the profit rate $\pi = .25$. In effect, we are asking ourselves what a capitalist would have to charge for his unit of corn or iron in order to cover his costs, including a period-by-period profit markup equal to the economy-wide ruling or natural profit rate, which, as we have seen, is 25 percent. Table 7 summarizes the analysis through five cycles of production prior to the present one.

What Table 7 shows is the amount of labor that must be directly expended in each period of production, starting from the present and working backwards, in order to produce one unit each of corn and iron in the present period. Reading the table from right to left, we see that .1 unit of labor is required in the present period to produce one unit of corn. This is 20 percent of all the labor embodied in that unit of corn output. In the period just past, $P - 1$, 14/100 units of labor were

TABLE 7. Period-by-Period Labor Requirements for Units of Corn and Iron

	$P-5$	$P-4$	$P-3$	$P-2$	$P-1$	P
Corn Sector	$.0092_l$ $.0554_c \longrightarrow .0923_c$ $.0185_i$ $.0138_l$ $.0035_c \longrightarrow .0346_i$ $.0035_i$	$.0144_l$ $.0865_c \longrightarrow .1442_c$ $.0288_i$ $.0230_l$ $.0057_c \longrightarrow .0574_i$ $.0057_i$	$.0242_l$ $.1352_c \longrightarrow .242_c$ $.0484_i$ $.036_l$ $.009_c \longrightarrow .09_i$ $.009_i$	$.038_l$ $.228_c \longrightarrow .38_c$ $.076_i$ $.056_l$ $.014_c \longrightarrow .14_i$ $.014_i$	$.06_l$ $.36_c \longrightarrow .6_c$ $.12_i$ $.08_l$ $.02_c \longrightarrow .2_i$ $.02_i$	$.1_l$ $.6_c$ $.2_i$
Total Labor	$.0092+.0138$ $= .023$ 4.6%	$.0144+.0230$ $= .0374$ 7.48%	$.0242+.036$ $= .0602$ 12.04%	$.038+.056$ $= .094$ 18.8%	$.06+.08$ $= .14$ 28%	$.1$ 20%
Iron Sector	$.0018_l$ $.0110_c \longrightarrow .0183_c$ $.0037_i$ $.0027_l$ $.0007_c \longrightarrow .0068_i$ $.0007_i$	$.0029_l$ $.0172_c \longrightarrow .0287_c$ $.0057_i$ $.0043_l$ $.0011_c \longrightarrow .0107_i$ $.0011_i$	$.0045_l$ $.027_c \longrightarrow .045_c$ $.009_i$ $.007_l$ $.002_c \longrightarrow .02_i$ $.002_i$	$.007_l$ $.042_c \longrightarrow .07_c$ $.014_i$ $.012_l$ $.003_c \longrightarrow .03_i$ $.003_i$	$.01_l$ $.06_c \longrightarrow .1_c$ $.02_i$ $.04_l$ $.01_c \longrightarrow .1_i$ $.01_i$	$.4_l$ $.1_c$ $.1_i$
Total Labor	$.0018+.0027$ $= .0045$ $.9\%$	$.0029+.0043$ $= .0072$ 1.44%	$.0045+.007$ $= .0115$ 2.3%	$.007+.012$ $= .019$ 3.8%	$.01+.04$ $= .05$ 10%	$.4$ 80%

expended in order to produce the corn, iron, and labor that are needed in the present period. That labor constitutes 28 percent of the labor embodied in a single unit of current corn output. And so on, as we move backwards one production period at a time.

In the six most recent cycles of production including the present one, 98.4 percent of all the labor required to produce a unit of iron has been expended. What is more, 90 percent of the total has been expended in the present period and the one just preceding. In the same six cycles, only 90.9 percent of the labor required for the production of a unit of corn has been expended, and a mere 48 percent has been expended in the present period and the one preceding. With a price of labor $w = .8$, and a profit rate $\pi = .25$, we can now see how the relatively more distant or roundabout application of labor in corn production as compared with iron production drives the price of corn up above the price of iron.[14]

To see exactly what is happening, we can compare two sums. The first sum is formed by taking what a capitalist would have had to pay in period $P - 5$ for the .023 units of labor, multiplied by his profit markup of 1.25 over the six production periods that have elapsed up to the present moment, added to what he would have had to pay in period $P - 4$ for the .0374 units of labor, multiplied by the profit markup over the five production periods that have elapsed, and so forth, all the way up to what he has paid at the beginning of the present period for the .1 unit of labor, multiplied by one period's profit markup. This complicated sum represents what he must sell the unit of corn for in order to recover his outlay plus an average rate of profit. The central point, of course, is that the money he paid for wages back in period $P - 5$ is simply sunk in the product until he can sell the finished unit of corn at the end of the present production period. If he isn't earning a steady 25

---

[14] Strictly speaking, since we have set $p_c = 1$, the price of iron is driven down. Another way of demonstrating the same principle would be to normalize the price system by setting $w = 1$, in which case, of course, the price of corn relative to the wage would be 1.25, and the price of iron relative to the wage would be .75.

percent all that time, then he hasn't invested his money in the wisest way. (Strictly speaking, it probably isn't *this* capitalist who paid those wages five production periods ago, but since it was *some* capitalist, who by our hypothesis received the same 25 percent profit, we must include it in the sum.) The sum through six production periods—P back to $P - 5$—looks like this:

$$(.023)(.8)(1.25)^6 + (.0374)(.8)(1.25)^5 + (.0602)(.8)(1.25)^4$$
$$+ (.094)(.8)(1.25)^3 + (.14)(.8)(1.25)^2 + (.1)(.8)(1.25) \cong .701.$$

The same sum can be formed of the cost, including profit markup, of the labor bestowed on the production of a single unit of iron in the six production periods $P - 5$ through P, namely:

$$(.0045)(.8)(1.25)^6 + (.0072)(.8)(1.25)^5 + (.0115)(.8)(1.25)^4$$
$$+ (.019)(.8)(1.25)^3 + (.05)(.8)(1.25)^2 + (.4)(.8)(1.25) \cong .546.$$

Eventually, if we were to carry this process out through endlessly many previous production periods, the cost (including profit markup) of corn would converge on 1, and the cost of iron would converge on .6.

As the calculations show, in the backwards summation through six production periods, the price of corn has already overtaken the price of iron, even though less of the total labor required for its production has been taken into account. The reason for this is that the labor that has been taken account of was bestowed at an earlier time, and hence has been more powerfully affected by the compounding of the profit rate.

Ricardo was painfully aware of the fact that the failure of prices to be proportional to labor values undermined his entire economic theory. So long as prices *are* proportional to labor values, and so long therefore as the distributional variables, w and π, are independent of the prices of commodities, it is possible unambiguously to analyze the distribution of the social surplus. We can separate out the effects on the economy of a change in technology, which will show up as a change in relative prices, and a change in the distribution of the surplus, which will show up as a rise of the wage and a fall of the profit rate, or vice versa. Since labor values are derived directly from the technical conditions of production, they are unaffected by the way in which the surplus is divided between workers and capitalists—which is to say, they are independent of the values taken on by w and π. If prices are *proportional* to these labor values, then obviously prices as well will be independent of the wage and profit rate.

The converse is also true, though it may not be quite so obvious. If prices are independent of the wage and the profit rate, then they remain the same no matter what value π takes on. In particular, then, let $\pi = 0$. In that case, the price equations (5) through (7) of System C reduce to:

$$100w + 2p_c + 16p_i \qquad = 300p_c, \qquad (5^{**})$$

$$90w + 9p_c + 12p_i \qquad = 90p_i, \qquad (6^{**})$$

and

$$20w + \quad p_c + \quad 2p_i + 2p_b = 40p_b. \qquad (7^{**})$$

If we choose the wage as numeraire and set $w = 1$, then these equations become identical with the labor value equations (2) through (4), with $p_c = \lambda_c$, $p_i = \lambda_i$, and $p_b = \lambda_b$. Thus, when the wage and the profit rate are independent of prices, the prices are proportional to (and, for the appropriate numeraire, equal to) labor values.

In a system of this sort, a rise in the wage is unambiguously an improvement in the real (i.e., physical) income of the workers. Changes in relative prices will be a consequence solely of changes in the facility of production of commodities. Thus, it will be possible always to distinguish between objective or technical changes on the one hand and social or distributional changes on the other. To put the same point differently, it will always be possible to distinguish between a redistribution of the existing physical surplus and a technological change that alters the size and composition of the surplus.

But as our analysis of System D reveals, this lovely idea of Ricardo's is doomed to failure, as he himself knew. Although there is a good deal more of importance in Ricardo's political economy, including his theory of rent and his analysis of the determination of the real wage, from a strictly theoretical standpoint, Ricardo's labor theory of natural price comes to a dead halt right here. Just as Adam Smith was unable theoretically to extend his correct analysis of the early and rude state to the case in which the accumulation of stock and the appropriation of land has taken place, so Ricardo is unable to provide an adequate analysis of the deviation of natural prices from labor values as a consequence of unequal times that elapse between the bestowal of labor on the production of commodities and their realization, or sale, in the market.

What is it about some systems that makes their natural prices independent of the distributional variables and proportional to the labor values? Why is it that prices *are* proportional to labor values in System C, but are *not* in Systems D and E and so many other systems besides? Is there something peculiar about the structure of System C that yields this proportionality? Because we are dealing at so high a level of abstraction, in which our only data are the quantities of labor and commodities required as inputs in each line of production, the answer can only lie in some quantitative feature of the relative proportions in which the different inputs are combined.

In System E, as we saw, trouble arose as a consequence of the fact that 80 percent of all the labor embodied in a unit of corn was bestowed on it in the current production cycle, whereas only 20 percent of the labor embodied in a unit of iron was labor *directly* required in production. What, we might ask, are the proportions of labor directly bestowed and labor indirectly bestowed in the several sectors of System C?

In the corn sector of System C, 100 units of labor are bestowed directly on the production of the corn output. The non-labor inputs consist of 2 units of corn and 16 units of iron. These embody $2(.4) + 16(1.2) = 20$ units of labor, which is thus indirectly required for production. The ratio of labor directly required to labour indirectly required is $5:1$. Analogous calculations reveal that the same ratio, $5:1$, obtains in the iron and theology books sectors as well. Intuitively, we might guess that when the ratio of labor directly required to labor indirectly required is the same in all lines of production, then variations in the wage rate, and consequently in the profit rate, will affect all commodities proportionally, and hence will not alter the price of one commodity relative to another. An increase in the profit rate will, of course, work itself out more heavily the farther back in the past we carry our calculations, but since the proportion of labor directly to labor indirectly bestowed is the same for all commodities, no differential advantage will accrue to one commodity relative to another.

If we look back at Systems D and E, we find, as expected, that the ratios of labor directly required to labor indirectly required in the several sectors are widely divergent. In System D, for example, the ratio of direct labor inputs to embodied labor in the corn sector is roughly 2.58 to 1, whereas the ratio in the iron sector is 5.537 to 1. In System E, which was constructed to illustrate precisely this theoretical point, the divergence is even more striking. The ratio in corn is 1 to 4, and in iron it is 4 to 1.

The fact is that our general theoretical intuition is correct. In linear models like those we have been examining, so long as there is a positive rate of profit, natural prices are proportional to labor values *if and only if* the proportion of labor directly required to labor indirectly required is the same in all lines of production.[15] Ricardo's labor theory of natural price holds true for *all and only* those surplus-producing economies with positive rates of profit in which the ratio of labor directly bestowed on commodities in production to labor embodied in non-labor inputs and thereby indirectly bestowed on, or transmitted to, commodities in production is the same in all sectors.

Thus far, our result may appear to be little more than a theoretical curiosity, for the condition that direct to indirect labor ratios be the same in all industries is thoroughly contrary to

---

[15] See Appendix A, Section V.2 for a proof of this extremely important proposition. It is necessary to specify a positive rate of profit because in an economy with a zero profit rate, commodities exchange in proportion to their labor values regardless of the proportions of labor directly and indirectly bestowed in the several sectors.

economic experience, and without apparent significance. Since it is generally the case that agriculture is relatively labor intensive and industry is relatively capital intensive, we would never expect to find an actual economy that even approximated equal ratios of direct and indirect labor across the board.

The result takes on a much deeper historical and theoretical significance however, when we discover, as we shall presently, that it serves as the starting point for Marx's theoretical investigations. The condition of equality of proportion of direct to indirect labor is arithmetically equivalent to what, in the terminology of Karl Marx, is called "equal organic composition of capital." Beginning precisely at the point where Ricardo's theory fails, Marx writes all of volume one of *Capital* from the point of view of, or on the assumption of, the proportionality of prices to labor values. Only after he has thoroughly explored this theoretical terrain does he go on, in volume three, to examine the general case in which prices deviate from labor values. Why he should choose to adopt this course will turn out to be a key to understanding his theory of capitalist exploitation.

With the formulation of the conditions under which Ricardo's theory of natural price fails, we have come to the theoretical dead end of his system. Ricardo himself devoted his last several years to unsuccessful attempts to analyze the problem, and in an unfinished essay written during the final weeks of his life, we can see him still turning the puzzle this way and that.[16] Before turning to Marx, however, we must devote a few pages to the two portions of Ricardo's system that we have thus far passed over in silence, namely his theory of rent and his theory of the determination of the wage.

3. LAND AND LABOR

(i) *Ricardo's Theory of Rent*

Our analytical story began with Adam Smith's observation that commodities fail to exchange in proportion to the labor directly

---

[16] See Ricardo (1951–73), vol. 4, pp. 357–412.

required for their production once we acknowledge accumulations of capital stock and private appropriation of land. We have now completed our examination of Ricardo's theoretical attempt to take account of the accumulation of capital, but we have not yet considered how he proposed to handle the fact of privately appropriated land. Strictly speaking, the Ricardian theory of rent is not directly relevant to our story, for the problem of rent is a side issue for Marx. Nevertheless, Ricardo's solution to the puzzle of rent is one of the analytical high points of the classical period, and is well worth a slight detour.

All commodities are produced, directly or indirectly, by the mixing of human labor with nature. Nature is, as Locke put it, a free gift from God, and so long as human need—or, more accurately, effective market demand—falls short of the abundant fecundity of God's gift, the part played by nature in production has no *economic* significance. When fertile land is plentiful, it will make no difference should one man lay claim to a portion of it and seek, by force of arms or writ of law, to exclude others from it. The rest will simply move on to new land, equally fertile, and mix their labor with it. Nor will anyone be willing to pay so much as a farthing for the sheer privilege of working a piece of land, so long as equally good land remains unclaimed.

Indeed, even if *all* the fertile land has been appropriated, Ricardo supposes, virtually no rent will be paid so long as three conditions are fulfilled: first, no single landholding must comprise so large a share of the whole that some cultivation of *it* will be required to satisfy existing effective demand (this guarantees that no single landowner has a stranglehold on the market for corn). Second, landlords and entrepreneurs must be perfectly self-interestedly rational (this guarantees that we can make a priori predictions of their behavior purely on the basis of a calculation of their economic interest). And third, no collusion must take place either among landowners or among entrepreneurs (this eliminates the possibility of monopolies or monopsonies that destroy the effects of market competition). If a landowner were to attempt to charge a rent for the use of his land, competition from other landowners, whose holdings were earning no rent and had no alternative uses, would drive the prevailing rent virtually to zero.

Let us now suppose that through population growth, the demand for food rises until all the available land of the best quality is under cultivation. As demand continues to grow, the market price of corn will rise above its natural price, and the entrepreneurs who have invested in corn production will earn a superprofit. At this point, two things will happen. First, it will become profitable, for the first time, to bring into cultivation less fertile lands, lands which require a greater application of capital (more labor, more fertilizer, more tools) per unit of output. It will be profitable because even though a bushel of corn grown and harvested on this land costs more to produce, still the unnaturally elevated price of corn permits entrepreneurs consigned to the less profitable land to earn at least the going rate of profit, and possibly more. But second, these newly arrived entrepreneurs, seeing the much greater rate of return earned by those farming the original, more fertile land, will offer to pay a rent to the owners of this land for its use, because they can afford to pay a rent and still do better than on the less fertile land, for the use of which they pay nothing.

Competition over time equilibrates the system so that the rent paid on the less fertile land just absorbs the extra return that would otherwise accrue to the entrepreneurs who grow their corn on it. In this way, a single system-wide profit rate is reestablished. Four things have changed: more corn is being grown; some of the corn is being grown with a new, less efficient technique; a rent is being paid on the most fertile land; *and the price of corn has risen.*

In fact—and this is for Ricardo the theoretical point of the entire exercise—the price of corn is determined by the technical conditions (or "facility of production") on the *least* fertile land. It is those conditions that determine how much an entrepreneur will be willing to pay in order to shift his production to the more fertile land, and it is thus those conditions that determine how large a rent will be paid for the more fertile land.

Now, in a competitive economy, there can be only one natural price for each commodity, and only one profit rate. By hypothesis, no rent is paid on the less fertile land. Hence, rent plays no role in the price of the corn grown on that land. But since the price charged for that corn must be the single price at which all corn sells, it follows that rent plays no role at all in the determination of the price of corn. And that being so, rent plays no role at all in the determination of *any* price in the economy!

This is a remarkable and thoroughly counterintuitive conclusion, which merits a bit of reflection. To the entrepreneur who must pay for his seed, his tools, his machines, his labor, *and* for the use of the land on which he raises his crop, it certainly appears that rent plays a role in the determination of price. The entrepreneur who prices his output without allowing for rental charges will quickly go broke, no matter what David Ricardo says. If rent is not a cost of production, what then is it?

Ricardo's answer, quite simply, is that rent is a deduction from profits. It is a diversion to the landlords of a portion of the profits earned by the entrepreneur. Adam Smith and the others have the matter exactly backwards. The price of corn is not driven up by the rentals paid to the landlords. No doubt the landlords will extract whatever rent they can, but in a competitive market entrepreneurs will consent to the payment of a rent only if they can thereby gain access to fertile land for the growing of corn which can be sold dear on the market. As Ricardo says in one of the best-known tags of classical political economy, "Corn is not high because a rent is paid, but a rent is paid because corn is high."[17]

Ricardo's theory of rent is thus, among other things, an addendum to his answer to the question: Who gets the surplus? In an economy in which arable land is scarce, a portion of the surplus is appropriated by the landlords in the form of the rentals they charge for the use of their land. The market is the mechanism by which they get their rentals, and the size of their share of the surplus is determined by the relationship between the conditions of production on the most fertile land and on land of lesser fertility.

[17] Ricardo (1951–73), vol. 1, p. 74.

TABLE 8. System F

	Labor Input	Corn Input	Iron Input	Output
Labor		62	31	310
First Corn Sector	100	2	16	300
Second Corn Sector	120	3	18	300
Iron Sector	90	9	12	90

To see exactly what role rent plays in a Ricardian system, let us suppose that the production of the 300 units of corn in System C entirely exhausts the supply of the most fertile land, and that with the further growth of population, 300 units in addition are now demanded. The short-term rise in the market price of scarce corn generates temporary superprofits in the corn sector, leading entrepreneurs to bring under cultivation less fertile land. On this second-quality land, we shall assume, 120 units of labor (instead of 100) must be combined with 3 units of corn (instead of 2) and 18 units of iron (instead of 16) to produce 300 units of corn. This is obviously a more costly method of producing corn, and so a rent arises on the first-quality land (which we shall suppose comprises 10 acres). Omitting the theology books industry from consideration as irrelevant to these calculations, we now have a new, more complex system consisting of three sectors of production rather than two, namely System F, given in Table 8.[18]

---

[18] For the sake of simplicity, I have left the level of output in the iron industry unchanged. The 18 units of iron required in the second corn sector can be imagined to come from what was, in System C, the surplus iron. We may suppose that capitalists have cut back their final demand for luxury iron just enough to free up the iron needed for investment in the second corn sector. The additional labor is supplied either by previously unemployed workers or, in long-run equilibrium, by an enlarged population. Their real-wage iron requirements can also be thought of as coming from reduced capitalist luxury consumption in just the right amounts. Since this is a linear model, and we are interested at this point in the characteristics of a static system, no harm is done by these simplifying assumptions.

Continuing our assumption that a single price for corn and a single profit rate reign in the system, we can write the new price equations, taking care to introduce into the equation for the price of the corn grown on the first-quality land a rent on the ten acres under cultivation. Letting ρ stand for the rental per acre, we have:

$$(100w + 2p_c + 16p_i + 10\rho)(1 + \pi) = 300p_c, \tag{8}$$

$$(120w + 3p_c + 18p_i)(1 + \pi) = 300p_c, \tag{9}$$

and

$$(90w + 9p_c + 12p_i)(1 + \pi) = 90p_i. \tag{10}$$

Equations (9) and (10) form a system of two equations in four unknowns: w, p_c, p_i, and π. Setting $p_c = 1$, and fixing w by specifying a real wage, say (.2 corn, .1 iron)/unit of labor, so that $w = .2p_c + .1p_i$, we can solve these equations for the profit rate and the relative price of iron. The results are:

$$p_c = 1$$

$$p_i \cong 2.59$$

$$w \cong .459$$

$$\pi \cong 1.865$$

Notice that the price of corn is determined by the conditions of production on the *less* fertile land—the land that does not earn a rent. Since it is more difficult to produce corn on this land, the price of corn is driven up, and so we find that corn has become more expensive.[19] Most significantly, the profit rate has fallen, as indeed we would expect when one of the basic commodities in the system is produced by a less efficient method.

---

[19] The price of corn appears not to change, inasmuch as we have chosen it as numeraire, but of course its relative price changes—the ratio in which it exchanges for iron or labor—and that is all that matters.

With w, p_c, p_i, and π now determined, we can solve (8) for ρ, obtaining as a result $\rho \cong 1.5372/\text{acre}$. The rental rate is thus a thoroughly dependent magnitude in the system. It cannot vary independently, for if ρ were to rise or fall, equation (8) would cease to be consistent with the determinate equation system (9)–(10).

In real terms, what has taken place is a transfer of a portion of the entrepreneurial profit into the hands of the landlords, who collectively hold a monopoly of a scarce resource—fertile land. The money wage has changed, but by an amount just sufficient to permit workers to purchase the same market basket of goods at the new prices.[20] It follows that there is no real opposition of interest between the landed class and the working class. The real conflict is between the landed gentry and the capitalist class.

As the demand for corn grows, it is quite possible that all of the second-quality land will be brought under cultivation without satisfying demand. Even less fertile land will then be cultivated. The even less facile mode of production employed on the least fertile land will result in a still higher price for corn, and this in turn will increase the rent on the most fertile land and introduce for the first time a rent on the land of second quality. The rentals will differ by just enough to maintain a single economy-wide price for corn. The profit rate will of course fall. In this way, a schedule of graduated rents can come into existence on lands of decreasing fertility. Always, there will be no rent paid on the least fertile land, and it will be the conditions of production on *that* land that will determine the price of corn.

The reason for Ricardo's fear of a "stationary state" emerges clearly from this analysis. Ricardo, like Smith, was persuaded that economic growth would come only from the productive investment of the revenues of the capitalist class, not from the expenditures of rental income, which he saw as being unpro-

---

[20] This is not an inference, of course, but simply a reflection of the *assumption* that the real wage does not change. We shall discuss Ricardo's reasons for this assumption presently.

ductively consumed in the maintenance of a grand style of manorial living. As population growth increased the demand for food, ever less fertile land would be called into cultivation. Rentals would rise and the profit rate would fall, and a larger and larger share of the social surplus would be transferred to the unproductive consumption of the landlords. The portion of the surplus devoted to new investment would shrink until, at the horrible limit, the entire annual surplus would go for rent, and scarcely enough would remain in profits to encourage entrepreneurs even to undertake simple reproduction.[21]

(ii) Ricardo's Theory of Wage Labor

Labour, like all other things which are purchased or sold, and which may be increased or diminished in quantity, has its natural and its market price. The natural price of labour is that price which is necessary to enable the labourers, one with another, to subsist and to perpetuate their race, without either increase or diminution.[22]

The central fact of capitalism is the historic separation of the working class from the means of production, and the consequent emergence of wage labor. Dobb has remarked that Ricardo's argument against Adam Smith's "adding-up" theory of price "turned on his bringing money itself within the circle of commodities, and in doing so postulating that the price of any commodity or group of commodities can only rise if more labour is required to produce it relatively to the amount of labour required to produce an ounce of gold."[23] It could even

---

[21] Ricardo failed to anticipate the dramatic improvements in the facility of production of foodstuffs, as a consequence of scientific and technological innovation. The extraordinary decline in the proportion of the workforce devoted to agricultural labor testifies to the transforming impact of technical change over the past two centuries. Nevertheless, recent experiences with shortages of fossil fuels, and the consequent transfer of mammoth quantities of revenues to essentially unproductive owners of scarce resources, suggest that Ricardo's analytical intuition was quite acute.

[22] Ricardo (1951–73), vol. 1, p. 93.

[23] Dobb (1973), p. 77.

more pointedly be argued that the heart of Ricardo's theoretical advance lay in his bringing *labor* itself within the circle of commodities.

Everything in Ricardo's discussion in the chapter "On Wages" makes it clear that labor is to be analyzed as a produced commodity. The quantity of labor available on the market adjusts itself to long-run fluctuations in effective demand, just as does the quantity of corn or iron. And the natural price of labor is determined by the quantity of labor directly and indirectly bestowed upon *its* production. Clearly, the treatment of labor itself as a produced commodity, both by society and by the theorists of political economy, constitutes a development of enormous historical and theoretical importance. Since this theoretical and historical development lies at the heart of *Capital*, we shall postpone an extended discussion of it until we come to Marx's political economy. At this point in our story, let us confine ourselves to those points that are essential to an understanding of Ricardo's theory.

Ricardo was able to incorporate wage labor into an analysis of the value-determination of produced commodities by adopting Thomas Malthus's views concerning the growth and fluctuation of population in response to variations in the real wage. In the opening paragraphs of the *Principles*, Ricardo observes that there are some commodities "the value of which is determined by their scarcity alone. No labour," he says, "can increase the quantity of such goods, and therefore their value cannot be lowered by an increased supply." Ricardo cites the now classic examples of "some rare statues and pictures, scarce books and coins, [and] wines of a peculiar quality, which can be made only from grapes grown on a particular soil." But he brushes these sorts of commodities aside impatiently, noting that they "form a very small part of the mass of commodities daily exchanged in the market."[24] Like his fellow analysts of the burgeoning capitalism whose revolutionary productivity was even then pouring forth such heaps of commodities as had never been seen before, Ricardo focuses his theoretical attention on

[24] Ricardo (1951–73), vol. 1, p. 12.

common consumer and capital goods—corn, iron, linen, woolens—not on the luxury goods that had formed the predominant part of the trade of an earlier age. Rather than argue the matter at length, Ricardo simply lays it down as a stipulated constraint on his system that "in speaking then of commodities, of their exchangeable value, and of the laws which regulate their relative prices, we mean always such commodities only as can be increased in quantity by the exertion of human industry, and on the production of which competition operates without restraint."[25]

There are, however, two items on the market whose quantity seems, at first sight, not to be capable of increase at will, but whose importance to the economy does not permit us to consign them to the residual category of old pictures and fine wines, namely *land* and *labor*. The available acreage of arable land and the labor force seem to be fixed quantities that must be treated as parameters of any economic model, not as variables. Ricardo's theory of value, or indeed any theory of value that explains price as determined by cost of production, depends upon a successful treatment of the prices of land and labor—rent and the wage.

Ricardo has handled rent by adopting the West/Torrens/Malthus analysis, according to which the rental charged by landlords plays no role in the determination of price. To deal with labor, Ricardo takes up Malthus's theory that population adjusts itself to food supply. The wage is construed as the *price* of labor, and a cost-of-production account is given of the determination of that price. When excess demand for labor (during a period of rapid economic expansion, for example) drives the market price for labor above its natural price for any significant period of time, the working class responds by bearing and rearing more children. After a period of disequilibrium, the augmented supply of labor drives the market price down to its natural price.

In weighing the plausibility of the Ricardo/Malthus theory of the wage, particularly in comparison with Marx's alternative

[25] Ibid.

account of the "reserve army of the unemployed," we ought to keep in mind that Ricardo was writing at the beginning of the nineteenth century, at a time when the secular growth of the labor force was more significant than short-term fluctuations attendant upon business booms and busts.

Prudent capitalists choose the most efficient techniques available for the production of their commodities, combining just as little corn, iron, linen, and labor as is absolutely required by the technology of the period. Competition ensures that there will be no waste, for the entrepreneur who allows his tools and raw materials to be used with less than maximal efficiency will be driven to the wall by competition in the market.

So too, we are to suppose, workers adopt a technique for the reproduction of their labor—a standard of living, we call it—that is maximally efficient. The worker who insists on eating steak rather than potatoes, and who prices her product—her labor—to suit will find herself unable to sell her product on the market. She will be out of a job, in short. Thus, the natural or equilibrium price of labor will be a wage just sufficient to support a subsistence standard of living.

But to this Swiftian tale, Ricardo adds the crucially important qualification that habit and custom, history and culture, in part determine what will count, at any moment, as *subsistence*. One passage will suffice to represent Ricardo's views on this subject, which are not very systematically developed:

> It is not to be understood that the natural price of labour, estimated even in food and necessaries, is absolutely fixed and constant. It varies at different times in the same country, and very materially differs in different countries. It essentially depends on the habits and customs of the people. An English labourer would consider his wages under their natural rate, and too scanty to support a family, if they enabled him to purchase no other food than potatoes, and to live in no better habitation than a mud cabin; yet these moderate demands of nature are often deemed sufficient in countries where "man's life is cheap," and his wants easily satisfied. Many of the conveniences now

enjoyed in an English cottage, would have been thought luxuries at an earlier period of our history.[26]

Ricardo shows no awareness that the collective definition of subsistence might be a matter over which classes could struggle, nor, needless to say, does he evince any recognition of the deep epistemological problems posed by the possibility that the cognition of certain elements of social reality is an object of class conflict.

One of the peculiar consequences of Ricardo's assimilation of the reproduction of the working class to the entrepreneurial production of commodities is that in his theoretical model, workers are the only producers who have a significant positive interest in employing suboptimal methods of production insofar as they are able! From an economic point of view, an improvement in the standard of living of the working class is a step backward to a less efficient method of production. A higher standard of living means less capital available for investment and growth.

Piero Sraffa, in his modern reconstruction of the Ricardian perspective, adopts an alternative way of analyzing the price of labor. He treats all wage payments as a distribution of a portion of the surplus, in the manner of neoclassical theory but *not* of classical or Marxian theory.[27] He then studies the relationship between the wage and the profit rate, allowing each to vary from zero to its maximum magnitude. If we look back at System C, for example, we can calculate that π reaches its maximum at $\pi = 5$, when $w = 0$. When $\pi = 0$, $w = 2.5$ units of corn. This mode of analysis has a number of implications, all of which seem to me to be unfortunate for a fruitful exploration of capitalist economies.

The first is that as far as the formal structure of the model is concerned, the wage rate can in principle sink to zero, leaving

[26] Ricardo (1951–73), vol. I, chap. 5. Note that Ricardo employs the phrase "man's life is cheap" in its literally correct sense, to mean not that people care little for human life but simply that the cost of reproduction of a human being is low.

[27] Sraffa (1960), pp. 9–10.

the workers to live on air. A rise in the wage above zero is construed as a reflection of some positive measure of political or bargaining power of the working class. But this is contrary to capitalist reality. As Ricardo and Marx quite correctly observe, at any specific moment in history there is a physically and socially defined conception of subsistence that determines a floor below which the real wage may not for long be allowed to fall.

Viewed from the perspective of Ricardo and Marx, labor/management bargaining takes two quite distinct forms. The first is a struggle over the distribution of what is acknowledged to be surplus, with capital seeking to drive labor's wage down to subsistence, and labor seeking to raise the wage above subsistence. The second is a struggle over the social definition of reality itself—a struggle over what shall count as part of subsistence. Are medical services *necessary*, or are they a luxury? Are pensions necessary, or are they too luxuries? Is meat a necessary part of a working-class diet? And so on. The periodic redefinition by the U.S. Bureau of Labor Statistics of a poverty-level standard of living for a family of four is merely the latest and most sophisticated version of this old struggle.

When scarcity of labor drives the market wage above the natural wage (as defined by the conditions of subsistence), workers strive to preserve their gain by redefining "subsistence." Capitalists meanwhile seek to drive down the natural wage by branding costly elements of the working-class real wage bundle as luxuries that are unnecessary and inimical to a satisfactory rate of capital accumulation. The importance of this direction of analysis lies precisely in its identification of the ways in which the collective social definition of reality supercedes merely technical production relations. This in turn introduces an historical dimension into what is otherwise a timeless analysis of objective input/output proportions. Sraffa's analysis confuses the two quite different forms of labor/capital struggle.

The second consequence of treating wages as a distribution from surplus is that wage goods (food, clothing, and shelter) must be construed formally as luxuries rather than as inputs into production. Food, on this construal, is not directly or indirectly *required* for the production of all commodities, even though labor is directly required in all industries, because it is in theory possible for workers to consume nothing at all. It follows that a change in the facility of production of corn will have no effect on the profit rate. Aside from the fact that this consequence is utterly false to Ricardo's intentions and underlying ideas, it is, I suggest, a quite unfortunate analytical implication to build into one's basic model.

Third, the Sraffa line of analysis construes labor as a scarce good whose supply is determined outside the economy, not as a produced commodity whose natural price is governed by the conditions of its reproduction and whose available quantity is regulated by market forces. In short, labor is, in Sraffa's model, exactly like land. Now, the Sraffa/Ricardo analysis of rent portrays it as a distribution of a portion of the surplus to landowners as a consequence of the scarcity of land of the best quality. When land of the best quality is not in short supply, competition together with the rational self-interest of the landowners drives rental charges to zero. But as far as any analytical feature of Sraffa's formal model is concerned, labor ought therefore to earn no wage at all. The workers, like the landowners, are the possessors of a factor of production that is in excess supply and has no alternative uses. In therefore ought to bear a zero price.

More generally, insofar as we distinguish skill levels, and admit alternate techniques of production using labor of differing skill levels, we can suppose that when all the most highly skilled workers have been employed at vanishingly low wages, a rent will arise on their scarce skills, and they will begin to receive this wage while their less-skilled brethren receive no wage at all for unskilled labor. The wage, like ground rent, will thus be seen as a distribution of the surplus, having no effect on prices. On this analysis, which is indeed implicit in the Sraffa approach, the only difference between landlords and laborers is the extra-economic fact that workers organize to drive the wage above its natural economic level, for example by unionization or other techniques for creating artificial scarcity, whereas landlords do not.

This is certainly a consistent way of handling labor and the wage, but it is, I suggest, quite unsatisfactory. First of all, it entirely ignores the purely physical or biological preconditions for the survival of the workers. Second, it belies the central fact that what is commonly accepted as a subsistence level of existence is socially determined. Third, it loses entirely the analytically powerful idea that the wage is related to the cost of reproduction of labor, an idea which is central to the entire classical tradition. For these reasons, I believe Sraffa is wrong to adopt the analytical line he does, and in the later portions of this book, I shall follow the Ricardo/Marx proposal to treat the wage as determined by the cost of reproduction of labor.

FOUR

* * * *

MARX'S THEORY OF EXPLOITATION AND SURPLUS VALUE

1. The Theoretical Presuppositions of Volume One of *Capital*

Our analytical narrative halted with Ricardo's failure to explain or account adequately for the deviations of natural prices from labor values in those cases in which the ratio of labor directly required to labor indirectly required varies from sector to sector. As we pick up the story again in volume one of *Capital*, we must make sure we understand precisely the level of Marx's understanding of Ricardo's problem and the theoretical perspective with which he begins his exposition.

First, however, we must introduce some new terminology, in order to make Marx's theoretical standpoint comparable with that of Ricardo. For analytical purposes, Marx defines a number of value categories and ratios. The principal categories are *constant capital*, symbolized by *c*, *variable capital*, symbolized by *v*, and *surplus value*, symbolized here by *s* (Marx used *m*, for *Mehrwert*, in the German). The fundamental analytical distinction, for Marx, is between capital outlays that necessarily contribute exactly their value equivalent to the output in production, no more and no less—hence *constant* capital—and capital outlays that depending on the circumstances, may contribute now more, now less to the value of the product—hence *variable* capital. Marx claims that labor power, and only labor power, is capable of creating new value. Hence only labor power can impart to the product a quantum of value different from what is embodied within it. So constant capital, c, is the labor value of all the production inputs save labor, and variable capital, v, is the labor value of the labor inputs. Surplus value, s, is the extra value imparted by the labor inputs to the output.

Marx defines three ratios that play a central role in his analysis. The ratio between the surplus value, s, and the value of the labor inputs, v, in a line of production—in other words, the fraction s/v—is called by him the "rate of surplus value." He also labels this ratio the "rate of exploitation." The ratio between the surplus value extracted from the economy and the labor value of the total capital input, including labor, which is to say the fraction $s/(c + v)$, is called the "value rate of profit." Finally, the ratio between the value of the non-labor inputs and the value of the labor inputs, in other words the fraction c/v, is labeled the "organic composition of capital."[1]

Let us begin with a fact which is now well known, but which was not known at all by the nineteenth-century readers of Marx, namely that virtually all the materials which eventually came to be published as volumes one, two, and three of *Capital* and as the three parts of *Theories of Surplus Value* were in existence, on paper, before volume one of *Capital* was published in 1867.[2] It follows that we are justified in assuming that Marx had clearly in mind any theoretical principles or presuppositions that can be found prominently set forth anywhere in the entire corpus. Generally speaking, it is unwise to treat a complex thinker as though he or she were thoroughgoingly consistent. Commentators frequently go wrong in supposing that the old Plato or the old Kant had directly present to his mind whatever he had put down on paper or tablet decades earlier. But Marx was working on the entire mass of materials

---

[1] Marx's value categories are actually rather confused in certain respects. For a detailed analysis and reconstruction of the major categories, with rigorous definitions of them in modern formal terms, see Appendix B.

[2] For a detailed account of the composition of *Capital*, see Rosdolsky (1977), part 1. The three parts of *Theories of Surplus Value* are usually referred to as volume four of *Capital*.

during the same relatively short span of time, and if there are solid *theoretical* grounds for imputing to him a position that finds adequate textual expression somewhere in the four volumes of *Capital*, then we can be reasonably confident that he really did intend to commit himself to it.

It is my contention that Marx understood the fundamental theoretical situation quite well. He knew that Ricardo's theory of natural price is valid for all *and only* those cases in which each sector of the economy exhibits the same organic composition of capital. Nevertheless, for deep and quite coherent reasons, he chose to limit the discussion in volume one of *Capital* to those special cases in which the ratios *are* equal and in which, therefore, commodities do in fact exchange precisely in proportion to the labor directly or indirectly required for their production. Marx deferred consideration of Ricardo's problem to volume three of *Capital*.

This interpretation of volume one is not original, by any means, but it is certainly controversial, and it is perhaps worth a few paragraphs to muster some textual evidence and hermeneutical argumentation in its support. I wish to advance three related propositions:

(1) Marx *says* that volume one of *Capital* has been written on the assumption that commodities exchange at their labor values.

(2) Marx *knows* that commodities exchange at their labor values if and only if (with a positive rate of profit), the organic composition of capital is the same in all lines of production. (The proposition that an economy has equal organic composition of capital is mathematically equivalent to the proposition that all sectors exhibit the same ratio of labor directly required to labor indirectly required, a fact which Marx appears *not* to have known.)[3]

(3) And finally, in volume one, Marx repeatedly shifts from calculations in terms of hours of labor time to

[3] See Appendix A, Section V.3 for a proof of this proposition.

calculations in terms of shillings and pence, a practice that makes sense only if commodities are exchanging at their labor values.

Let us take a look at the evidence.

(1) Marx *says* that volume one of *Capital* has been written on the assumption that commodities exchange at their labor values.

Marx lays the theoretical basis for the introduction of the concept of surplus value in the chapter of volume one entitled "Contradictions in the Formula of Capital." The central idea, as we shall see presently, is that in an economy in which all commodities exchange at their (labor) values, there seems to be no explanation for the fact that capitalists regularly exit from each cycle of production and exchange with augmented holdings. The argument does not absolutely *require* the assumption that natural prices equal labor values, but such an assumption makes the precise theoretical point being argued much cleaner and more striking. In that chapter, after considering the efforts of previous authors to trace capitalist profit to such sources as a general upping of prices above values, Marx observes: "It is true, commodities may be sold at prices deviating from their values, but these deviations are to be considered as infractions of the laws of the exchange of commodities, which in its normal state is an exchange of equivalents, consequently, no method for increasing value."[4] Two pages later, he summarizes his argument in these words: "The creation of surplus-value, and therefore the conversion of money into capital, can consequently be explained neither on the assumption that commodities are sold above their value, nor that they are bought below their value."[5] Several chapters later, he develops the analytical notion of the "rate of surplus value" by means of a detailed example in the course of which he uses

[4] Marx (1967a), pp. 158–159.
[5] Ibid., p. 161.

money prices despite the fact that he is talking about a ratio between quantities of labor. Marx simply asserts: "The calculations given in the text are intended merely as illustrations. We have in fact assumed that prices = values. We shall, however, see in Book III. [i.e., volume three of *Capital*], that even in the case of average prices the assumption cannot be made in this very simple manner."[6] Much later in volume one, in a chapter dealing with "Changes in Magnitude in the Price of Labour-Power and in Surplus-Value," Marx again flatly states: "I assume (1) that commodities are sold at their value; (2) that the price of labour-power rises occasionally above its value, but never sinks below it."[7] Finally, when Marx arrives, in volume three, at a direct confrontation with the original Ricardian problem of the deviation of natural prices from labor values, he states: "In Books I and II we dealt only with the *value* of commodities. On the one hand, the *cost-price* has now been singled out as a part of this value, and, on the other, the *price of production* of commodities has been developed as its converted form."[8]

(2) Marx *knows* that commodities exchange at their labor values if and only if (with a positive rate of profit) the several sectors of the economy exhibit equal organic composition of capital.

A certain amount of editorial hindsight is required before we can impute to Marx knowledge of the relevant proposition. First of all, as I have already pointed out, Marx seems not to have known that an economy exhibits equal organic composition of capital in all sectors if and only if all sectors have the same ratio of labor directly required to labor indirectly required. Second, although it is reasonable to suppose that he was in

[6] Ibid., p. 220n.
[7] Ibid., p. 519. Compare Adam Smith's remark that "the market price of any particular commodity, though it may continue long above, can seldom continue long below, its natural price" (1937, chap. 7).
[8] Marx (1967c), p. 163.

some sense implicitly aware of the fact that commodities exchange at their values when there is a zero rate of profit, regardless of organic composition, I am not sure that he ever formulated this proposition explicitly.[9]

Third, Marx seems *not* to have understood the difference between saying that commodities exchange *at* their values and saying that commodities exchange *in proportion to* their values. To say that commodities exchange *at* their values is to say (confusedly) that the price of a commodity *is* its labor value, a statement that ignores the difference between the units in which one measures labor values and the units in which one measures prices. To say that commodities exchange *in proportion to* their values is to say (quite properly and meaningfully) that the ratio of the labor value of commodity A to its price equals the ratio of the labor value of commodity B to *its* price, for all A and B. The two statements can be made to coincide simply enough, by setting the price of a unit quantity of

[9] There are a number of passages in which Marx manifests an implicit awareness of the principle involved. For example, in chapter ten of volume three of *Capital*, Marx writes: "Suppose, the labourers themselves are in possession of their respective means of production and exchange their commodities with one another. In that case these commodities would not be products of capital. The value of the various means of labour and raw materials would differ in accordance with the technical nature of the labours performed in the different branches of production. Furthermore, aside from the unequal value of the means of production employed by them, they would require different quantities of means of production for given quantities of labour, depending on whether a certain commodity can be finished in one hour, another in one day, and so forth. Also suppose the labourers work an equal average length of time, allowing for compensations that arise from the different labour intensities, etc. In such a case, two labourers would, first, both have replaced their outlays, the cost-prices of the consumed means of production, in the commodities which make up the product of their day's work. These outlays would differ, depending on the technical nature of their labour. Secondly, both of them would have created equal amounts of new value, namely the working-day added by them to the means of production. This would comprise their wages plus the surplus-value, the latter representing surplus-labour over and above their necessary wants, the product of which would however belong to them. . . . The exchange of commodities at their values, or approximately at their values, thus requires a much lower stage than their exchange at their prices of production, which requires a definite level of capitalist development" (1967c), pp. 175–177. See also Engels's gloss on this passage in the supplement to volume three, pp. 895ff.

the commodity chosen as numeraire equal to that commodity's labor value rather than to 1, but Marx clearly did not grasp this technical point, as is made manifest by his improper formulation of the "conservation principles" in chapter ten of volume three. Finally, for reasons that are bound up in rather complex ways with his attempted solution of the problem of the deviation of natural prices from labor values, Marx many times made incorrect assertions about the relation of prices to values in industries with "average" organic composition of capital. Nevertheless, once we have taken these theoretical errors and shortcomings into account, I think we can impute to Marx a clear knowledge of the analytical conditions under which commodities exchange at their values.

The evidence is found, for the most part, in the second part of *Theories of Surplus Value*, in Marx's analysis and critique of the political economy of Ricardo. In the chapter entitled "Ricardo's and Adam Smith's Theory of Cost-Price (Refutation)," Marx analyzes at length a number of examples of economies in which natural prices deviate from labor values because of unequal organic compositions of capital in different lines of production. He says, for example: "This is far more applicable to those commodities into whose composition the various organic constituents enter in the average proportion, and whose period of circulation and reproduction is also of average length. For these, cost-price and value coincide, because for them, and only for them, average profit coincides with their actual surplus-value."[10] Much earlier, in discussing

---

[10] Marx (1968), p. 199. As we shall see later on, Marx thought that the total quantity of surplus value extracted in the economy as a whole in a given cycle of production from all the direct labor inputs exactly equals the total money profit accumulated by all the capitalists in that cycle (a proposition that is, strictly speaking, meaningless unless some stipulation is made concerning the relation of the numeraire to the unit in which labor value is calculated). The competitive equalization of the profit rate, he argued, has the effect of distorting prices away from labor values, so that in capital-intensive industries, profits exceed surplus value, while in labor-intensive industries they fall short. It seemed intuitively obvious to Marx that in industries of "average" organic composition—industries, that is, whose proportion of constant to variable capital equals the proportion in the economy as a whole—the prices of the commodities produced in those industries would suffer

Rodbertus, Marx writes: "The amount of surplus-value produced by capitals of *equal* size varies *firstly* according to the correlation of their organic components."[11] Later in that lengthy discussion, Marx flatly asserts: "With the commodities of the particular sphere of production where the ratio of variable capital to the total sum of capital advanced (assuming the rate of surplus-value to be given) corresponds to the average ratio of social capital—value equals average price."[12]

From this it follows, of course, that if every line of production were to exhibit an organic composition equal to the

---

no distortion, and hence would exactly equal their labor values. Marx was wrong, however, as the following example shows:

SYSTEM J

corn sector:	20 labor	5 corn	0 iron	5 tools	⟶	35 corn
iron sector:	10 labor	0 corn	0 iron	5 tools	⟶	40 iron
tool sector:	10 labor	0 corn	30 iron	0 tools	⟶	12.5 tools

The real wage in System J is .5 corn/unit of labor. The labor values in the system are $\lambda_c = 1$, $\lambda_i = .5$, $\lambda_t = 2$, and $\lambda_w = .5$. If we set the price of corn equal to 1, then the remaining prices are $p_i \cong .567$ and $p_t \cong 2.675$. Quite obviously, prices are not proportional to labor values. The organic composition of the economy as a whole (this is the only thing Marx can possibly mean by "average organic composition") is 40 constant capital:20 variable capital (in calculating organic composition, one measures not the total direct labor input but the labor value of the direct labor input—the "necessary" labor, as Marx calls it), and this exactly equals the organic composition of the iron industry, which is 10 constant capital:5 variable capital. However, inspection reveals that the price of iron deviates from the labor value of iron. What is more, if the price of iron is set equal to the labor value of iron, thereby effectively deflating the price system by a factor of approximately .8818, then the surplus value extracted from the labor inputs in the iron industry is *not* equal to the profit earned in the iron industry, as Marx claims it should be. The problem, as Marx sometimes dimly saw, is that prices, even in an industry like iron whose organic composition mirrors that of the economy as a whole, are shaped by the organic composition of the other industries which produce the commodities that serve as inputs. A variation in the relative employment of iron, tools, and corn, while leaving the aggregate constant capital in the iron industry unchanged, might produce a complex distortion of prices.

[11] Marx (1968), p. 28. See also p. 34.
[12] Ibid., p. 70.

"average"—which is to say if all lines of production were to exhibit the same organic composition—then prices would equal values throughout the economy. Marx many times makes the same assertion in various forms.

(3) Marx writes volume one of *Capital* as though commodities exchange at their labor values.

The evidence for this assertion consists simply in observing that in passage after passage, Marx speaks indifferently of money prices or labor time without ever bothering to remind us of what he so obviously well knows, that money prices may deviate from labor values. Once the concept of surplus value has been introduced, for example, Marx invokes the rhetorically powerful device of dividing the workday into necessary labor time and surplus labor time, defining the former as the time during which the worker performs the labor necessary to reproduce his or her conditions of existence, and the latter as that variable quantity of extra labor which creates the new value appropriated by the capitalist.

In the chapter on "The Rate of Surplus-Value," to choose one example among many, Marx begins by defining the ratio (surplus value)/(variable capital) in terms of pounds and shillings. He then defines the ratio (surplus labor)/(necessary labor), and asserts that the two ratios are equal, and "express the same thing in different ways."[13] All such equations of labor-time ratios to monetary ratios presuppose that commodities exchange at their labor values—that the consumption goods which the workers purchase with their wages sell at prices neither above nor below their values.

2. Surplus Value and the Critique of Capitalist Exploitation

We may now have established *that* Marx wrote all of volume one of *Capital* from a theoretical perspective that entirely overlooks Ricardo's most serious problem, but we have not yet

[13] Marx (1967a), p. 218.

explained *why* he did so. The answer, which is rather complex, is that Marx perceived an anterior problem with the classical theoretical position, so deep and far-reaching that it afflicts even the special case in which the proportionality of prices to labor values holds. His first task, Marx believes, is to expose that problem and to reconstruct the classical theory accordingly.

He is willing to postpone consideration of the deviation of prices from values for three reasons: first, because he believes that this new problem pertains to the underlying reality of capitalism, whereas the deviation of prices from values is merely one of the superficial ways in which capitalism manages to mystify its appearances so as to conceal the reality of exploitation from our view; second, because there is so much theoretical gold to be mined from the deeper problem and its solution that Marx will need an entire volume simply to lay out his results, before he even gets to subsequent and subsidiary problems; and third, because Marx believes that the solution to the deeper problem carries within it the solution to the Ricardian problem of the deviation of prices from values.

What is the deeper problem? Paraphrasing Heidegger (and also Leibniz), we may say that Marx poses to Ricardo and the classical economists the challenge: Why is there in general profit, and not nothing?

The problem is this. Assume that in the sphere of circulation, all commodities exchange at their values—neither above nor below (which, strictly speaking, is to say that the prices are proportional to labor values). Each capitalist purchases his inputs—corn, iron, lumber, tools, labor—at their labor values. He combines them in the production process—or, more precisely, he commands that they be combined—and he then takes the finished product back into the marketplace, where, by hypothesis, it sells at *its* labor value. When the cycle is completed, the capitalist recovers a quantum of money equal in labor value to the value embodied in his commodity, equal therefore presumably to the value embodied in the inputs into that commodity, and hence equal in value to what he paid for those inputs. But nothing more. Whence therefore the profit,

the increment of new value which, as we all know, each capitalist successfully claims as his right at the end of each cycle
of production and circulation?

At the close of chapter five of *Capital*, volume one, entitled "Contradictions in the General Formula of Capital," Marx
poses his problem with a mocking Aesopian tag:

> The conversion of money into capital [which is to say, the
> appearance of an increment, of a *profit*] has to be explained
> on the basis of the laws that regulate the exchange of
> commodities, in such a way that the starting-point is the
> exchange of equivalents. Our friend, Moneybags [*Geld-
> besitzer*], who as yet is only an embryo capitalist, must buy
> his commodities at their value, must sell them at their
> value, and yet at the end of the process must withdraw
> more value from circulation than he threw into it at start-
> ing. His development into a full-grown capitalist must
> take place, both within the sphere of circulation and with-
> out it. These are the conditions of the problem. *Hic Rhodus,
> hic salta!*[14]

To the first sentence of this paragraph, Marx appends a
long note which, at one and the same time, expresses the depth
of his insight into the problem and also the degree of the
confusion to which he is still subject. It is worth examining the
note in its entirety:

> From the foregoing investigation, the reader will see that
> this statement only means that the formation of capital
> must be possible even though the price and value of a
> commodity be the same; for its formation cannot be at-
> tributed to any deviation of the one from the other. If
> prices actually differ from values, we must, first of all, re-
> duce the former to the latter, in other words, treat the dif-
> ference as accidental in order that the phenomena may be

[14] Ibid., p. 166. ("Here is Rhodes! Jump here!" refers to a braggart who
claimed to have made a great jump in Rhodes.)

observed in their purity, and our observations not interfered with by disturbing circumstances that have nothing to do with the process in question. We know, moreover, that this reduction is no mere scientific process. The continual oscillations in prices, their rising and falling, compensate each other, and reduce themselves to an average price, which is their hidden regulator. It forms the guiding star of the merchant or the manufacturer in every undertaking that requires time. He knows that when a long period of time is taken, commodities are sold neither over nor under, but at their average price. If therefore he thought about the matter at all, he would formulate the problem of the formation of capital as follows: How can we account for the origin of capital on the supposition that prices are regulated by the average price, i.e. ultimately by the value of the commodities? I say "ultimately" because average prices do not directly coincide with the values of commodities, as Adam Smith, Ricardo, and others believe.[15]

The footnote begins clearly with the statement that the origin of profit must be explained without appeal to the deviation of natural prices from labor values. Capitalists will earn a profit even in those special circumstances under which prices coincide with labor values. Hence, any explanation of the origin of profit must abstract from the quite separate fact that natural prices, under most conditions of reproduction, diverge from labor values.

Now Marx begins to confuse the deviation of natural prices from labor values with the entirely separate phenomenon of the fluctuation of market prices around natural prices. This fluctuation, which has nothing whatsoever to do with the problem under discussion, can indeed be described, albeit somewhat inaccurately, as an oscillation around the mean, and Marx is perfectly correct in saying that in long-run equilibrium, commodities sell at their natural (i.e., "average") prices.

[15] Marx (1967a), p. 166.

But at this point, Marx seems to realize that he has strayed from the original point of the footnote, and so, rather confusedly, he pulls himself back to the subject of the deviation of natural prices from labor values, concluding with the remark (mistaken with regard to Ricardo, certainly) that "average [i.e., natural] prices do not directly coincide with the values of commodities, as Adam Smith, Ricardo, and others believe."

Despite the multiple confusions, the central point of the note is perfectly clear and quite correct. No explanation of the origin of capitalist profit can be allowed which traces it to the fact that natural prices deviate from labor values. Such an explanation would imply that in economies exhibiting equal organic composition of capital, entrepreneurs would reap no profit from their investments, an implication, Marx rightly insists, that is quite false.[16]

If the quantum of new value which the capitalist appropriates as his profit cannot be discovered in the sphere of circulation, where equals exchange for equals (and, by the hypothesis

---

[16] By parallel reasoning, it should be noted, we must reject as unacceptable any explanation of the origin of profit that traces it to the capitalists' tendency to squeeze more labor time, and more intensive laboring, from their workers than they and the workers contract for in the marketplace. Despite the enormous power and emotional impact of his accounts of the quasi-political struggles in the workplace between capital and labor, Marx is committed to the proposition that exploitation occurs, and hence profits arise, even in the most benign capitalist setting, in which capitalists scrupulously extract from their workers only as much, and as intense, laboring as was anticipated and agreed upon when the wage bargain was struck. This fact, as we shall see, contributes to the power of Marx's explanation of the origin of profit, but also creates enormous theoretical obstacles to any sort of formal treatment, within a Marxian model of price formation, of domination in the workplace.

One of the reviewers of this work for the Press has questioned the interpretation offered here of the lengthy footnote at the end of chapter five of volume one of *Capital*, suggesting instead that the entire note is unambiguously, and unconfusedly, about the deviation of market prices from natural prices. But I do not believe that can be the correct interpretation, for the note is appended to a sentence that reads: "The conversion of money into capital has to be explained on the basis of the laws that regulate the exchange of commodities, in such a way that the starting-point is the exchange of equivalents." But it is not the deviation of market price from natural price that raises questions about the "exchange of equivalents." It is the deviation of natural prices from labour values that does so.

of volume one, where commodities exchange at their labor values), then, Marx argues, it must be the case that the new value arises outside the sphere of circulation. Within circulation, it is only the *exchange* value of commodities that matters. Their individuating qualitative particularity, those concrete characteristics that make commodities *useful* in this way or that, figure not at all in the processes or calculations attendant upon exchange. But when the capitalist removes his purchases from the market and repairs to the factory, then for a time the exchangeable nature of the commodities retreats to the background and their specific qualities as fuel, raw materials, or tools come to the fore.

Now, by the methods of computation that underlie the classical theory of price, commodities on which a certain quantity of labor has been bestowed transmit or pass on that embodied labor to the commodities produced from them or with their aid.[17] As they are consumed or used up in production, the labor embodied in them is progressively transmitted to their products, until when they are entirely used up or worn out as means of production, their value is exhausted.[18] It would seem, therefore, that nothing is to be gained in our pursuit of the secret of profit by the move from the sphere of circulation to the sphere of production. In circulation, equals exchange for equals and no extra quantum of value, no profit, is thereby generated. In production, the labor embodied in the inputs, and already fully accounted for in their purchase price, is transmitted piecemeal to the outputs, with neither gain nor loss in the factory of average efficiency. How can any increment of extra value arise here? "In order to be able to extract value from the

---

[17] See, for example, Ricardo (1951), vol. 1, chap. 1, section 3: "of the durable implement only a small portion of its value would be *transferred to the commodity*" (emphasis added).

[18] This statement, which has the sound of a description based upon observation, is of course in reality a tautology following necessarily from the accounting procedures employed to impute to the cost of each unit of output some appropriate portion of the cost or value of the inputs. The classical economists, including Marx, generally adopt the simplest form of straight-line depreciation, despite the fact that Marx at least recognizes some of the difficulties with such accounting procedures.

consumption of a commodity," Marx writes with deliberate and bitter irony, "our friend, Moneybags, must be so lucky as to find, within the sphere of circulation, in the market, a commodity, whose use-value possesses the peculiar property of being a source of value, whose actual consumption, therefore, is itself an embodiment of labour, and, consequently, a creation of value. The possessor of money does find on the market such a special commodity in capacity for labour or labour-power."[19]

In this remarkable passage, Marx suddenly explodes all of classical political economy. In the space created by the explosion there appears for the first time the pivotal concept of Marx's critique of capitalism: *exploitation*. The deeper logic of Marx's argument is very peculiar indeed, and we shall have a great deal to say about it later. For the present, let us simply rehearse the surface, so to speak, of Marx's explanation of the origin of profit.

Labor, as measured in units of time—hours, say—is the substance of value. It is what value in itself *is*. This Marx takes here either as given by classical political economy or else as having been proved by the hasty arguments at the opening of chapter one. Objects *have* value by virtue of embodying labor. (I pass over for the moment the crucially important qualification that this labor must be, in Marx's terms, abstract homogeneous socially necessary labor.) When a commodity is produced, human labor is embodied or "congealed" in it. When that commodity is consumed, the labor embodied within it is yielded up. If the commodity is consumed unproductively (not consumed, that is to say, in the efficient production of a new commodity), then the labor embodied within it is extinguished and drops out of the economic system. If the commodity is productively consumed, then the labor embodied within it is transmitted to the product.

Farmers sell corn and weavers sell cloth. But wage earners have nothing to sell save their labor power, which is to say they sell, or rent out, their capacity to labor. The capitalist who hires a worker buys for the day her ability to labor. When

[19] Marx (1967a), p. 167.

the capitalist "consumes" what he has bought, by setting the worker to work in his factory, the worker, by laboring, bestows new labor, new value, on the commodity being produced. The old "dead" labor embodied in the worker's labor power—the labor that in previous periods produced the food, clothing, and shelter that the worker had to consume in order to be ready to work this day—is used up and extinguished. If the worker labors for more hours each day than it took to produce her own laboring capacity for that day, then she will create a quantum of new value that is greater than was embodied in her labor power. If she labors for fewer hours, then she will create less new value than is extinguished by her laboring.[20]

Suppose that a worker's capacity to labor for one day contains or embodies a quantum of value equal to six hours of laboring. If the worker works for six hours, she just manages to create as much new value as is extinguished by the productive consumption of her labor power. But should the capitalist manage to extract eight or even ten hours of laboring from her, as most assuredly he will, then the total new value freshly created and embodied in the product will be one-third or even two-thirds greater than the old value embodied in the labor power and used up in the course of the workday. Assuming the capitalist has paid a price for the labor power equal, but *only equal*, to its value—which is to say, a price equal to six hours of laboring—he will indeed exit the production process with a quantum of new value. The products which he takes from his factory back into the market will be worth more than (i.e., will embody more labor value than) the totality of all the

---

[20] There is obviously a theoretical glitch in Marx's argument. In order to maintain strict parity between labor power as a commodity and other commodities, Marx *ought* to say that when the worker's labor power is productively consumed, its value is transmitted to the finished product. Then, *in addition*, some new value may be created, depending on how long the worker labors and how much value is already embodied in her labor power. But such a characterization of the situation does not comport with Marx's claim that all productive laboring is the creation of new value.

commodities, including labor power, that he purchased during his last trip to the market and that he brought with him into his factory.

One question remains to be answered before the argument is complete. How is the value of labor power itself determined? By this I of course mean *not* how we discover or ascertain what the value of labor power is, but rather what it is that confers upon labor power the value it has. Marx's answer, like Ricardo's before him, is that the value of labor power is determined precisely as the value of all commodities is determined, by the quantity of labor that has been bestowed, directly and indirectly, on its production. The worker eats food, wears clothes, inhabits a dwelling, and in general consumes some set of commodities in order to stay alive and replenish her physical and spiritual powers so that she may be able to labor for another day. Allowing something for depreciation of the worker's capital stock (her body) which must in time be replaced (by her children), we arrive at whatever historically and culturally determined standard of living is *required* on average to maintain and reproduce the worker's labor power. The labor directly and indirectly required to produce the market basket of commodities that constitutes a subsistence living is the labor embodied in labor power. The *value* of labor power is simply equal to the quantity of labor embodied in it. Under the conditions Marx has posited for volume one, according to which commodities exchange at their values, the money wage, or natural price of labor power, is simply equal to the labor value of that labor power.[21]

---

[21] The worker buys food, clothing, and shelter as "inputs" into her productive activity," the reproduction of her labor power. But she also expends a good deal of labor time cooking the food, mending the clothes (or perhaps making them), and caring for her dwelling. This labor time does *not* play any role in the determination of the value of labor power. If workers purchase labor services on the market—the services of a doctor, a tailor, a plumber, say—that labor *does* enter into the value of labor power. Why is this, and what is its significance? The simple answer is that only what Marx calls abstract socially necessary labor time, labor time that has acquired the status of value by virtue of its role in the production of commodities, enters into the

Now Marx can answer the question, Why is there in general profit in a capitalist system, and not nothing, even under those special circumstances in which commodities do indeed exchange at their labor values? The extra quantum of value, or as Marx will hereafter call it, the surplus value (*Mehrwert*), consists precisely in the value created by the workers during those hours of laboring which they perform over and above what is required in the economy to reproduce the labor power which is being used up as they labor. Since in at least one sense, "exploitation" is "the extraction from a productive input of more value than is contained within it," the labor power of the workers is, in a capitalist economy, *exploited*.

Marx defines the *rate of surplus value* as the ratio of the surplus value extracted from a unit of labor power to the value of that labor power. If 6 hours a day are required to reproduce a worker's labor power and yet the worker labors for 10 hours, then the *rate of surplus value* is 4:6 or 66 2/3 percent. Profits are simply the surplus value produced by the workers and appropriated by the capitalists. Having purchased all the inputs into the production process, including the labor power, at their fair and full value, they naturally and (by bourgeois law) rightfully lay claim to ownership of the finished commodities. It is obvious on reflection that in such a system, there

---

determination of the labor value of those commodities. The extra-systematic laboring of workers off the job, although indispensable for their survival (if they do not cook their own food, who will?), does not exist economically and contributes nothing to the production of value. The significance of this fact is that by virtue of the bizarre and paradoxical construal of workers as "producers" of a commodity called "labor power." the entire family structure and private world on which bourgeois society and the capitalist economy rests is systematically ignored in classical political economy. The exploitation of women and children within the family, the maintenance of a several-tiered wage structure premised on the existence of the household as the primary unit of consumption, and much more are concealed in the simple fact that the labor within the family does not figure in the subsistence wage. A number of socialist feminist theorists are currently attempting to develop models of intrafamily exploitation that can be incorporated into the Marxian model of capitalist exploitation. See Folbre (1982).

will be a positive rate of surplus value if and only if there is a positive rate of profit.

3. LABOR AS THE SUBSTANCE OF VALUE

Marx's answer to the question, Whence profit?, rests upon a conception of labor as the substance of (exchange) value. This conception first appears in the opening pages of chapter one. The following lengthy abstract contains the heart of Marx's statement of the case:

> Exchange-value, at first sight, presents itself as a quantitative relation, as the proportion in which values in use of one sort are exchanged for those of another sort, a relation constantly changing with time and place. Hence exchange-value appears to be something accidental and purely relative, and consequently an intrinsic value, *i.e.*, an exchange-value that is inseparably connected with, inherent in commodities, seems a contradiction in terms. Let us consider the matter a little more closely. . . .
>
> Let us take two commodities, *e.g.*, corn and iron. The proportions in which they are exchangeable, whatever those proportions may be, can always be represented by an equation in which a given quantity of corn is equated to some quantity of iron: *e.g.*, 1 quarter corn = x cwt. iron. What does this equation tell us? It tells us that in two different things—in 1 quarter of corn and x cwt. of iron, there exists in equal quantities something common to both. The two things must therefore be equal to a third, which in itself is neither the one nor the other. Each of them, so far as it is exchange-value, must therefore be reducible to this third. . . . [T]he exchange-values of commodities must be capable of being expressed in terms of something common to them all, of which thing they represent a greater or less quantity.
>
> This common "something" cannot be either a geometrical, a chemical, or any other natural property of commodities. Such properties claim our attention only insofar

as they affect the utility of those commodities, make them use-values. But the exchange of commodities is evidently an act characterised by a total abstraction from use-value . . . .

If then we leave out of consideration the use-value of commodities, they have only one common property left, that of being products of labour. But even the product of labour itself has undergone a change in our hands. If we make abstraction from its use-value, we make abstraction at the same time from the material elements and shapes that make the product a use-value; we see in it no longer a table, a house, yarn, or any other useful thing. Its existence as a material thing is put out of sight. Neither can it any longer be regarded as the product of the labour of the joiner, the mason, the spinner, or of any other definite kind of productive labour. Along with the useful qualities of the products themselves, we put out of sight both the useful character of the various kinds of labour embodied in them, and the concrete forms of that labour; there is nothing left but what is common to them all; all are reduced to one and the same sort of labour, human labour in the abstract.

Let us now consider the residue of each of these products; it consists of the same unsubstantial reality in each, a mere congelation of homogeneous human labour, of labour-power expended without regard to the mode of its expenditure. All that these things now tell us is, that human labour-power has been expended in their production, that human labour is embodied in them. When looked at as crystals of this social substance, common to them all, they are—Values.[22]

The importance to Marx of this argument can be judged by his well-known remark, in a letter to Engels written just after the completion of volume one, that "[One of] the best

[22] Marx (1967a), pp. 36–38.

things in my book [is] the *double character of labor*, according to whether it is expressed in use value or exchange value."[23]

The argument itself is notoriously weak. Commodities, Marx says, cannot establish stable exchange relations with one another unless they share a common characteristic in stable quantitative proportions. Commodities, upon inspection and reflection, are seen to have nothing in common save the characteristic of being products of human labor—labor, furthermore, that can appropriately be considered abstract, homogeneous, and socially necessary. Hence, such abstract labor is the substance of value.

But commodites *do* have something else in common, besides the fact that they are all products of human labor. They all satisfy human needs and desires—in short, they are sources of subjective satisfaction or utility.[24] To be sure, the needs or desires that they satisfy are extremely varied, but so too are the labors that produce them. If it is possible to abstract from the variations in those labors, and ground a theory of price determination on the concept of labor in general, then why can we not abstract from the variations in needs and desires, and ground a theory of price determination on the concept of satisfaction in general? Since we know, as Marx could not, that the decade following the publication of *Capital* would see the introduction of no fewer than three versions of a subjective utility theory of natural price, we can hardly feel comfortable with Marx's first justification of the thesis that labor is the substance of value.

Marx's real argument comes not in the opening pages of chapter one, which can best be construed as a rehearsal of the theoretical presuppositions presented to Marx by the then-dominant Ricardian school, but rather in chapter six, "The

[23] MEW (1958–66), vol. 31, p. 326. See also the letter of 8 January 1868, in which Marx adds a third contribution—the treatment of time wages and piece wages (ibid., vol. 32, p. 11).
[24] E. Böhm-Bawerk, in a famous critique of Marx entitled *Karl Marx and the Close of His System*, makes the same point. See Böhm-Bawerk (1974), p. 75.

Buying and Selling of Labour-Power."[25] The theoretical legitimation of the distinction between labor and labor power, of the concept of surplus value, and of the associated concept of exploitation, according to Marx, consists ultimately in the fact that with them, *and with them alone,* can we solve the qualitative and quantitative riddle of the origin of profit in a capitalist economy.

Moneybags must be so lucky, Marx says, as to find a commodity whose use value possesses the peculiar property of being a source of value, and so he does, in "capacity for labor" or labor power. "Moneybags must be so lucky": we may read this bitter remark with Marx's observation, much later on in volume one, that "to be a productive labourer is . . . not a piece of luck, but a misfortune."[26] Marx invites us to imagine, in madcap Alice-in-Wonderland fashion, that the fundamental wage-labor relation between capital and labor is no more than a historical and ontological accident. Had the divine artificer cast the world in a slightly different mold, it might have been corn or iron or linen which was so unfortunate as to be the substance of value. In that case, we may suppose, the miseries of the working class would have been borne by fields of grain, or lodes of iron ore, and workers would not suffer the indignity of exploitation!

Perhaps the misfortune of producing that commodity whose usufruct is the substance of value is not, by itself, enough to bring down on one's head the sufferings of exploitation. Perhaps this fact must be conjoined to a second accident, namely that with regard to the product of the working classes, but with regard to no other product, we can distinguish between the commodity itself and the commodity's employment, between labor power and labor. In the space that opens up between these two, there appears *surplus labor time,* the source of that surplus value whose realization in the market is profit.

---

[25] Note that the Moore/Aveling/Engels translation of Marx's *Capital* divides certain chapters, so that, for example, what I am here calling chapter six is actually the third subsection of chapter four in the German.
[26] Marx (1967a), p. 509.

4. ABSTRACT HOMOGENEOUS
SOCIALLY NECESSARY LABOR

Thus far, we have been speaking as though Marx's account of the embodiment of human laboring in commodities proceeds in essentially the same way as that of Ricardo. In fact, of course, there is a fundamental difference between Marx's conception of labor and that of his predecessors. In contrast to Ricardo and the other previous labor-value theorists, Marx argues that it is not concrete human laboring, but labor in the abstract, homogeneous labor, that becomes embodied in commodities and forms the substance of their value. The following passages capture Marx's position:

> Some people might think that if the value of a commodity is determined by the quantity of the labour spent on it, the more idle and unskilful the labourer, the more valuable would his commodity be, because more time would be required in its production. The labour, however, that forms the substance of value, is homogeneous human labour, expenditure of one uniform labour-power. The total labour-power of society, which is embodied in the sum total of the values of all commodities produced by that society, counts here as one homogeneous mass of human labour-power, composed though it be of innumerable individual units. Each of these units is the same as any other, so far as it has the character of the average labour-power of society, and takes effect as such; that is, so far as it requires for producing a commodity, no more time than is needed on an average, no more than is socially necessary. The labour-time socially necessary is that required to produce an article under the normal conditions of production, and with the average degree of skill and intensity prevalent at the time. . . .
>
> We see then that that which determines the magnitude of the value of any article is the amount of labour socially necessary, or the labour-time socially necessary for its production. . . .

On the one hand all labour is, speaking physiologically, an expenditure of human labour-power, and in its character of identical abstract human labour, it creates and forms the value of commodities. On the other hand, all labour is the expenditure of human labour-power in a special form and with a definite aim, and in this, its character of concrete useful labour, it produces use values.[27]

The stipulation that we speak in terms of socially necessary labor carries with it the peculiar—and, on Marx's part, deliberately paradoxical—consequence that a quantum of laboring may *retroactively* become socially unnecessary, and hence not form a part of the value-substance congealed or crystallized in the commodity on whose production it has been expended. A capitalist may hire workers, set them to work in a factory using techniques of average efficiency, work them at average intensity, complete his production process in a manner of average efficiency, and yet find, upon bringing his wares to market, that through no fault of his own there has been a shift in demand that deprives him of customers. His inability to sell his goods, to "realize their value," retroactively deprives the laboring of his workers of its socially necessary character. It turns out that they have *not* been embodying new value in the goods they have been making—at least, not the quantum of new value that the time, intensity, and efficiency of their laboring might have led us to suppose.

As Marx explains in considerable detail, a lengthy and complex historical and social development must take place before it is meaningful to employ the concept of "abstract homogeneous socially necessary laboring." A progressive standardization of the labor process and of the commodities produced must be combined with a progressive destruction of traditional craft skills, a separation of workers from ownership of the means of production, a freeing of entrepreneurs from all state restrictions on prices, wages, location and technique of production, and so forth.

[27] Ibid., pp. 39 and 46.

Equally important, and not at all emphasized by Marx, the concept of abstract homogeneous socially necessary labor is a *theoretical* concept. It is formed not by abstraction from observations, but by a process of a priori reasoning within a model of a competitive capitalist economy that is equilibrated by a system of natural prices, a single wage rate, and a uniform rate of return on the value of capital invested.

Imagine two automobile production workers, John and Mary, who perform identical assembly-line tasks in plants of identical (and average) efficiency, working at identical (and average) intensity. John, we may suppose, works for Ford, and Mary for Chrysler. Under these assumptions, John and Mary embody in the automobiles that pass them on the line equal quantities of abstract homogeneous socially necessary labor.

Now suppose that the vice president in charge of the truck division of Ford adopts a new technique of truck production which—thanks to his incompetence—is substandard for the industry, with the result that the truck division (which is *not* the division in which John works) starts to produce trucks at a higher than average cost in labor time.

John, of course, has not altered his actual laboring activity in the slightest, nor have the other workers who, together with him, assemble Ford sedans. However, the Ford Motor Company as a whole has dropped below average efficiency by the standards of the industry, thanks to the unwise decision by the vice president of the truck division. Consequently, John is no longer embodying as much abstract homogeneous socially necessary labor in *his* product as Mary is in hers!

Lee Iacocca's misreading of the tastes of the American people may subsequently cause Chrysler to accumulate large parking lots of unsold cars, in which case it will turn out, retroactively, that Mary was embodying even less abstract homogeneous socially necessary labor in her product than was John.

The point of this somewhat puckish example is to force us to recognize that "abstract homogeneous socially necessary labor" is essentially a theoretical notion. In this case, it is invoked as an accounting notion for the purpose of imputing the costs of production to output. Saying that laboring has retroactively become socially unnecessary is a deliberately provocative way of saying that the rational firm will "write off" the cost of such labor, after discovering that the goods produced with it cannot be sold.

The statement that a yard of linen cloth embodies a certain quantum of abstract homogeneous socially necessary labor is, as Marx shows us, *not* a statement that can be given meaning in abstraction from the historical process by which commodity production comes into being. Nor is it a statement whose meaning can be separated from the entire social and economic context within which full-scale commodity production takes place. Furthermore, its truth depends on the conditions of production throughout the economy, not simply in the linen industry. This follows from the fact that the quantity of labor embodied in a yard of linen is in part a function of the labor value of the capital inputs into the linen industry, and hence is in part a function of the conditions of production in every industry whose output serves, directly or indirectly, as input into the industries that produce the capital inputs into the linen industry.

But even after we posit the historical development of capitalist commodity production, we still cannot treat statements about the embodiment of quanta of abstract homogeneous socially necessary labor in commodities as *descriptive*. It is a mistake, as Marx frequently tells us, to go looking in feudal, or slave, or other pre-capitalist societies for such distinctively capitalist economic phenomena as capital, profits, and wage labor. But it is equally a mistake to go looking for them in a capitalist economy, if by "looking" we mean "inspecting the bits and pieces of evidence presented to our senses." Even in a capitalist economy, we can *find* such theoretical entities only by means of a thoroughgoing theoretical interpretation of the facts in the context of a model of a competitive economy equilibrated by a uniform rate of return on the value of invested capital.

This point is important enough to warrant some development. Marx frequently writes as though the quantity of abstract labor congealed in a commodity were a characteristic of that commodity open to inspection, although he knows better than anyone how mystified and fetishistic such a way of thinking is. He also writes as though one could ascertain the amount of abstract labor embodied in a commodity by examining the input requirements of the entire industry of which the individual commodity is a product. But that too is a form of fetishism, or perhaps it is simply a theoretical error. As we have several times seen, the quantity of abstract labor embodied in a commodity is a function of the input requirements of *all* the industries that contribute, directly or indirectly, to its production. A change in the efficiency of production of some other industry that indirectly supplies inputs into the given commodity will alter the quantity of abstract labor "embodied" in it, even though it obviously works no physical change in the commodity. Nothing short of a theoretical analysis of the structure of the entire economy will suffice to yield the answer to the simple question, How much abstract homogeneous socially necessary labor is congealed in a commodity?[28]

Marx frequently analyzes examples couched in terms of the money costs of the several inputs into the production of a commodity. Usually he works in terms of percentages, assuming, for example, that a money capital of 50 (meaning 50 percent) is invested in wages and a money capital of 50 (i.e., the other 50 percent) is invested in non-labor inputs, yielding a total return of 120 (i.e., a profit of 20 percent). Now, this procedure is acceptable in the special case of equal organic composition of capital, for then the prices are proportional to the labor values. But in general, as he well knows, prices deviate from labor values, and it is quite unacceptable to analyze the embodied labor of commodities in terms of the money costs of the production of the commodity.

---

[28] It is, I realize, quite provocative and controversial to speak of Marx himself as having suffered from a fetishistic misunderstanding of the nature of embodied labor. Nevertheless, I believe that an examination of the texts bears me out. For a detailed look at the problem, with emphasis on the technical confusions to which this fetishistic thinking gives rise in Marx's theory, see Appendix B.

What this means—and it is a problem Marx never confronted—is that we cannot allow the market to serve as our calculator of labor values. We cannot treat prices—not even natural, or equilibrium, prices—as measures of embodied labor. Only a full-scale theoretical analysis of the sort developed by the economist Wassily Leontief will enable us to compute the quantities of abstract homogeneous socially necessary labor required for the production of individual commodities.

FIVE

MARX'S THEORY OF
NATURAL PRICE

1. The Quantitative
Determination of Surplus Value

Marx has answered the *qualitative* question: What is profit? Profit is surplus value, extracted from the workers. But we have not yet addressed his answer to the *quantitative* question: How much profit is appropriated by the capitalists? Marx's answer to the first question carries with it implicitly an answer to the second. The total profit in the sort of capitalist economy we are examining in volume one of *Capital* must be exactly equal to the total surplus value extracted from the labor inputs into production anywhere in the system.

By way of illustration, let us return to System C in which, we may recall, $\lambda_c = .4$, $\lambda_i = 1.2$, and $\lambda_b = .6$. (See Table 3.) Three hundred units of corn, 90 units of iron, and 40 units

Table 3. System C

	Labor Input	Corn Input	Iron Input	Books Input	Output
Labor		42	21	0	210
Corn Sector	100	2	16	0	300
Iron Sector	90	9	12	0	90
Books Sector	20	1	2	2	40
Total Input	210	54	51	2	

of books are produced in three single-product industries. The economy as a whole employs 210 units of labor. In order to make a quantitative test of the claim that profit is simply surplus labor extracted from workers, we must calculate both the total profit appropriated in the system as a whole and the total amount of surplus labor time extracted from the working class as a whole.

In analyzing System C, we arbitrarily assumed that the workers earn a money wage large enough to enable them to consume .2 units of corn and .1 unit of iron for each unit of labor they sell. Since the labor value of a unit of corn is .4 and the labor value of a unit of iron is 1.2, the labor value of the real wage must be $(.2)(.4) + (.1)(1.2) = .2$. What this means, quite simply, is that it takes two-tenths of an hour of labor somewhere or other in the system to produce the corn and iron required to replenish a worker's ability to labor for one hour. Put another way, in System C it takes only 20 percent of the workday to reproduce the worker's capacity to work for another day.

Two-tenths of a unit of labor are required to reproduce 1 unit of labor. But when that unit of labor is consumed productively, it contributes a full unit of new labor value to the output. It follows that .8 units of surplus value are extracted from each unit of labor consumed productively in the system. The system requires 210 units as a whole, and so $(.8 \times 210) = 168$ units of surplus labor are extracted from the labor inputs.

The total profit appropriated in System C in one cycle of production can be found by taking the aggregate price of all the inputs, including the labor inputs, and multiplying it by the profit rate. With the price of corn set equal to 1, the price system, we found, is:

$$p_c = 1$$

$$p_i = 3$$

$$p_b = 1.5$$

$$w = .5$$

$$\pi = 2$$

As Table 3 shows, 210 units of labor, 12 units of corn, 30 units of iron, and 2 units of books are used as inputs. The total profit is therefore:

$$\text{total profit in C} = (210w + 12p_c + 30p_i + 2p_b) \times 2$$
$$= [(210)(.5) + (12)(1) + (30)(3)$$
$$+ (2)(1.5)] \times 2$$
$$= 420.$$

Thus far, however, no comparison can be made between surplus labor value and profit, for they are measured in different units. In order to compare the two, we must somehow make the *prices* of commodities commensurable with their *labor values*. We can accomplish this by choosing labor time as our money, and by selecting our units so that the price of corn, say, is set equal to its labor value. In other words, we can stipulate that $p_c = .4$ hours. This has the effect of deflating the entire nominal monetary system by 60 percent.

When we carry out this deflation, we discover that the total profit in C, measured in labor-hour units rather than in corn units, is just $(420 \times .4)$, which is to say 168. In System C, at any rate, Marx is right. Total profits just equal total surplus labor extracted from the labor inputs.

A closer examination of System C shows that not only in the system as a whole but also in each industry, the profit appropriated exactly equals the surplus value extracted from the labor inputs into that industry. In the iron sector, for example, 90 units of labor are used up, yielding a surplus value of $(90)(1 - .2) = 72$ hrs. The profits in the iron sector equal the price of total input times the profit rate, or:

$$\text{total profit in iron} = [(90)(.5) + (9)(1) + (12)(3)] \times 2$$
$$= 180.$$

When this is adjusted by the deflation factor, to make prices and labor values commensurable, we find:

$$\text{total profit in iron} = (180 \times .4)$$
$$= 72.$$

TABLE 9. Physical Surplus in System C

	Corn Sector	Iron Sector	Books Sector
Output	300	90	40
Capital Inputs	⟨12⟩	⟨30⟩	⟨2⟩
Wage Inputs	⟨42⟩	⟨21⟩	0
Surplus Output	246	39	38

which just equals the surplus labor value extracted from the labor inputs.

What is true for System C in particular is, as we might expect, true for all systems in which the ratio of labor directly required to labor indirectly required is the same in all lines of production. In all such systems, with a suitable selection of units, it turns out that the profit generated in each sector exactly equals the surplus labor value extracted from the labor inputs into that sector, and hence by aggregation that total profits equal total surplus value.[1]

We began our investigation of Ricardian and Marxian political economy with an examination of the notion of a physical surplus. What can Marx's analysis tell us about the composition and appropriation of the physical surplus generated in each cycle of reproduction?

Following the classical train of thought, we have been construing the surplus as the collection of commodities that remains after the workers have spent their wages for food, clothing, and shelter. To compute the physical surplus, therefore, we must first specify the real wage. (It is not enough to specify the money wage, for from that information alone, we cannot determine what actual market basket of goods the workers will buy with their wages.) In the present instance, once we set the real wage at (.2 corn, .1 iron)/unit of labor, we can calculate the physical surplus by subtracting capital inputs and wage inputs from output, as shown in Table 9.

[1] For a formal proof of this proposition, see Appendix A, Section V.4.

Examination of the composition of the physical surplus reveals two equalities, each of which is significant for the classical perspective. First of all, the money profit appropriated by the capitalists just equals the price of the physical surplus:

price of physical surplus:

$$(246 \times 1) + (39 \times 3) + (38 \times 1.5) = 420.$$
$$\quad\ \text{corn} \qquad\quad \text{iron} \qquad\quad \text{books}$$

Secondly, the labor value of the physical surplus just equals the surplus labor extracted from the workers in the production process:

labor value of surplus:

$$(246 \times .4) + (39 \times 1.2) + (38 \times .6) = 168.$$
$$\quad\ \text{corn} \qquad\quad \text{iron} \qquad\quad \text{books}$$

Thus, in System C, the workings of the market distribute the physical surplus to the capitalists, who buy it with their money profits at the end of each cycle of production. If they turn out not to want corn, iron, and theology books in precisely the proportions generated as surplus, their market demand will result in temporary imbalances, which will lead eventually to an adjustment of the sizes of the three sectors. In long-run equilibrium, after these market fluctuations have been smoothed out, the capitalists will be able to spend their money profits for exactly the combination of corn, iron, and theology books they desire.

This equality between the total profits and the price of the physical surplus is hardly surprising, of course. It is simply one way of saying that the system is in equilibrium. Hence, the significant fact is that no matter what shape the capitalists' demand for surplus goods takes, there is always some level of activity of the several industries which will exactly satisfy their demand.

The second equality is, in its way, more striking. What it tells us is that the physical surplus generated in the economy as a whole is actually the embodiment or congelation of the surplus labor time expended by those who do the work of producing the corn, iron, and books in the system. This equality is perfectly general. It does not depend on the organic composition of capital, or on any of the other constraints we have been presupposing. In any economy, the labor value of the physical surplus exactly equals the surplus labor performed by those who sell their labor for wages. Hence, a society that assigns a portion of that surplus, however small, to a class of men and women who do not labor to produce it is a society founded on exploitation.[2]

Having established the concepts of surplus value and exploitation, Marx proceeds to deploy them over many hundreds of pages in a wide-ranging critique and exposé of the structure and variations of capitalist accumulation. Through the extraordinarily dramatic device of dividing the workday into necessary labor time (the time required to reproduce the labor being consumed) and surplus labor time (the time that workers labor over and above what is socially necessary to reproduce their conditions of existence), Marx is able to organize and illuminate a mass of historical and contemporary data concerning the bitter ongoing struggle between workers and capitalists over the length of the workday, the intensity and conditions of the labor process, the introduction of machinery, and of course the wage.

2. Prices and Values: The Mystification of Capitalism

The introduction of the distinction between labor and labor power, and with it the associated concepts of surplus value and exploitation, enabled Marx to explain the origin of the profit which capitalists annually accumulate and reinvest. What is more, these analytical weapons permitted him to mount a powerful attack on the legitimacy of capitalist appropriation. Indeed, so rich are the conceptual possibilities of the concept

---

[2] For a formal proof of this proposition, see Appendix A, Section V.5.

of surplus value that Marx scarcely exhausts its implications in the long first volume of *Capital*. Nevertheless, the careful reader will have noted that when we come to the end of volume one, we have still moved not at all beyond the point Ricardo had reached in his search for a theory of natural price.

In volume one, Marx adopts the simplifying assumption that each industry exhibits the same proportions of living to dead labor. In Ricardian terms, this means that each line of production employs the same proportions of labor directly required to labor indirectly required. In Marxian terms, all industries have the same organic composition of capital. However we choose to express it, Marx assumes precisely those special conditions under which the Ricardian theory of natural price holds.

But as Ricardo and Marx both knew, the theory fails in the general case. The problem, as we have seen, is that entrepreneurs guide their economic decisions by the goal of maximizing their rate of return on the (money) value of the total capital they invest in some line of production. In calculating whether a certain industry offers an attractive investment opportunity, a capitalist figures on the basis of the capital he must lay out, regardless of whether it be laid out for labor or for non-labor inputs. As capital is moved from sector to sector in pursuit of the highest rate of return, it is the money rate of profit that tends to be equalized.

As Marx analyzes the problem, the situation is this: all workers earn the same money wage, and spend it on roughly the same market basket of goods. Consequently, all workers, regardless of what industry they are employed in, must on average work the same number of hours per day to reproduce their conditions of existence. Furthermore, the workday is the same length throughout the economy. Consequently, each worker puts in the same number of hours of surplus labor time each day—time during which he or she is creating surplus value that can be appropriated by the capitalist. Putting these assumptions together, we can conclude that in Marx's terms, the ratio s/v, which he calls the rate of surplus value or rate of exploitation, is uniform throughout the economy.

Now, save under the most restrictive and special of conditions—what Marx calls "equal organic composition of capital"—it is obvious that industries are going to differ widely in the proportions in which they combine labor and non-labor inputs. Agriculture, for example, might use a great deal of labor relative to raw materials, machinery, and tools, while oil refining, with modern semiautomated refineries, might use very little living labor relative to capital. This would mean that the labor value of the non-labor inputs was large in oil and small in agriculture. Therefore, the "value rate of profit," $s/(c + v)$, would be very small in oil, and very big in farming.

To put the same point in a different way, a capitalist investing in corn would extract a great deal of surplus labor value from his workers per million dollars he invested, while another capitalist investing in oil might extract very little surplus labor value. (Indeed, in some modern refineries, an enormous multi-million dollar plant may be run by a skeleton crew of workers who simply keep an eye on the dials and gauges!)

But capitalists are quite uninterested in something called surplus labor value. They care only about the percentage return on their investment—on the profit rate. If oil is paying a lower return than corn, they will switch into corn, and vice versa. So, with the wage constant, and the profit rate equalized by the movements of capital in and out of industries, the only thing that can shift, so as to make the equations balance, is the price of commodities.

But—and this is the point of the whole story—the labor values of commodities depend only on the technical conditions of production, and hence are unaffected by changes in the profit rate or the movement of capital. So, with prices shifting to balance the system, and labor values unaltered, prices will move away from labor values. In short, it will no longer be the case that prices are proportional to labor values, and the labor theory of value will be refuted.

We can illustrate the propositions just enunciated (and others besides, as we shall see) by an analysis of a three-sector model: Using the data contained in Table 10, we can form a system

TABLE 10. System G

	Labor Input	Corn Input	Iron Input	Tools Input	Output
Labor		30	15	0	150
Corn Sector	80	128	2	3	240
Iron Sector	20	16	1	5	60
Tools Sector	50	6	27	4	16

of equations, as before, relating the direct and indirect labor requirements in each sector to the labor embodied in the output. When this is done, and the equations are solved, we find (using λ, as before, to stand for labor value), that:

$$\lambda_c \cong .9344$$

$$\lambda_i \cong 1.2168$$

$$\lambda_t \cong 7.3712$$

In order to calculate the "organic composition of capital" in the corn, iron, and tool sectors, we must first specify the real wage, because the organic composition, c/v, depends on the amount of labor time, v, that must be expended to reproduce the real wage.

Using the same assumptions with which we have been working, let us set the real wage at .2 units of corn, and .1 unit of iron per unit of labor. In the corn sector, for example, where 80 units of labor are employed, the total real wage will amount to 16 units of corn and 8 units of iron.

In Marx's terminology, v_c, the value of variable capital in the corn industry, will therefore be equal to $16\lambda_c$ plus $8\lambda_i$, or $[(16)(.9344)] + [(8)(1.2168)]$, which is to say 24.69. The labor value of the constant capital in the corn sector, c_c, is calculated by adding up the labor value of each of the non-labor inputs—the corn, the iron, and the tools. If we carry out these calculations for all three industries, we can find the organic composition of capital in corn, in iron, in tools, and finally

TABLE 11. Organic Composition of System G

	Constant Capital (c)	Variable Capital (v)	Organic Composition (c/v)
Corn Sector	24.69	144.15	.1713
Iron Sector	6.17	53.02	.1164
Tool Sector	15.43	67.94	.2271
System G	46.29	265.11	.1746

in the economy as a whole. The results are summarized in Table 11.

Thus, the tool sector has the highest organic composition of capital, the corn sector has the second highest, with a ratio close to the ratio for the economy as a whole, and the iron sector has the lowest, with a ratio slightly more than half that of the corn sector. (Notice, by the way, that although the ratio in any single industry is determined solely by the proportions of the several inputs and by their labor values, and hence is independent of the level of activity at which the industry is run, the system-wide ratio depends on the activity levels as well.)

System G, with its wide variations in the ratio of labor to non-labor inputs, is more like what we would expect to find in an actual economy. What are the prices, the money wage, and the profit rate in System G? To answer that question, we must go through the same exercise as before. Setting the price of corn equal to 1 arbitrarily, and using the real wage already stipulated of .2 corn and .1 iron per unit of labor, we can form a set of price equations and solve them. When we do so, we find the following:

$$p_c = 1$$

$$p_i \cong 1.364$$

$$p_t \cong 7.455$$

$$w \cong .3364$$

$$\pi = 1/3$$

TABLE 12. Value Rates of Profit in System G

	Surplus Value (s)	Constant Capital (c)	Variable Capital (v)	Value rate of Profit [s/(c + v)]
Corn Sector	55.31	24.69	144.15	.3276
Iron Sector	13.83	6.17	53.02	.2337
Tool Sector	34.57	15.43	67.94	.4147

The first thing we notice when we examine the results we have obtained thus far is that prices are not proportional to labor values in System G:

$$p_c/\lambda_c \cong 1.0702$$

$$p_i/\lambda_i \cong 1.12097$$

$$p_t/\lambda_t \cong 1.0114$$

Furthermore, the value rate of profit, $s/(c + v)$, varies from industry to industry, as Table 12 shows. Thus, the value rate of profit in the corn sector is not too far from the money rate of profit, 1/3, but the value rates of profit in iron and tools are very wide of that mark. In System G, and in all other economies that fail to exhibit equal organic composition of capital, the central tenets of the value theory of volume one of *Capital* fail. Thus far, we have simply arrived back at the point at which Ricardo's political economy broke down.

Now Marx makes his move. The prices at which commodities exchange in the market are merely the surface of the capitalist market, the *appearance*. The underlying reality is the extraction of surplus value from the workers in the sphere of production. As Marx says in a letter to Engels in the year following the publication of volume one, "*profit* is for us first of all only *another name* or another category of *surplus value*. . . . [S]*urplus value* gets the form of *profit*, without any *quantitative* difference between the one and the other. This is only the illusory form in which surplus value appears".[3]

[3] MEW (1958–66), vol. 32, p. 71. Emphasis in original.

The classical economists, to be sure, had drawn a similar distinction between appearance and reality in their account of the relationship between fluctuating market prices and the "centers of gravity" or natural prices toward which they tended. Indeed, this distinction, as we have seen, was central to the development of the concept of equilibrium, on which virtually all subsequent economic theory has rested.

But the classical economists did not go deep enough, Marx argued. They took the natural prices, determined as they were by a uniform profit markup over the long-run cost of production, to be the fundamental reality. And they made this mistake because they failed to penetrate the inner essence of profit as surplus value.

The truth, Marx asserted, is this: profit, ground rent, and interest all originate as surplus value extracted from workers in the process of production. The total amount of surplus value generated in the economy as a whole in a single cycle of production is determined by the *difference* between the number of hours of labor performed by wage laborers and the number of hours of socially necessary labor directly or indirectly required to reproduce the work force (to feed, clothe, and house them and their families) for another time period. Competition moves capital around in search of the highest rate of return on the total money value of invested capital, with the result that natural prices in general deviate from labor values. Furthermore, a number of subordinate classes—landowners, retail merchants, bankers and financiers, and so forth—appropriate a portion of the total surplus value in the form of rent, merchant profit, interest, etc.

As a result of the workings of a fully developed capitalist market system, the underlying fact of exploitation—the extraction of surplus value from the workers—is thoroughly concealed from view. Even the most "scientific" observers of capitalism fail to perceive the inner connection between profits and exploitation. The way is opened to the rationalization of profit as the reward for abstinence (or "waiting"), for entrepreneurial skill, or for risk taking.

So long as we deal with a simple, perspicuous case of equal organic composition of capital, the value rate of profit in each sector, $s/(c + v)$, exactly equals the money rate of profit, π, and the total surplus value extracted in each line of production, s, exactly equals the profits earned in that sector (with the wage, w, taken as numeraire). It is, in this case, transparently clear where profits come from. But in the general case, the link between profits and exploitation is thoroughly obscured.

How is the reality of this link to be reestablished? Marx's answer is quite striking, and in its way philosophically rather profound. Capitalist production is socialized production, he says. The division of labor first described by Smith has transformed the activities of many individuals into a thoroughly interconnected system of social production and exchange. It is therefore only at the aggregate level of the total economy that the link between profits and exploitation can be reestablished. This formal fact corresponds to the economic fact that it is the capitalist class as a whole that exploits the working class, not individual identifiable capitalists who somehow exploit individual workers.

The link between profits and exploitation postulated by Marx is a simple equation at the aggregate or society-wide level. The profits appropriated in any single industry may exceed or fall short of the surplus value extracted from the workers in that industry, but in the society as a whole, the total profits earned by all capitalists must exactly equal the total surplus value extracted from the entire working class. (Or, more precisely, the total of profits, rents, interest, and other unearned income in the society as a whole must exactly equal the surplus value extracted from the workers.) Marx adds a second thesis, that the total price of all the commodities sold in a single time period must equal the total labor value of those commodities, even though the price of an individual commodity may fall above or below its labor value.

The passage in which Marx asserts these equalities appears in the tenth chapter of volume three of *Capital*: "Consequently, the sum of the profits in all spheres of production must equal the sum of the surplus-values, and the sum of the prices of production of the total social product equal the sum of its value."

Marx's central idea seems clear enough, on first examination, and in fact he deploys it countless times in the pages of volume three of *Capital* and throughout the three volumes of *Theories of Surplus Value*. Surplus value *is* surplus labor extracted from the workers in the course of production. That surplus value is congealed in the commodities produced, and is then translated into money, or realized, when the commodities are sold. The total quantity of surplus value generated throughout the economy equals the total profit appropriated by the capitalists and by the other parasite classes associated with or dependent on them. The rents collected by landlords who let their land to agricultural capitalists, the interest charged by financial capitalists who lend money capital to entrepreneurs, the merchants' profits made by middlemen in the sphere of circulation—all this is simply a portion of the surplus value spread around but not thereby either increased or diminished in aggregate quantity. *Au fond*, there is no way for profit to be created save by the extraction of surplus labor from productive workers.

The distribution of surplus value is warped and biased by the relentless capitalistic search for the highest possible rate of return on the *monetary* value of invested capital. As a consequence of this process, capitalists appropriate profits that bear only the most indirect relation to the amount of surplus labor time they extract from their workers. To the capitalists themselves, of course, it would seem absurd to suggest that their profits come only from the money they lay out for labor. A prudent capitalist calculates his profit on the total value of his investment—on the money he has spent for raw materials, for rent, for machinery, for electricity, and for tools, as well as on what he has spent for wages. Indeed, a financier who does his own books and sweeps up after himself may not have any employees at all! Yet he still collects interest on the money he lends. So the equilibrating of the price system by the search for profit has the unintended but quite significant effect of concealing from everyone's eyes the true source of profit.

Marx's notion, although powerful and compelling, is as it stands not quite coherent, and it requires some slight reformulation before we can examine it analytically. The problem is one of units or dimensions. Surplus value is measured in units of time—hours of averagely efficient laboring. But profits are measured in monetary units—dollars, pounds, or francs. The statement that the total surplus value in the society as a whole equals the total profit appropriated by the capitalists is therefore, strictly speaking, meaningless.

A second associated problem with the simple assertion (total surplus value) = (total profits) is the fact that under certain circumstances, it can be used trivially as a way of choosing a numeraire, or standard of money, for the economy. Recall our analysis of the price and profit equations of System C and similar systems. There are always two more variables than there are equations, namely the variables representing the prices of the commodities, the variable representing the money wage, and the variable representing the profit rate. What we did, it will be recalled, was to posit a real wage, thereby permitting us to substitute the price of the real wage for the variable w, and then to make a second reduction in the number of variables by choosing one commodity (corn, in the case of System C) and arbitrarily setting its price equal to 1. Now, from a mathematical point of view, setting the price of corn equal to 1 is actually the same as adding a new equation, namely:

$$p_c = 1. \tag{4*}$$

When we add this equation to System C, we have four equations instead of three, and this exactly equals the number of variables (with the wage already eliminated). Thus the system balances, and can be solved.

Once we think of the matter in this way, it may occur to us that equation (4*) is not the only equation we can add to the system in order to reduce the gap between equations and variables. Needless to say, we can choose iron or books as numeraire, and add $p_i = 1$ or $p_b = 1$ as the fourth equation. But we are not by any means restricted to simple equations of this sort.

We might choose to stipulate that the sum of the prices of one unit of corn, one unit of iron, and one unit of books exactly equals 1. This would mean adding as our fourth equation:

$$p_c + p_i + p_b = 1. \qquad (4^{**})$$

Indeed, we might even add an equation stating that the total surplus value produced in the system equals the total profit appropriated by all the capitalists in the system. Such an equation would look a good deal more complicated than equation (4^*), and even than equation (4^{**}), but it would be a perfectly legitimate, arbitrary way of closing the system and choosing a numeraire. We might equally well decide to fix our numeraire by adding, as our fourth equation, the proposition that the total labor value of all the commodities produced in the society exactly equals the total price for which they are sold. This too would be a rather complicated equation, but like (4^*), (4^{**}), and the (total surplus value) = (total profit) equation, it would be nothing more than an arbitrary device for choosing a money unit.

But Marx's mathematical instincts, as usual, are more acute and reliable than his mathematical practice. Instead of merely adding the arbitrary normalizing equation, (total surplus value) = (total profits), or the equally arbitrary normalizing equation (total labor values) = (total prices), Marx actually asserts them both! This has the effect of adding *more* equations than there are unknowns. The system of equations is no longer *under*determined. It is now *over*determined.

All of this is mathematical jargon for saying that Marx has said something significant, not something trivial. By asserting both equations at the same time, he has made a very powerful claim about the relation between surplus value and profits, a claim that could be wrong, but whose truth would really constitute a legitimate foundation for a successful theory of natural price.

There is a simple, more elegant way of combining Marx's two assertions that has the virtue of avoiding problems about incompatible units. Instead of reading Marx as making two claims, one about prices and values and the other about profits and surplus value, we can instead construe him as making one proportionality assertion, namely:

(total profits)/(total surplus value) = (total prices)/(total values).

Since the top half, or numerator, of each fraction is measured in money, and the bottom half, or denominator, is measured in hours, the dimensions of the two halves of the equation match. Each one is measured, so to speak, in units of dollars per hour.

This is Marx's solution to Ricardo's problem of the deviation of prices from labor values. The price of corn may diverge from the labor value of corn. The price of iron may diverge from the labor value of iron. The total surplus value extracted from the books industry may not match the total profit appropriated in the books industry. But at the aggregate level of the economy as a whole, the ratio of total profits to total surplus value will exactly equal the ratio of total prices to total values. Put even more clearly and simply, if we choose our numeraire by setting total prices equal to total values, then, Marx asserts, the total profit in the system will exactly equal the total surplus value.

The time has come to find out whether Marx is right. Marx himself offers nothing resembling a proof for his assertion. Indeed, it is not even clear whether Marx recognized that a proof was called for. Nevertheless, we have succeeded in interpreting his claims in such a way that it ought to be possible to confirm them or disconfirm them directly by an examination of sample economic systems. Let us therefore return to System G, which, it will be recalled, is an economy in which Ricardo's simple labor theory of natural price does *not* work. Is Marx's conjecture true for System G? Is the ratio of total profits to total surplus value equal to the ratio of total prices to total values of commodities produced?

Total profits are calculated by multiplying the system-wide money profit rate, 1/3, by the total price of all the capital outlays, including those for labor. In other words,

total profits:

$$(150w + 150p_c + 30p_i + 12p_t)(1/3) = 110.28 \text{ money units.}$$

Total surplus value is calculated by subtracting the total number of hours of necessary labor from the number of hours of labor worked in the entire economy. In other words,

total surplus value: $150(1 - \lambda_w) = 103.71$ units of labor.

Total prices are computed simply by adding up the price of everything produced in the system, namely,

total prices: $240p_c + 60p_i + 16p_t = 441.12$ money units.

Finally, total values are computed in the same way, using labor values instead of prices. Thus,

total values:
$$240\lambda_c + 60\lambda_i + 16\lambda_t = 415.20 \text{ units of labor.}$$

With this information computed, we can now check Marx's claim.

(total profits)/(total surplus value)

$\cong 1.063$ money units/unit of labor.

(total prices)/(total values)

$\cong 1.062$ money units/unit of labor.

What is more, when we compute the economy-wide value rate of profit, we find that it exactly coincides with the money rate of profit:

$$S/(C + V) = 103.71/(265.118 + 46.29) \cong .333 = \pi.$$

So, in System G, Marx's solution to the problem of the deviation of natural prices from labor values holds true. Even though the organic composition of capital varies from sector to sector, thereby causing natural prices to deviate quite significantly from labor values, the ratio of total profits to total surplus value exactly equals the ratio of total prices of all produced commodities to the total of their labor values. When a price numeraire is chosen so as to make total prices equal total labor values, then the total profits in the system equal the total surplus value extracted from the working class.[4]

Marx's revision of the classical labor theory of value is an enormously powerful analytical and critical tool. It enables him to explain the formation of natural or equilibrium prices—something that neither Ricardo nor his followers had ever been able to do—and also at the same time to mount a devastating critique of capitalism. Capitalist accumulation, Marx demonstrates, is nothing but exploitation. Capitalism is an enormous machine for pumping surplus labor out of the working class.

Previous economic systems had of course rested on exploitation. No one disputed that! But capitalism seemed to rest on equal exchanges, freely entered into in the marketplace. The slave owner forces his slaves to work the land, feeding them just enough to keep them alive and appropriating the entire product of their labors. The feudal lord requires the serfs to labor for several days each week on the manor lands, thus directly appropriating such surplus labor as the peasants are capable of performing. But under capitalism, matters appear to be quite different. In the free market, it is all "Freedom, Equality,

---

[4] Marx speaks a good deal about industries exhibiting "average" organic composition of capital, thereby echoing statements by Ricardo concerning his search for an "invariant standard of value." (Compare Ricardo's remark in the chapter "On Value" in the *Principles:* "May not gold be considered as a commodity produced with such proportions of the two kinds of capital as approach nearest to the average quantity employed in the production of most commodities?" (1951–73, vol. 1, p. 45). In fact, as Marx did not quite realize, it is a weighted average rather than merely an average that is required. The weights are precisely the levels of activity at which the several industries are operated. Specifically, if $y_1, y_2, \ldots, y_n$ are the activity levels at which industries 1, 2, . . . , n operate in System K, then the $n + 1$st normalizing equation that makes total profits equal total surplus value is $y_1 p_1 + y_2 p_2 + \cdots + y_n p_n = y_1 \lambda_1 + y_2 \lambda_2 + \cdots + y_n \lambda_n$. In System G, with the price of corn = 1, total prices $\cong$ 441.12 units of corn, while total labor values $\cong$ 415.20 labor hours. Adding the $n + 1$st equation above has the effect of deflating all prices by a factor $\cong$ .94124. Since the choice of a numeraire is arbitrary, this deflation, although awkward, is legitimate. Total profits $\cong$ 110.28 corn. Total surplus value $\cong$ 103.71 labor. Multiplying profits by the deflating factor, we have [(110 corn)(.94124 labor/unit of corn)] $\cong$ 103.7999 units of labor, which, within the limits of accuracy of our calculations, just equals the total surplus value.

Property, and Bentham!"[5] Where is the exploitation? Where is the appropriation of surplus labor?

But Marx knows better: "The essential difference between the various economic forms of society, between, for instance, a society based on slave-labour, and one based on wage-labour, lies only in the mode in which this surplus-labour is in each case extracted from the actual producer, the labourer."[6]

The dirty secret of capitalism is that profit is nothing but surplus value, abstract homogeneous socially necessary labor performed by the workers and appropriated by the capitalists and their subordinate classes. The proof of this proposition lies in the demonstration that at the aggregate, or society-wide, level, the total profit appropriated by the capitalists is exactly equal to the surplus value embodied by the workers in their product.

In previous societies, the ruling class extracted surplus labor, but not in the form of surplus *value*, which is peculiar to capitalism. In order for surplus labor to manifest itself in the form of surplus value, the goods produced by the workers must become commodities, which is to say, they must be produced for capitalist exchange in a competitive market situation. Thus Engels, in a letter to Paul Lafargue, points out that the feudal lord "lives off the surplus labor of others, but does not transform the product of this surplus labor into surplus value. He does not sell it, he consumes it, distributes it, squanders it."[7]

In Marx's theoretical reconstruction of classical theory, the extraction of surplus labor in the process of production, the embodiment of that surplus labor in commodities as surplus value, the realization of surplus value in the sphere of circulation as profit, and the movement of surplus value throughout the economy, all constitute the reality that lies beneath the surface appearance of "Freedom, Equality, Property, and Bentham." The genius of Marx's theory of surplus value consists precisely in the fact that the very same theoretical innovation

---

[5] Marx (1967a), p. 176.
[6] Ibid., p. 217.
[7] MEW (1958–66), vol. 36, p. 195.

that permits him to explain the origin of profit—namely, the distinction between labor and labor power—also enables him finally to bring the century-old search for a satisfactory theory of natural price to a close.

3. Is Marx Right?

The theory we have just examined is a complex variant of, or revision of, the Ricardian labor theory of natural price. It can be summarized (albeit somewhat inadequately) in four propositions:

> *First*, that labor is the substance of value, which is to say that the exchange value of commodities is at base determined by the quantity of abstract, homogeneous, socially necessary labor embodied in them,
> *Second*, that profit, rent, and interest are surplus value,
> *Third*, that competition and capitalists' pursuit of the highest possible rate of profit distort natural prices away from labor values so as to equalize the money rate of profit throughout the economy.
> And, *fourth*, that despite the distortions arising from competition, the aggregate society-wide quantum of surplus value extracted from the working class is, for suitable independently chosen numeraire, equal to the total unearned income appropriated by the capitalist class and its dependent classes in the form of profits, rents, and interest.

The critical theses are the first, second, and fourth: that labor is the substance of value; that profit, rent, and interest *are* surplus value; and that at the aggregate level total surplus value equals total profit. The third thesis concerns the processes by which the equalization of the profit rate equilibrates the price system. Marx was obviously enormously interested in this process, for he works through dozens of examples in great detail, consuming scores of pages with numerical calculations. In fact, however, his results follow quite directly from his premises,

TABLE 13. System H

	Labor Input	Corn Input	Iron Input	Output
Labor		.1.5	0	15
Corn Sector	13	5	1	20
Iron Sector	2	10	5	11

and would have been acceptable to the economists of his day had they accepted those premises, for he is simply reiterating the common behavioral assumptions of the classical tradition.

Let us begin in reverse order, by examining more closely the claim that aggregate profit quantitatively equals aggregate surplus value, or, more precisely, that the ratio of total profit to total surplus value equals the ratio of total prices to total values. We have already seen that this thesis is true for System G, despite the fact that System G does *not* exhibit equal organic composition of capital, and hence that in System G natural prices are not proportional to labor values.

Consider first the little corn/iron system given in Table 13. Setting up and solving a system of labor value equations in the usual manner, we find that in System H:

$$\lambda_c = 1$$
$$\lambda_i = 2$$

If we fix the real wage at .1 unit of corn per unit of labor, the labor value of the real wage becomes .1, from which it follows that .9 units of surplus labor are extracted from each unit of labor input. With the wage known, we can set up and solve the price equations for the system. Choosing corn as numeraire, and setting $p_c = 1$, we find:

$$p_i \cong 5.922$$
$$w = .1$$
$$\pi \cong .636$$

If we now test Marx's hypothesis in System H, we find:

(total profits)/(total surplus value) $\cong$ 2.453 corn/unit of labor

and

(total prices)/(total values) $\cong$ 2.027 corn/unit of labor,

which does not check at all. Furthermore, the value rate of profit for the system as a whole, $S/(C + V)$, is roughly .474, which is not even close to the money profit rate of .636. So Marx's ingenious hypothesis fails completely for System H.

Nor is this result an isolated anomoly. If one simply constructs little two- and three-sector systems (or larger ones) and grinds out the values of the variables representing labor values, prices, and profit rates, the likelihood is rather small that one will hit upon a system that obeys the principle of the conservation of surplus value (as we may call it).

This is really a rather devastating discovery! In the thousands of pages of political economy that Marx wrote and rewrote during the 1860s, one finds countless passages in which he appeals to the thesis that profit, rent, and interest are merely surplus labor value redistributed. The entire critical claim that capitalist accumulation rests upon the exploitation of the working class depends on this thesis. If there is no regular relationship between accumulating capital on the one hand and surplus labor extracted from the workers on the other, then what theoretical grounds are there for asserting that the one is really the other mystified?

Nothing we have said thus far calls into question the distinction between labor and labor power, and the associated concept of surplus value. But Marx needs the quantitative conservation principle if he is to establish the proposition that profit *is* surplus value. He himself quite well understands that his entire theoretical enterprise would be severely damaged were he to have to give up the claim that profits, rents, and interest are simply surplus labor value transmuted, redistributed, but neither increased nor diminished in quantity.

We know, of course, that the conservation principle will hold for any system exhibiting equal organic composition of capital in all lines of production. We also know that it will hold trivially of any system in which the profit rate is zero, and the entire physical surplus is appropriated by the workers, for in those cases, profits are zero, surplus value is zero, and prices exactly equal labor values. And we know, by experimentation, that in at least one case, namely System G, the conservation principle holds despite the fact that the several sectors do not have even approximately equal organic composition. But we do not yet have any analytical insight into the reasons why the principle holds for System G. Consequently, we cannot yet define the theoretical constraints under which it is valid.[8]

[8] The treatment of the conservation principle in this chapter and elsewhere is not precisely correct, a fact that I realized only after the book was in page proof. Strictly speaking, the equation asserting the equality of total prices and total labor values (formally, $yp = y\lambda$) should be construed as an arbitrary specification of the numeraire, and hence true by stipulation. It is thus formally on a par with the specification of the numeraire by the equation $p_c = 1$, which is used throughout this book. The equation asserting the equality of total profits and total surplus value (formally, $yp - yAp - yLbp = yL - yLb\lambda$) is then a substantive assertion true under the conditions indicated in this chapter. With this emendation, the formal proof of Case C in Appendix A Section V.4 can be simplified. If the price system is normalized by means of $p_c = 1$ or other similar stipulation, then the proportionality (total profits)/ (total prices) = (total surplus value)/(total values) accurately renders Marx's principle of the conservation of surplus value.

BALANCED GROWTH AND THE CONSERVATION OF SURPLUS VALUE

1. Why Did Marx Believe That Total Profits Equal Total Surplus Value?

Before we proceed to the detailed analysis of the conditions under which the principle of the conservation of surplus value is true, let us ask why Marx thought it was true, keeping in mind that he did not have available to him the sort of analytical formalism that we have been employing throughout this book. (The technique of solving simultaneous equations was known in Marx's day, but it was not applied to the calculation of labor values until almost a century later.)

Marx devotes scores of pages to detailed explorations of the ways in which the surplus value extracted from the workers is redistributed among the several subclasses of the capitalist class. He many times reiterates his conviction that the total society-wide quantum of surplus value extracted from the workers in a single period of production equals the total money profit appropriated by the capitalist class. And yet, nowhere have I been able to find even a single passage in which he presents a coherent argument for his principle of the conservation of surplus value.

There is very little to be gained from an endless citation of texts. In chapter nine of volume three of *Capital*, for instance,

Marx works through an elaborate numerical example, but his calculations are entirely vitiated by his failure to value the inputs as well as the outputs at their equilibrium *prices* rather than at their labor values. Marx knows that the input prices will in general already show the distortions produced by the equalization of the profit rate in the presence of unequal organic compositions of capital, but he does not know how to take account of that fact arithmetically.[1]

Why then *does* Marx think that total profits equal total surplus value? I should like to offer the judgment, without anything that can be called conclusive textual confirmation, that Marx assumes the truth of his conservation principle because he himself suffers from precisely the fetishistic confusions that he labors so hard in volume one to expose. Virtually everywhere save when he is actually dealing directly with the mystifications of the concept of value, Marx speaks as though the quantity of labor embodied in a commodity were a physical magnitude, a mass of value that resides in the commodity and constitutes one of its objective characteristics. Repeatedly, he talks as though surplus value were a homogeneous ectoplasmic stuff that could be transferred, through the workings of the market, from one owner to another.

One of the ways in which Marx reveals the fetishistic character of his thinking about surplus value is in his remarks about the notion of an "average" profit. It seems obvious to him that we can speak of "averages" only insofar as there exists some objective substance whose various quantitative manifestations are being averaged. Consider for example the following two

---

[1] Consider, for example, this passage from chapter nine: "We had originally assumed that the cost-price of a commodity equalled the *value* of the commodities consumed in its production. But for the buyer the price of production of a specific commodity is its cost-price, and may thus pass as cost-price into the prices of other commodities. Since the price of production may differ from the value of a commodity, it follows that the cost-price of a commodity containing this price of production of another commodity may also stand above or below that portion of its total value derived from the value of the means of production consumed by it" (Marx [1967c], pp. 164–165).

passages, the first from *Theories of Surplus Value* and the second from *Capital*:

> If *profits* as a percentage of capital are to be equal over a period, say of a year, so that capitals of equal size yield equal profits in the same period of time, then the *prices* of the commodities must be different from their *values*. The sum total of these *cost-prices* of all the commodities taken together will *be equal to their value*. Similarly the total profit will be equal to the total surplus-value which all these capitals yield, for instance, during one year. If one did not take the definition of value as the basis, the *average profit*, and therefore also the cost-prices, would be purely imaginary and untenable. The equalisation of the surplus-values in different spheres of production does not affect the absolute size of this total surplus-value; but merely alters its *distribution* among the different spheres of production. The *determination of this surplus-value* itself, however, only arises out of the determination of value by labour-time. Without this, the average profit is the average *of nothing*, pure fancy. And it could then equally well be 1,000 per cent or 10 per cent.

✳ ✳ ✳

> Wherever an average profit, and therefore a general rate of profit, are produced—no matter by what means— such an average profit cannot be anything but the profit on the average social capital, whose sum is equal to the sum of surplus-value. . . . It is evident that the average profit can be nothing but the total mass of surplus-values allotted to the various quantities of capital proportionally to their magnitudes in the different spheres of production. It is the total realised unpaid labour, and this total mass, like the paid, congealed or living, labour, obtains in the total mass of commodities and money that falls to the capitalists.[2]

[2] Marx (1968), p. 190; Marx (1967c), p. 174.

There are, of course, countless passages in which Marx *uses* the conservation principle to explain a variety of economic phenomena, but these passages do not constitute a defense of the principle, for they all proceed from Marx's unquestioning assumption of its truth.

The same mind-set is encountered in Marx's exposition of his analytical framework of categories and ratios, as I have tried to show in Appendix B below. Once we start thinking of surplus value as an objective physical (or "meta-physical") quantum of congealed or crystallized labor, embodied in the commodities emerging from a production process, then we may quite naturally be drawn to the conclusion that it can be *redistributed* by the processes of realization and circulation, but can neither be increased nor decreased in magnitude.

But this way of thinking is crazy! The surplus value generated in an economy is not some ectoplasmic stuff spewed forth as a joint product in the corn, iron, or tool industry! It is simply the difference between the quantity of abstract homogeneous socially necessary labor required, directly or indirectly, to reproduce the conditions of existence of the working class and the aggregate quantity of abstract homogeneous socially necessary labor performed by that class.

More generally, the labor value of a commodity is not a natural property of that commodity. It is a theoretical magnitude defined by reference to, and acquiring meaning only within, a model of a total economic system. In order even to conceptualize the labor value of a commodity, we must abstract from the endless individuating particularities of the place, pace, skill level, style, material, and accidents of production.

It makes no sense to point to an actual pair of pants and say, "That pair of pants contains three hours of abstract homogeneous socially necessary labor," as though some supernatural substance called abstract labor had, by the skill of the tailor, been sewn into the lining and the cuffs. Statements about the labor value of individual commodities are actually, in misleading form, statements about the structure of the entire industry of which the individual commodity is a product. Indeed, strictly speaking, it does not even make sense to point to the entire output of the garment industry and say, "Those garments in the aggregate embody so much abstract labor," as though that were a concrete fact about the garment industry alone. Such assertions, depending as they do on the conditions of production in all the industries that directly or indirectly supply inputs into the garment industry, are in fact statements about the structure of production of the entire model.

It is thus a prime instance of fetishistic thinking to imagine that in each line of production—indeed, in each factory—a quantum of surplus value is extracted from the workers, which may be appropriated by the capitalists in that line of production, or may be shifted and spread this way and that, but can never be augmented or diminished by the processes of circulation. Marx talks as though aggregate surplus value *must* be equal to aggregate profit because profit just *is* surplus value. There is no way for any surplus value to leak out of the system, nor is there any other source for it save the surplus labor time of the workers.

But now the full extent of the problem becomes evident. For it is Marx himself who has taught us to think in terms of abstract homogeneous socially necessary labor time. It is he who has imported into political economy the categories of fetishism from the sociology and anthropology of religion. And it is he who bitingly stigmatizes as crazy, *verrückt*, just the sort of thinking into which he appears to have fallen here.[3]

Marx's belief in the principle of the conservation of surplus value seems in the first instance to have rested on his conviction that surplus value is an actual quantity of labor moving hither and yon throughout the economy as a consequence of

---

[3] See, for example, Marx (1967a), p. 76: "When I state that coats or boots stand in a relation to linen, because it is the universal incarnation of abstract human labor, the craziness [*die Verrücktheit*] of the statement is self-evident. Nevertheless, when the producers of coats and boots compare those articles with linen, or, what is the same thing, with gold and silver, as the universal equivalent, they express the relation between their own private labour and the collective labour of society in the same crazy form."

the processes of circulation. But there is a secondary consideration that may have misled Marx into supposing that the aggregate quantity of surplus value must equal the aggregate profit in the economy as a whole. It will be recalled that in System C, and more generally in any economic model like the ones we have been studying, regardless of the organic composition of capital, the following two equalities hold:

total surplus value = labor value of the physical surplus.

total profits = price of the physical surplus.

I think it is at least possible that Marx was misled by these two confusingly similar equalities into supposing that total profits must equal total surplus value.

We are left with the fact that Marx's conservation principle *does* hold for System G, despite the fact that in that system, prices deviate widely from labor values, but that it does *not* hold for System H. What is peculiar about the structure of System G that produces this result? And more generally, what are the conditions under which a system will conform to Marx's principle of the conservation of surplus value?

2. The Conditions of the Validity of the Principle of the Conservation of Surplus Value

We can in fact say something substantive about the conditions under which the conservation principle holds, but the subject is rather tricky, and will take us a bit further into modern economic theory than we might wish to venture.[4] Nevertheless, the complications are worthwhile, for by means of them we

---

[4] What follows is derived from several sources. The fullest analytical exploration of this issue of which I am aware is to be found in Abraham-Frois and Berrebi (1976), pp. 195–229. See also Pasinetti (1977), pp. 122–150, especially pp. 127–134.

can bring to light an exciting connection between Marx's political economy and some of the most sophisticated advances of twentieth-century theory.

Let us begin by recalling the source of the problem that Ricardo and Marx wrestled with—the problem of the deviation of natural prices from labor values. It was Ricardo's conviction, taken from Adam Smith among others, that the ultimate determinant of the relative prices of commodities was simply the amount of labor bestowed upon them in the course of their production—either directly, in the current production period, or indirectly, by having been bestowed in earlier production periods on commodities that were subsequently employed in production in the current period.

The physical surplus of commodities produced in each cycle, Ricardo thought, was distributed through the market to capitalists, landlords, and workers by means of the profits, rents, and wages that they received. Having conceived the matter in this way, Ricardo concluded that changes in the distribution of the annual surplus—which is to say, fluctuations in the wage rate and the profit rate—should have no effect on the relative prices of commodities, for *how* the surplus is divided up ought to have nothing to do with how much labor must be expended in producing its component parts.

This conviction of Ricardo, we now know, is not universally correct. Generally speaking, in a capitalist economy natural prices will deviate from labor values as a consequence of variations in the temporal pattern of bestowal of labor upon production. The only way to guarantee that price ratios will not deviate from ratios of labor requirements is to require that the proportion of labor directly required to labor indirectly required be the same in all lines of production. And this requirement, as we know, is equivalent to Marx's stipulation in volume one of *Capital* that all sectors exhibit the same organic composition of capital.

Under this extremely restrictive constraint, it is of course true that the ratio of total profits to total surplus value equals the ratio of total prices to total values. But since it was precisely the deviation of prices from values in the absence of equal organic composition of capital that prompted Marx to enunciate his principle of the conservation of surplus value, this result is neither interesting nor reassuring.

There is, however, another class of cases, of considerably greater interest, for which Marx's conservation principle holds. Recall that in his early *Essay on Profits*, Ricardo flirted briefly with the intriguing notion of an economy regulated entirely by an independent corn sector whose inputs and output consist solely of corn. (The idea is that workers eat only corn, entrepreneurs use only seed corn as input, and output consists of corn.) Ricardo reasoned, quite correctly, that in this economic fantasy world, none of the vexing problems of economic theory arises.

First of all, since the only things bought and sold in this world are corn and labor, there is only one relative price, namely the amount of corn paid to each worker per unit of labor. Nor is there any problem aggregating economic magnitudes, for everything is measured in terms of corn. One unit of corn costs, trivially, 1. One unit of labor costs whatever the going wage is. Profit, measured also in units of corn, consists simply in the portion of the crop remaining after next year's seed corn has been set aside and the workers have been given their corn ration. The profit *rate*, theoretical determination of which loomed as such a problem in classical political economy, is in this elementary economy merely the ratio of surplus corn to the corn advanced for seed and wages.

In such a world, Marx's conservation principle is trivially true. To see exactly why this is so, let us suppose that we do in fact have an economy in which corn is the only output, and corn and labor the only inputs. Since corn is the only commodity in the system, we can assign it any price we wish. Let us, for the sake of simplicity, set its price equal to its labor value, which we will call λ.

We can further simplify things by setting the total output of corn in one production cycle equal to unity, and the total quantity of labor employed in one cycle of production also equal to unity. We can do this because it is arbitrary what physical units we use to measure corn and labor (bushels, tons, silo-fulls, or annual outputs, it makes no difference). Finally, let us assume that s units of corn ("s" for "seed") are used as input and w units of corn are consumed by the workers as their wage. (Once we have arbitrarily specified the annual corn output as 1, we cannot in general make any assumptions about the magnitudes of s and w, save, of course, that each is less than 1.) We then have the following set of facts, by stipulation:

A CORN-LABOR ECONOMY

Physical Data
Annual output of corn:	1
Annual input of corn:	s
Annual input of labor:	1

Labor Values
Labor value of corn:	λ
Labor value of the wage:	$w\lambda$
Labor value of the seed:	$s\lambda$

Prices
Price of corn:	λ
Money wage:	$w\lambda$
Price of the seed:	$s\lambda$

The total labor value of the output minus the labor value of the capital employed in producing it is clearly equal to the total labor directly employed in production. In other words:

$$\lambda - s\lambda = 1. \tag{11}$$

If we now subtract from the left side of this equation the price of the corn consumed by the workers and from the right side the labor value of that corn (the two, it will be recalled, being equal by stipulation), we will have, on the left, the total profit remaining to the capitalists, and on the right, the surplus labor value extracted from the laborers, which is to say:

$$\lambda - s\lambda - w\lambda \text{ [total profit]} = 1 - w\lambda \text{ [total surplus value]} \tag{12}$$

And that, quite simply, completes the proof. In a one-commodity world, when the price of the one commodity is set equal to its labor value, total profit equals total surplus value.[5]

If we wish to follow the earlier procedure, and set the price of corn equal to 1, then we can express the same equality in terms of the pair of ratios discussed earlier, by rearranging the equation thus:

$$\frac{[\text{total profit}]}{[\text{total surplus value}]} \quad \frac{1 - s - w}{1 - w\lambda} = \frac{1}{\lambda} \quad \frac{[\text{total prices}]}{[\text{total values}]}$$

So far, we have nothing more than a theoretical curiosity. The class of economies for which Marx's conservation principle holds has now been enlarged, but not in a manner that seems to hold any economic interest. To the economies exhibiting equal organic composition of capital have now been added one-commodity economies. But one-commodity economies are, if possible, even farther from economic reality than economies with equal organic composition!

Suppose, however, that a multi-sector, multi-commodity economy could be organized in such a manner that it functioned *as though* it were a single-sector, single-commodity economy. Suppose, that is to say, there were some way of balancing the proportions of the several sectors so that from a purely formal point of view, the entire economy acted like a large, complex single sector. We could expect Marx's conservation principle to hold for such an economy, despite the fact that the individual sectors did not exhibit equal organic composition of capital, and despite the fact that there were many commodities, not just one, being produced.

In order to see more clearly what is involved in treating a multi-commodity economy as though it were a one-commodity economy, let us think for a bit about a one-commodity economy in which the commodity is suits of clothes. (This is not, I grant, a terribly realistic example, inasmuch as it requires

---

[5] For those who find this "proof" a trifle casual, a formal demonstration of the same proposition may be found in Appendix A, Section V.4.

us to suppose that workers eat suits of clothes, and capitalists use suits of clothes as capital for making more suits of clothes, but it will serve to make the logical point that is at issue here.) In this suit economy, the only input is suits, and the only output is suits.

A suit of clothes, we may imagine, consists of a jacket, a vest, and two pairs of pants (an old-fashioned example). Obviously, therefore, in this economy, twice as many pairs of pants are produced as jackets or vests, for the unit of production is *suits*, not separates. Such an economy can be run at various levels of activity, simply by augmenting or constricting the scope of production, but always the jackets, vests, and pants will enter the production process as inputs and exit as outputs in the proportions 1 jacket/1 vest/2 pairs of pants.

Now let us imagine a three-sector economy that produces jackets in one sector, vests in a second sector, and pants in a third sector, using the same technology as our one-sector suit economy, with jackets, vests, pants, and labor as inputs. In general, such an economy would *not* be a one-commodity economy, and nothing in general could be said about the relative levels of activity at which the several industries were operated. But if this three-sector economy were always to be operated precisely in the proportions 1 part jackets/1 part vests/2 parts pants, then we could just as well treat it as though it were our old familiar suit economy. In other words, so long as the proportions were maintained, we could construe the three-sector economy as a quasi-one-sector economy. In this three-sector economy, the outputs would always bear the proportions 1 jacket/1 vest/2 pairs of pants, *and so would the inputs*. (This last is the crucial point.) And consequently, Marx's conservation principle would hold.

Now we may take the last step, and generalize what we have learned. In order for a multi-sector economy to function as a quasi-one-commodity economy, it must be possible to treat the several commodities as though they are simply component parts of a single composite commodity, into which the individual commodities enter in fixed, unvarying proportions. We must be able to think of the economy not as combining iron, corn, and coal with labor to produce more iron, corn, and coal, but rather as combining a composite iron/corn/coal commodity with labor to produce more of the same iron/corn/coal composite commodity.

Clearly it will make sense to construe the economy in this fashion only if the total output of each commodity bears the identical proportionate relation to the total quantity of itself required as input anywhere in the system. To see what this means, let us return for a last look at our suit economy. Suppose that the economy as a whole uses ten suits total as inputs (either as raw materials for the new suits, or as food for the workers), and turns out fifteen suits at the end of each period of production. The profit rate is obviously 50 percent. Ten jackets, ten vests, and twenty pairs of pants will be used up in each production cycle, and fifteen jackets, fifteen vests, and thirty pairs of pants will emerge as the end product. In short, the ratio of suit output to suit input, namely 3:2, is matched by the ratio of jacket output to jacket input, vest output to vest input, and pants output to pants input.

The same equality of proportion will have to obtain in the general case of a quasi-one-commodity economy. If iron, corn, and coal are used in a fixed iron/corn/coal ratio as input and appear in the same iron/corn/coal ratio as output, then the ratio of corn output to corn input must match the ratios of iron output to iron input and coal output to coal input, and all three ratios must equal the economy-wide profit rate.

Under these conditions, with a multi-sector economy behaving as a quasi-one-commodity economy, Marx's principle of the conservation of surplus value will hold. This proposition is true regardless of how many sectors the economy has, of course, so long as the proportions of gross output to aggregate input remain the same for each commodity.

If we return now to System G, in which, it will be recalled, Marx's principle held even though there was no equal organic composition of capital, we will find that what we have is actually a quasi-one-commodity economy. (See Table 10.) If we total up the inputs required anywhere in the system, including the corn and iron consumed by the workers at a wage of .2

TABLE 10. System G

	Labor Input	Corn Input	Iron Input	Tools Input	Output
Labor		30	15	0	150
Corn Sector	80	128	2	3	240
Iron Sector	20	16	1	5	60
Tools Sector	50	6	27	4	16

corn and .1 iron per unit of labor, we find the following:

INPUTS AND OUTPUTS FOR SYSTEM G

total corn input:	180	total corn output:	240
total iron input:	45	total iron output:	60
total tool input:	12	total tool output:	16

It is obvious upon inspection that the ratio of output to input is the same for each commodity, namely 4:3. From this, it ought to follow that the profit rate is 1/3, as indeed it is. We can see now why System G conforms to Marx's conservation principle. In effect, the entire economy is a single complex sector, using as input 3 units of a complex commodity consisting of (60 corn, 15 iron, and 4 tools), and spewing forth 4 units of the same complex commodity as output.

We have now expanded even further the class of economies conforming to the conservation principle. Restricting ourselves to the sorts of linear reproduction models with which we have been concerned in this book thus far, we can now see that this class includes:

All economies with a zero profit rate
All economies with equal organic composition of capital
All single-commodity economies
All quasi-single-commodity economies

Does this exhaust the class of economies for which the conservation principle holds? There are in fact certain extremely special circumstances under which the money profit rate of the economy exactly equals the value profit rate (i.e., the ratio

$S/(C + V)$, even though the conservation principle, as such, does not hold. But these circumstances do not seem to have any economic significance, and it is not even very easy to characterize them without invoking some quite technical mathematics.[6]

We can state, therefore, that *if* the profit rate is zero *or* there is equal organic composition of capital *or* there is only one commodity produced in the economy *or* the structure of outputs and inputs makes the economy a quasi-one-commodity world, *then* the ratio of total profits to total surplus value equals the ratio of total prices to total values.

Thus far, this result may seem little more than a curiosity, for we might expect to find systems exhibiting the proportions of System G about as often as we find systems exhibiting equal organic composition of capital. Now, however, things become rather interesting. Let us reflect for a bit on the subcategories of economies for which the conservation principle holds.

The case of a zero profit rate is obviously of no interest to anyone concerned with a critique of capitalism, for profits are the distinguishing mark of capitalism. And the case of a one-commodity economy is just a curiosity, historically important because of Ricardo's *Essay on Profits*. The case of equal organic composition of capital is of great historical significance because it is the case in which Ricardo's theory of price is valid, and also the case which Marx limited himself to in volume one of *Capital*. But equal organic composition of capital is so restrictive a condition that we can hardly base a critique of capitalism on its characteristics.

The last case—the quasi-one-commodity world—turns out to have much greater economic significance than appears on first inspection. Let us begin by comparing the case of the quasi-one-commodity world with the case of equal organic composition. The organic composition of an industry is a function of the technology of the economy as a whole (including the real wage). Once we specify the proportions of inputs to output in each line of production, including the real wage, the organic composition of any particular industry is determined.

---

[6] See Abraham-Frois and Berrebi (1976), pp. 218–226.

We can increase the level of activity at which one sector is operated, and decrease the level at which another is operated, all without altering in the slightest the organic composition of any industry. (The aggregate organic composition of the economy as a whole, on the other hand, *is* in part a function of the relative levels of activity at which the several sectors are operated. Decrease the agricultural sector in size, and expand the petrochemical sector, and you will almost certainly increase the proportion of capital to labor in the economy as a whole.) In particular, therefore, the equilibrating force of competition will have no effect whatsoever on the organic composition of the individual sectors of an economy.

The case of the quasi-one-commodity economy is quite different. An economy has a quasi-one-commodity structure when the total output of each commodity bears the same proportionate relationship to the aggregate input of that same commodity required anywhere in the system. The amount of corn produced as output depends on the level of activity at which the corn sector operates. Double the corn sector while the rest of the economy remains unaltered, and you will not change the labor values of any of the commodities, nor will you change the equilibrium prices and the profit rate. But you will most certainly change the ratio of corn output to aggregate corn input. (A quick experiment with System G will make this clear.)

It is therefore somewhat misleading to describe an *economy* as exhibiting a quasi-one-commodity structure. If, by System G, we mean the technology plus the real wage, then System G as such is not a quasi-one-commodity economy. Rather, System G operated at a quite particular choice of activity level for each sector is a quasi-one-commodity world. If we were presented with an economy having exactly the same technology and real wage as System G, but operating at different output levels, it might very well not be a quasi-one-commodity economy. But we could transform it into a quasi-one-commodity world by adjusting the output levels until they fit those of System G! (Strictly speaking, we would only have to adjust them until they were all the same multiple of the levels of System G. If we double all of System G, or reduce it by one-third, or increase all of it across the board by 17 percent, we won't change the fact that gross output bears the same proportion to aggregate input for each commodity.)

And now it may begin to dawn on us that perhaps there are a great many other economies which do not have a quasi-one-commodity structure, but which can be transformed into quasi-one-commodity economies merely by altering the output levels of the several industries. Is this so? Indeed it is! In fact, if we restrict ourselves to economies in which there are no luxury goods sectors (no theology books sectors, no ostrich feathers sectors, no yacht or Jacuzzi sectors), then *every economy can be transformed into a quasi-one-commodity economy by suitable adjustments of the output levels of its several sectors.*[7]

This carries us quite a way, despite the condition that there be no luxury sector in the economy, but there is still one more step to take. Is there any theoretical reason to expect a real economy to adjust itself to the precise proportions required to transform it into a quasi-one-commodity world? Once again, the answer, remarkably, is yes.

Let us recall the three assumptions on which Marx, following Ricardo, bases his analysis: first, that competition is unfettered; second, that the workers live at whatever is historically and socially defined as subsistence; and third, that capitalists are perfect accumulators, reinvesting their entire profit in expanded production. "Accumulate, accumulate! That is Moses and the prophets! 'Industry furnishes the material which saving accumulates' [quoting Smith]. Therefore, save, save, *i.e.,* reconvert the greatest possible portion of surplus-value, or surplus-product into capital! Accumulation for accumulation's sake, production for production's sake: by this formula classical economy expressed the historical mission of the bourgeoisie."[8]

If capitalists are perfect accumulators and workers live at subsistence, then there will be no luxury sectors of the economy to speak of, for there will be no demand for their output. Assuming (as Marx does) that the labor is available for

---

[7] For a proof of this proposition, see Appendix A, Section V.6.
[8] Marx (1967a), p. 595.

economic growth, it follows that the entire resources of the economy will be devoted to the achievement of a maximum rate of expansion. At first, of course, the precise mix of physical surplus may fail to match the market demand of capitalists seeking new capital goods for their expansion. But over time, assuming that there is no technological change, the economy will settle into a shape permitting maximum growth.

Once that happens, regardless of the shape in which the economy began, the relative proportions of the several sectors will guarantee that Marx's principle of the conservation of surplus value holds.

This is really an extremely powerful result. To be sure, it rests on the dramatically simplifying assumption that there is no technological change (an abstraction that removes this theory very far from the real world, but not at all from modern economic theory!). It rests, too, on a number of simplifying assumptions about the behavior of workers and capitalists, and the supply of labor. But since these are simplifications and assumptions that were, for the most part, shared by all the classical economists, Marx cannot fairly be taxed too heavily with them.

Is this a result with which Marx himself would have been happy? It is very difficult to tell. On the one hand, it would appear that Marx can defend something approximating his conservation principle for a very significant set of cases of capitalist economies embarked on maximum-growth paths. On the other hand, since the focus of Marx's critique of capitalist dynamics was precisely *unbalanced* growth, with its attendant crises of overproduction, we must suppose that he would be unhappy to learn that his solution to the problem of the deviation of prices from values works *only* in the case of trouble-free balanced maximum growth.

TECHNICAL AFTERWORD TO CHAPTER SIX
A NUMERICAL EXAMPLE

A fully formal treatment of the theses just summarized can be found in Appendix A, but some readers may find it useful to see an example in the style of the analysis presented thus far. Let us turn back to System H, the little corn/iron economy of Table 13 in which, it will be recalled, the conservation principle did not hold.

Assume a real wage of .1 corn/unit of labor. Then labor values are:

$$\lambda_c = 1$$
$$\lambda_i = 2$$
$$\lambda_w = .1$$

Prices, with $p_c = 1$, are:

$$p_i \cong 5.9223462$$
$$w = .1$$

The profit rate $\cong .636347$.

TABLE 13. System H

	Labor Input	Corn Input	Iron Input	Output
Labor		1.5	0	15
Corn Sector	13	5	1	20
Iron Sector	2	10	5	11

TABLE 14. System H'

	Corn Input	Iron Input	Output
Corn Sector	.315	.05	1
Iron Sector	.927273	.454545	1

In order to transform System H into a quasi-one-commodity world, it is convenient to divide the corn sector through by 20 and the iron sector through by 11, giving us the inputs per unit output. Combining the corn required by the real wage with the other corn inputs, and dividing through, we get the result given in Table 14.

Since we are seeking the relative activity levels, we can set the activity level of the corn sector equal to 1. We are then looking for an activity level of the iron sector, y_i, such that:

(corn output)/(corn input) = (iron output)/(iron input),

which is to say:

$$1/(.315 + .927273y_i) = y_i/(.05 + .454545y_i).$$

When we solve this equation for y_i, keeping in mind that y_i must be positive, we find:

$$y_i \cong .31934.$$

Multiplying the iron sector by y_i, we obtain the result given in Table 15.

TABLE 15. System H''

	Labor Input	Corn Input	Iron Input	Output
Corn Sector	.65	.25	.05	1
Iron Sector	.058	.29	.145	.31934

(Corn output)/(corn input) $= 1/(.065 + .0058 + .25 +$
$.29) = 1.637$, which within the limits of calculation $= (1 + \pi)$.

(Iron output)/(iron input) $= .31934/(.05 + .145) = 1.6376$,
which within the limits of calculation, also $= (1 + \pi)$.

When Sraffa carries through this sort of transformation of a
system into a quasi-one-commodity system (or, as he calls it,
a "Standard System"), he normalizes the scale of the system
by holding the total direct labor inputs constant. In the present
case, this means multiplying both sectors by 21.186, in order
to obtain a system that employs 15 units of labor, while pre-
serving the quasi-one-commodity structure. If we make this
final adjustment, we obtain the result given in Table 16.

The effect, as we can see by comparing System H''' with the
original System H, is slightly to enlarge the corn sector while
slightly shrinking the iron sector. If we now check System H'''
for Marx's conservation principle, using the prices, labor values,
and profit rate originally calculated (none of which has been
altered by these proportionate increases and decreases of the
the sizes of the sectors, of course), we find:

$$\text{(total prices)/(total values)} = 61.2552/34.7178$$
$$= 1.76437$$

and

$$\text{(total profits)/(total surplus value)} = 23.804/13.5$$
$$= 1.76326$$

which, within the limits of calculation, are equal.

TABLE 16. System H'''

	Labor Input	Corn Input	Iron Input	Output
Corn Sector	13.7710	5.2966	1.0593	21.1864
Iron Sector	1.2288	6.1440	3.0720	6.7657

When competitive pressures begin to move System H in the direction of a quasi-one-commodity structure, the actual composition of capitalist demand will not match the existing store of physical surplus, even though the total price of the physical surplus equals the total profit in the hands of the capitalists. For example, capitalists in the corn sector will appropriate, in one cycle of production, a total profit of 7.77765. Capitalists in the iron sector will appropriate, in the same cycle, a total profit of 25.334.

Now, the corn producers know that they must invest .611 corn units of money to produce each additional unit of corn, and therefore with their profit, they can expand production by approximately 12.73 units. The iron producers know that it costs them 3.6192 to produce 1 unit of iron, so they will seek to expand production by approximately 7 units. They have enough *money* to buy the necessary inputs at equilibrium prices, to be sure, but will the physical quantities of corn and iron be available in the right amounts? No! Total additional capitalist demand for corn will equal 10.5 units, whereas only 3.5 units of surplus corn are available. Total additional capitalist demand for iron will equal 3.8183, far short of the 6 units available. The result, obviously, will be a temporarily high price for corn and a temporarily low price for iron, resulting in rises and falls of the profit rate in those sectors, movement of capital from iron into corn, and in the end an equilibration of the system at relative activity levels that permit balanced maximum growth. At these levels, the ratio of total prices to total values will exactly equal the ratio of total profits to total surplus value; the value rate of profit for the economy as a whole, $S/(C + V)$, will equal the money profit rate, π, and this profit rate will equal the rate of growth, g.

It should now be clear why an economy that includes luxury sectors cannot always be transformed into a quasi-one-commodity world. A luxury good forms a part of the final demand of the economy, but plays no role in production, save perhaps as an input into its own production or the production of other luxury goods (see the theology books sector in System C). Now, if the aggregate input of a commodity is zero, then the ratio of gross output to aggregate input will be undefined. And if there *is* some positive input, then the ratio of output to input *may* conform to the proportions required for the quasi-one-commodity structure, but it will only be an accident should that happen. The lack of dependence of the rest of the economy on the luxury sector separates its proportions from the general proportions of the system as a whole.

ENVOI

* * * * *

SOME DOUBTS ABOUT MARX'S
THEORY OF VALUE
AND EXPLOITATION

Our story is finished. With the precise delineation of the conditions of validity of Marx's principle of the conservation of surplus value, we have brought to completion the century-long theoretical development that began with Adam Smith's observations about the determinants of exchange in the "early and rude state" preceding the appropriation of land and the accumulation of capital. But though the story is ended, its meaning remains unclear.

For Smith and Ricardo, the deeper aim of a theory of natural price was a coherent account of the reproduction of the produced means of production, the distribution of the social surplus, and the shape and pace of economic growth. For Marx, however, these desiderata were secondary to his primary goal, which was to demonstrate and explain the exploitative foundations of capitalist accumulation. It is not the purpose of this book to debate the adequacy of Marx's account of exploitation, but with the aid of the analytical clarifications we have achieved, it is possible at least to raise some questions that contemporary students of *Capital* may find it useful to address.[1]

---

[1] There is already a considerable literature on the issues to be discussed in this concluding chapter. See, for example, Bowles (1983), Roemer (1982), Wolff (1981), Vegara (1979), Nell (1982), among others.

The key to Marx's theory of exploitation is the claim that labor power, and labor power alone, is exploitable. To test this claim, let us return yet one more time to System C, the corn/iron/theology books model which we used to introduce the Ricardian theory of natural price. The system, it will be recalled, had the structure given in Table 3.

In analyzing System C, we began by asking how much labor is required by its technology, directly or indirectly, to produce a single unit of corn, of iron, and of books. We answered that question by translating the input requirements of the system into a system of simultaneous equations. The specifications for the corn sector, for example, yielded the equation:

$$100 + 2\lambda_c + 16\lambda_i + 0\lambda_b = 300\lambda_c. \qquad (2)$$

This equation says that the labor embodied in the 300 units of corn output equals the sum total of the labor embodied in the 2 units of corn input, the 16 units of iron input, *and the 100 units of labor directly required*. The key to the construction of equation (2), and of all the other labor value equations we have written, is the distinction between labor directly required and labor indirectly required. When writing the labor value equation for the corn sector, we enter the 100 units of labor at par, so to speak, since those 100 units are required directly. The 2 units of corn and 16 units of iron are construed as so much embodied labor, labor that has been expended at an earlier time and thus is required *indirectly* by the 300 units of corn output.

TABLE 3. System C

	Labor Input	Corn Input	Iron Input	Books Input	Output
Labor		42	21	0	210
Corn Sector	100	2	16	0	300
Iron Sector	90	9	12	0	90
Books Sector	20	1	2	2	40
Total Input	210	54	51	2	

Suppose we now ask a question that neither Ricardo nor Marx thought to ask, but which does not at all seem precluded by the objective specifications of the model: How much *corn* is required, directly or indirectly, to produce a single unit of iron, of books, of labor, or of corn itself? In short, what is the "corn value" of a unit of each of the commodities produced in the system?[2]

Why should we suppose that corn is in fact required indirectly as well as directly to produce iron, books, labor, or corn itself? we might ask. Iron is required to produce iron, and corn is required to produce iron, so obviously corn is required indirectly to produce iron. What is more, iron and corn are required to produce books, labor, and corn itself, so corn is in fact an input, both directly and indirectly, into every single commodity in the system.

Since corn is required indirectly as well as directly as an input into every commodity in System C, we could presumably undertake to calculate the *quantity* of corn required, directly or indirectly, to produce one unit of, say, iron. We could do this by constructing an infinite backwards series of the corn inputs directly required in the present period, the corn inputs directly required in the period just previous, and so on. Or, alternatively, we could define variables standing for "the corn value of iron," "the corn value of labor," "the corn value of books," and even "the corn value of corn," and then try to translate the input/output data of System C into a system of corn value equations.

A rather deeper question might be asked. What makes us suppose that the infinite series of direct and indirect corn inputs converges to some finite quantity, as in fact the series of labor inputs does? Alternatively, what makes us think that a system of "corn value" equations would have an economically meaningful solution? The question is rather technical, but the

---

[2] I attempted to explore the implications of this question in an essay published in *Philosophy & Public Affairs* (1981). Since then, I have learned that the same question was asked, and many of the same conclusions drawn, by Josep Vegara in a very interesting work entitled *Economia politica y modelos multisectoriales*. See Vegara (1979), chap. 3, especially section 3.5.

answer is not. So long as corn is indeed required either directly or indirectly for the production of each commodity in the system, the infinite series defining the corn value of iron, the corn value of books, or the corn value of corn itself will converge, and the system of corn value equations will have an economically meaningful solution (these are actually two equivalent ways of saying the same thing).[3]

There is nothing special about corn, of course. We could just as easily have chosen to ask about the iron values of the system. (But not the book values, for theology books are *not* required directly or indirectly as an input into all other commodities.)

When we first introduced the notion of labor values, we chose to calculate them not by summing infinite series, but by solving systems of simultaneous equations. Let us see how we would set up such a set of equations for the purpose of calculating the corn values of the commodities produced in the System C.

In order to avoid confusion, let us introduce a new symbol for "corn values," namely γ. Using subscripts in the same manner as before, we can then define three new variables:

γ_i = the corn value of iron (i.e., the quantity of corn directly or indirectly required for the production of one unit of iron)

γ_b = the corn value of books (i.e., the quantity of corn directly or indirectly required for the production of one unit of books)

γ_l = the corn value of labor (i.e., the quantity of corn directly or indirectly required for the production of one unit of labor)

However unfamiliar the notion of a "corn value" may be, the underlying idea is exactly like that of "labor value." It takes labor indirectly as well as directly to produce iron and we can

---

[3] A proof of this proposition can be found in Appendix A, Section V.7.

therefore ask how much labor is required, indirectly as well as directly, to produce one unit of iron. That quantity is, quite simply, what we mean by the "labor value of iron." So too, it takes corn indirectly as well as directly to produce iron and we can therefore ask how much corn is required, indirectly as well as directly, to produce one unit of iron. That quantity is what we mean by the "corn value" of iron.

Are we then to suppose that a unit of iron has embodied, congealed, or crystallized within it, some quantum of corn? We shall have to postpone the answer to that question for a bit, but at this point, suffice it to say that we can speak perfectly meaningfully about the amount of corn directly and indirectly required to produce a unit of iron without slipping into potentially mystifying talk about "congealed corn."

How would we go about constructing a "corn value" equation for the iron industry of System C, using the input/output data listed in Table 3? Following the procedure used in formulating the labor value equations, we begin by assuming that the total quantity of corn required directly and indirectly to produce 90 units of iron, which we can represent as $90\gamma_i$, equals the amount of corn directly and indirectly required to produce the labor inputs into the production of that iron, plus the amount of corn directly and indirectly required to produce the corn and iron inputs, *plus* the 9 units of corn required as direct corn inputs. In short:

$$9 + 90\gamma_l + 12\gamma_i + 0\gamma_b = 90\gamma_i. \text{ [Iron industry]} \qquad (13)$$

Using the same procedure, we can now write corn value equations for the books industry and for the "labor industry," namely:

$$1 + 20\gamma_l + 2\gamma_i + 2\gamma_b = 40\gamma_b. \text{ [Books industry]} \quad (14)$$

$$42 + 0\gamma_l + 21\gamma_i + 0\gamma_b = 210\gamma_l. \text{ [Labor industry]} \quad (15)$$

There are several things to note about this system of corn value equations. First of all, there is no equation representing the corn industry. A variable, γ_c, standing for the quantity of corn directly and indirectly required to produce one unit of corn, nowhere appears in the equations we have written. We can, of course, write an equation for the corn industry:

$$2 + 100\gamma_l + 16\gamma_i + 0\gamma_b = 300\gamma_c. \text{ [Corn industry]} \quad (16)$$

But this equation merely permits us to determine the value of γ_c. We do not need it to determine the values of the other variables, for equations (13) through (15) form an independent, determinate system of three equations in three unknowns.

It follows that a change in the conditions of production in the corn industry will have no effect on the corn values of the other commodities produced in the system, even though corn is a direct input into all the other sectors. In this way, of course, the price of corn occupies a role that is formally identical to that of the wage in our original labor value calculations.

The second point of importance is that in order for the corn value equations to form a determinate system, labor must be construed as a produced commodity whose conditions of production are fixed. The roles of labor and corn are here reversed: the real wage must be taken as specified for purposes of analysis of the system, but the conditions of production of corn can be left indeterminate.

It is easy enough to understand why this reversal takes place. We are attempting to calculate the quantities of corn required directly or indirectly for the production of labor, iron, and books in System C. The corn directly required enters our calculations at par—one unit of corn directly required contributes one unit of corn value to the finished product. Hence, with regard to those corn units, it makes no difference to our calculations how much corn they have cost to produce, for no matter what their cost, we value them at one per unit. Had the available stocks of corn descended as manna from heaven, or been washed up on the shores of the community, so that they cost nothing to produce, the resulting corn value calculations would be the same as if the corn were produced by a technique requiring a variety of labor and non-labor inputs.

When we solve the corn value equations, we obtain the following results:

$$\gamma_i \cong .3913$$

$$\gamma_l \cong .23913$$

$$\gamma_b \cong .17277$$

$$\gamma_c \cong .10725$$

What these numbers say is that it takes approximately four-tenths of a unit of corn, directly and indirectly, to produce one unit of iron; slightly less than a quarter of a unit of corn, directly and indirectly, to produce one unit of labor; and so forth.

The most significant result of our little exercise is the discovery that it takes *less* than a unit of corn to produce a unit of corn. Indeed, under the conditions of production specified in our model, it turns out to require scarcely more than one-tenth of a unit of corn to produce a unit of corn. But when we set up our corn value equations, we entered each unit of corn at par. So in a manner of speaking (indeed, in more than merely a manner of speaking), almost nine-tenths of a unit of "surplus corn value" is extracted from each unit of corn input. At the same time, of course, *no* surplus corn value is extracted from the *labor* inputs. Each labor input costs (i.e., requires) .23913 units of corn, directly and indirectly, to produce, and that is precisely how it is entered into the equations. When we are calculating corn values, labor is treated exactly like iron or books.

Notice that the extraction of surplus corn value from the corn inputs does not require anything resembling a distinction between corn and "corn power." We need not tell a story about how the entrepreneur buys a bushel's corn power and then sets the corn to work in such a way as to extract a full bushel's corn value from it. The appearance in the model of surplus corn value results directly from the fact that corn inputs are valued at par in the equations, while all other inputs are valued at their corn values.

In this case, it takes less than a bushel of corn to make a bushel of corn. Will that *always* be true, or is this simply an accidental result of some special feature of System C? The answer is that this is no accident. *So long as some physical surplus of any commodity is produced anywhere in the system, it will take less than one unit of corn to produce one unit of corn.*[4]

When we analyzed Marx's explanation for the appearance of profit even in economies exhibiting equal organic composition of capital, we found that the quantity of surplus labor extracted from the labor inputs into System C exactly equaled the labor value of the physical surplus generated by the system as a whole each year. Indeed, we showed that this equality in no way relied on the special organic structure of the economy, but held good for every possible productive economy of the sort we were examining. Is there any significant relationship between the surplus *corn* value and the physical surplus?

None whatsoever, if it is the *labor value* of the physical surplus that is at issue. The surplus corn value extracted in System C as a whole simply equals the aggregate corn input minus the corn value of that input, or:

$$\text{surplus corn value} = 54 - 54(.10725)$$
$$\cong 48.209.$$

The (labor) value of the physical surplus, as we saw, equals 168.

When we calculate the *corn* value of the physical surplus, on the other hand, we find:

$$\text{corn value of physical surplus} = 246\gamma_c + 39\gamma_i + 38\gamma_b$$
$$\cong 48.209.$$

So, an analysis of System C in terms of the quantity of corn directly and indirectly required in production yields exactly the same results as an analysis in terms of labor. In labor value terms, the value of the physical surplus equals the surplus value extracted from the labor inputs. It looks, therefore, as though the labor inputs are exploited in capitalist production. In corn value terms, the value of the physical surplus equals the surplus corn value extracted from the corn inputs. So it also looks as though the corn inputs are exploited in capitalist production.

[4] A proof of this proposition can be found in Appendix A, Section V.8.

It should by now be obvious that there is nothing special about corn. We could have carried out the same calculations in terms of iron (but *not* in terms of books, for it does not take any books at all to produce corn, iron, or labor, either directly or indirectly). So long as we select a commodity, A, which serves, directly or indirectly, as an input into the production of all other commodities, it will be true that the "A-value" of the physical surplus exactly equals the "surplus A-value" extracted from the A-inputs![5]

This proposition is perfectly general. It does not depend, for example, on the fact that both labor and corn are *direct* inputs into the production of every commodity. We can easily imagine an economy in which coal enters into the production of iron, and iron enters into the production of corn, so that coal is *indirectly* required for corn production, but not *directly* required. Nevertheless, we could perfectly well calculate the "coal value" of corn in such a system. Nor is it necessary that a commodity be a direct input into itself in order to prove that the quantity of that commodity required to produce one unit of itself is less than 1. (Labor, note, is not required directly to produce labor, but nevertheless we can show that less than a unit of labor is required to produce a unit of labor.)

In fact, as the reader will by now quite well recognize, *all* of the results developed in the preceding sections with regard to labor values and prices can be duplicated no matter which commodity we pick out as "substance of value." For example, we can quite easily define "corn-organic composition of capital" as the ratio between the corn value of the non-corn inputs and the corn value of the corn inputs. We can then show, by exactly the same argument (with the symbols for labor and corn adjusted), that with a positive rate of profit, the prices in a system will be proportional to corn values if and only if the system exhibits equal corn-organic composition of capital.

Indeed, we can even reproduce the results concerning balanced growth and the conservation of surplus corn value. In other words, we can show that when the proportions of the

[5] Ibid.

several sectors are adjusted so as to make the economy into a quasi-one-commodity world, then the ratio of total profits to total prices will exactly equal the ratio of total surplus corn value to total corn values of the commodities produced. To show this last proposition, however, we must be careful to specify a labor "industry" that produces a "physical surplus" of labor in the proper proportion to aggregate labor inputs.

Extending the analysis of corn values in a manner exactly parallel to that for labor values, we can treat the inputs required for corn production as a "wage," and conceive of them as variable. The system of price equations with some commodity chosen as numeraire will then exhibit one degree of freedom. Needless to say, it will be the case that the price of corn varies inversely with the profit rate, apparently thereby "showing" that there is a conflict of interest between capitalists and corn suppliers!

By reproducing, for corn or iron or coal, all the striking results that Marx derived concerning labor, we have, it seems to me, raised questions about the foundations of Marx's critique of capitalism and classical political economy.

This line of argument may strike the serious student of Marx as bizarre, quite possibly even as absurd. How can one seriously undertake to analyze a capitalist economy in terms of corn values, embodied corn, corn organic composition of capital, and surplus corn value?

First of all, it may by objected that Marx couches his analysis in terms of abstract homogeneous socially necessary labor, whereas we have spoken only of corn, or in the most general terms of a commodity, A, "identified as substance of value." Might one not argue that the historical/theoretical process whereby concrete, particular laboring is transformed into abstract homogeneous labor singles labor out as unlike the other inputs into the production process, and hence makes it the only suitable choice as "substance of value"?

As we observed in the discussion of Diana and Orion earlier, commodity production and exchange and the establishment of a system of natural prices presuppose an extensive historical transformation of useful objects into *commodities*. The products of wage labor must become standardized no less than the laboring. If a capitalist employs his corn inputs with less than an average efficiency, he will not be able to recover their full cost when he sells his product in the market, any more than he will be able to recover the full cost of inefficiently employed labor. What is more, the development of a market in corn, with a single economy-wide natural price, requires a historical process of standardization of corn which effectively eliminates those regional or craft variations that in a pre-capitalist economy might enable the connoisseur to distinguish corn of one region from corn of another.

The very abstractness of our calculations must have made it obvious that we were no more concerned with actual, spatially locatable, and materially specifiable corn and iron than with concrete particular laborings. So this objection will not stand inspection.

A more serious objection to the corn-value fantasy is that calculations in terms of labor values are legitimated by the fact that labor alone is required for the production of all commodities. But this will not do either, for under the assumptions of the analysis we have been pursuing, so are corn and iron. It takes labor to produce corn. But it takes corn to produce labor. It takes labor to produce the corn that is required to produce the labor. True, but it takes corn to produce the labor that is required to produce the corn that is required to produce the labor. And so on. Each commodity that is required directly or indirectly in the production of all others has this peculiar regressive feature.

What is more, as we have just seen, the infinite regressive series of earlier and earlier direct inputs converges to a finite, economically meaningful sum, whether it is labor inputs, corn inputs, or coal inputs that one is summing. So long as the economy is capable of reproducing itself, and of producing *some* physical surplus, no matter of what sort, all those infinite series will converge. Even more significantly, it will take less than a unit of whatever commodity we are summing, directly and indirectly, to produce a unit of that commodity. And the value of the physical surplus in the system, measured in terms of that commodity, will exactly equal the surplus value of that commodity extracted from the inputs of it into the economy as a whole.

A second, more serious objection to the claim that corn, iron, and coal are formally on a par with labor is that although many inputs are required directly or indirectly for the production of all commodities in the system under examination, only labor is *directly* required. Therein lies the formal peculiarity of labor. In the little two- and three-sector models we have been using for purposes of theoretical analysis, both corn and labor are direct inputs into every sector. But in the real world, the variation in capital inputs is enormous. There is scarcely likely to be any single raw material, machine, or tool that is universally employed. *Labor*, on the other hand, will most certainly play an essential role in *every* production process.

It is not clear exactly what this argument is intended to demonstrate. The quantity of labor *directly* required for the production of a commodity is not an economically significant datum, save in Adam Smith's "early and rude state of society." Neither Ricardo nor Marx imagines that the ratios in which commodities exchange have anything to do with the quantities of labor *directly* required for their production. From a purely analytical point of view, it is simply an accident that every production process uses labor.

Indeed, if we analyze an economy at a sufficiently high level of aggregation—say, into an agricultural sector, an industrial sector, and a luxury sector—then we can confidently anticipate that *every* sector will use some of the output of the industrial sector, for that will represent *all* the tools, machinery, and manufactured goods produced anywhere in the system.

So labor is not the only commodity directly or indirectly required for the production of all other commodities in the world we have been examining, and at some suitable level of analysis, it is not even the only commodity directly required for the production of every other commodity. Nevertheless, it might still be claimed that labor is analytically unique inasmuch as it, and it alone, is an input directly and indirectly required for the production of every output *in every logically possible capitalist system.*

After all, it could be said, no one food is a staple of the working class diet in every society. In some societies, rice plays that role, in others potatoes, in still others wheat or maize. What is more, no one capital input is required for production in *every* possible capitalist economy. There are societies that have functioned without iron, without coal, even without wood. But in all capitalist economies, labor is directly or indirectly required for the production of all outputs. So in the enlarged logical space of all possible capitalist economies, labor is formally distinguishable from all other inputs.

This argument too is faulty, but for somewhat subtler reasons. The problem is essentially one of classification and disaggregation. If we treat *food* as a single category for purposes of analysis, then it will of course be true that in all possible capitalist societies both food and labor are directly or indirectly required for all outputs. ("Possible" here is not meant to encompass science-fiction fantasies of societies in which workers can live without eating.) On the other hand, if we disaggregate food into rice, beef, maize, and so on, then no one subcategory will be directly or indirectly required for the production of all commodities in all possible capitalist societies.

But it is also true that if we disaggregate laboring into tailoring, carpentering, tool and die making, and so on, then no one subcategory of labor will be directly or indirectly required for the production of all commodities in all possible capitalist societies. In other words, we can make labor appear to be analytically unique by construing it as homogeneous and all other general categories of inputs as heterogeneous. But although this corresponds to Marx's theoretical inclination, it is not at all clear why so heterogeneous a theoretical practice should be adopted.

We might think to get around this last difficulty by classifying labor into low-skill, median-skill, and high-skill labor.

It will then be true, of course, that in all possible capitalist societies, low-skill labor will be directly or indirectly required for the production of all commodities (omitting, for the sake of simplicity, the quirky possibility that in some society the low-skill labor might be employed only for the production of luxury goods and services). But the actual concrete physical activities classified as "low-skill" will vary considerably from society to society. We could equally well classify food into subsistence, medium-quality, and luxury food, in which case it would be the case that subsistence food, like low-skill labor, would be directly or indirectly required for the production of all commodities in all possible capitalist societies. But the actual physical foods classified as subsistence food would, as Ricardo long ago pointed out, vary considerably from society to society.

✳ ✳ ✳

If we reflect for a moment on the content and direction of our analysis, it is not difficult to understand how we have arrived at this curious set of conclusions. We began with a generalized characterization of the cyclical processes by which societies reproduce their material conditions of existence. We then sought to formalize that characterization by means of several systems of simultaneous equations. Following Marx, we sought to establish certain propositions concerning what *really* takes place in a capitalist economy, below the misleading surface of prices, wages, and profits, and thereby to legitimate the introduction of certain powerfully loaded theoretical terms, such as "surplus value" and "exploitation." Explicit in our initial non-formal discussion of reproduction, and implicit in our move to formalism, was the assumption that labor plays a distinctive role in the process of reproduction, and that wage labor plays a special role in a capitalist economy. *But little or nothing of the distinctiveness of that role found its way into the formal structure of our model of a capitalist economy.* In the logical space we have been investigating, all commodities, *including labor*, exhibit the same formal structure. The identification of labor as "substance of value" is arbitrary and without theoretical significance unless it can be shown that labor is in some way formally distinguishable from all other commodities. To say that it is *formally* distinguishable is to say that its role in the system of production and exchange exhibits formal peculiarities which are independent of the conventions of notation.

When we look at the systems of equations that we constructed from the data of System C and its fellows, we find that labor is distinguished only notationally from corn, iron, or cloth. In the labor value equations, to be sure, the labor inputs are valued at par, unlike the non-labor inputs. But that distinction, we found, was a *consequence* of our decision to treat labor differently (by calculating "labor" values), not a *justification* of the decision. It turned out that we could just as easily have chosen to calculate corn values or iron values, in which case corn and iron would have been treated in a manner formally identical to the manner in which labor was treated in the labor value equations.

In the price equations, labor appears as an input with a price, and the equilibrium profit rate is construed as a markup on the total cost of all inputs, labor included. Only an arbitrary notational convention differentiates the price of labor (w) from the price of a commodity i (p_i).

Marx's view, of course, is that labor *is* formally distinguished from all other commodities by virtue of the possibility of distinguishing between labor and labor power. The capitalist, he argues, buys the worker's labor power, and then undertakes to extract labor from it in the workplace. A struggle ensues between worker and capitalist over how much labor, of what intensity, and directed to what tasks, the worker shall actually deliver up in the factory. As he had long since made clear in the writings of his youth, Marx viewed agricultural and industrial labor under capitalism as a painful, exhausting, alienating activity that prudent workers would shun so far as was within their power. Through the striking device of the division of the workday into necessary and surplus labor time, Marx was able to organize a large body of historical material on labor-management struggles. The theme of the story is always the same: capital's attempt to extract more labor from the

177

labor power it has purchased, through its control of the workplace and the work process, and labor's increasingly stubborn effort to resist capital's encroachments.

Marx is clearly correct in his emphasis on the historical conflict over hours and working conditions. But as he himself would have been the first to acknowledge, the capitalist's effort to extract *more* or *more intense* labor from his workers than was bargained for in the marketplace must not be identified as the *ground* or *source* of profit. To adopt such a line of analysis would commit Marx to the totally unacceptable conclusion that in a benign capitalism, in which workers labor only for the time and with the intensity agreed upon when the wage contract is struck, there would be no profit and no exploitation!

There is in fact no place in the formal analysis at which the labor/labor power distinction gets introduced. The technical conditions of production specify quantities of *labor* required for unit outputs of individual commodities, and though it would be technically possible to convert all those quantities of labor into quantities of labor power (by *assuming* a given number of hours of labor as extractable from a unit of labor power), nothing would be gained thereby.

A number of recent authors have addressed themselves to the task of formally modeling the relations of domination in the workplace which Marx considered fundamental to capitalism.[6] As more and more theorists take up this challenge, it may finally prove possible to complete the analytic reconstruction of Marx's political economy in a way that preserves his deepest and most powerful insights. But that is more appropriately the subject of a separate book.

[6] See Nell (1982) and Bowles (1983) for especially suggestive treatments.

A FORMAL ANALYSIS OF RICARDIAN AND MARXIAN POLITICAL ECONOMY

SECTION I: SOME IMPORTANT FACTS ABOUT MATRICES

I.1 When a matrix has been brought into row-echelon form by a series of elementary operations, the *rank*, *r*, of the matrix is equal to the number of non-zero rows. If we construe each row of a matrix as a vector, then the rank of the matrix is equal to the number of linearly independent rows.

I.2 For a square matrix, A, of order n [i.e., having dimensionality $(n \times n)$] and having rank $k \leq n$:
   (a) $k =$ the number of linearly independent rows (and columns) of A.
   (b) $|A| = 0$ iff $k < n$.
   (c) A^{-1} exists iff $k = n$.

I.3 Consider the system of linear equations: $Ax = b$. This system has a unique solution if and only if A is non-singular (of rank n), namely,

$$x = A^{-1}b.$$

If we form the augmented matrix $[A, b]$ having n rows and $n + 1$ columns, where A is the "coefficient matrix" of the system $Ax = b$, then in general:
   (a) The system has *no* solution if $r[A, b] > r[A]$, which is the case when b is linearly independent of the columns of A.

(b) The system has a *unique* solution if $r[A, b] = r[A] = n$.
(c) The system has an *infinite* number of solutions if $r[A, b] = r[A] = k < n$.

I.4 In the particular case of a system of homogeneous linear equations, of the form $Ax = 0$, $r[A, 0] = r[A]$, because the null vector is linearly dependent on any set of vectors. Hence a solution to $Ax = 0$ always exists.

(a) When $r[A] = n$, there is a single solution, namely the trivial solution $x = 0$, for then A^{-1} exists, and so, by premultiplying both sides of the equation by A^{-1}, we have $A^{-1}Ax = 0$, or $Ix = 0$, or $x = 0$.
(b) When $r[A] = k < n$, then there are infinitely many non-trivial solutions.

I.5 *Eigenvalues and Eigenvectors*

Consider the special case of the equation $Ax = b$ in which $b = \lambda x$, where λ is a scalar. In other words, the matrix A transforms the vector x into some scalar multiple of itself. Given the square matrix A of order n, we can now ask for all those vectors, x, which satisfy the equation.

To solve this problem, we transform the equation into a linear homogeneous equation, thus:

$$[\lambda I - A]x = 0.$$

We know that this system always has the trivial solution $x = 0$. For non-zero solutions to exist, it is necessary and sufficient that $r[\lambda I - A] < n$, which is to say:

$$|\lambda I - A| = 0.$$

More fully, this is:

$$\begin{vmatrix} (\lambda - a_{11}) & -a_{12} & \cdots & -a_{1n} \\ -a_{21} & (\lambda - a_{22}) & \cdots & -a_{2n} \\ \cdot & \cdot & \cdot & \cdot \\ \cdot & \cdot & \cdot & \cdot \\ \cdot & \cdot & \cdot & \cdot \\ -a_{n1} & -a_{n2} & \cdots & (\lambda - a_{nn}) \end{vmatrix} = 0.$$

This is called the *characteristic equation* of A (*eigen* is German for, among other things, *characteristic*). Expanded, this equation becomes a polynomial in λ of degree n. Hence, the equation in general has n roots (in the domain of complex numbers), and these roots are called the *eigenvalues* or *characteristic roots* of A. Note that the eigenvalues of A may be all distinct from one another, or all the same, or there may be some repetitions. If an eigenvalue is repeated h times, it is said to have *multiplicity* h. A root with multiplicity 1 is said to be a *simple* root.

Thus, given a square matrix A of order n and of rank $k < n$, we know that there are exactly n numbers, λ, for which nontrivial solutions exist to the equation

$$Ax = \lambda x.$$

Since there are n (not necessarily distinct) eigenvalues associated with A, it follows that there are n linear homogeneous systems of the form

$$[\lambda_1 I - A]x = 0,$$

$$[\lambda_2 I - A]x = 0,$$

$$[\lambda_3 I - A]x = 0,$$

and so forth.

The vectors $x \neq 0$ satisfying these systems are called the *eigenvectors associated with the eigenvalues* λ_1, λ_2, and so forth. Obviously, if there is one vector satisfying the equation $[\lambda_i I - A]x = 0$, then there are an infinite number of vectors satisfying the equation, for:

If

$$Ax = \lambda_i x$$

then

$$\alpha Ax = \alpha \lambda_i x$$

and

$$A(\alpha x) = \lambda_i(\alpha x).$$

Everything that has been said so far about A could be said about the transpose of A, A'. The eigenvalues of A' are identical with the eigenvalues of A. However, the eigenvectors associated with the eigenvalues of A' are *not* in general the same as the eigenvectors associated with the corresponding eigenvalues of A. Thus, we can write the linear homogeneous system of equations:

$$A'y' = \lambda y$$

or

$$[\lambda I - A']y' = 0,$$

which, by transposition, yields

$$y[\lambda I - A] = 0.$$

Eigenvectors x are called *right-hand eigenvectors* of A. Eigenvectors y are called *left-hand eigenvectors* of A. (The fundamental duality of the physical quantity structure and price structure of a linear reproduction economy is grounded in the relationship between the left-hand and right-hand eigenvectors associated with the same [maximum] eigenvalue of the unit input coefficient matrix.)

I.6 Convergence Conditions for Square Matrices and the Existence of an Inverse

We can speak of the powers of a square matrix, A, namely $A^0 = I$, A, A^2, A^3, and so forth. A is said to be *convergent* when:

$$\lim A^n = 0 \quad \text{as } n \to \infty.$$

Note that to say that A^n tends to the null matrix, 0, is to say that all the elements of A^n tend to zero.

It is a theorem that for a positive real number k, kA is convergent if $k < (1/|\lambda_m|)$, where λ_m is the eigenvalue of A which is maximum in modulus.[1]

Now consider:

$$[I - kA][I + kA + [kA]^2 + \cdots + [kA]^n]$$
$$= I + kA + [kA]^2 + \cdots + [kA]^n - kA$$
$$- [kA]^2 - \cdots - [kA]^n - [kA]^{n+1}$$
$$= I - [kA]^{n+1}.$$

$$\text{As } n \to \infty, [kA]^{n+1} \to 0;$$

[1] See the proof for this theorem in Pasinetti (1977), pp. 265–266.

so

$$[I - kA][I + kA + [kA]^2 + \cdots] = I.$$

But this shows, first, that $[I - kA]$ has an inverse, so long as $k < (1/|\lambda_m|)$, and second, that the inverse can be calculated by summing the power series of $[kA]$.

I.7 Non-Negative Indecomposable Square Matrices

A matrix, A, is said to be *positive*, $A > 0$, when all the elements of A are positive numbers. A matrix, A, is said to be *non-negative*, $A \geqq 0$, when none of the elements of A is negative. A matrix, A, is said to be *semipositive*, $A \geq 0$, when none of the elements is negative, and at least one element is positive.

A square matrix, A, is said to be *partially decomposable* or *reducible* when it is possible, by a process of interchanging some rows *and the corresponding columns*, to bring the matrix into the form:

$$\begin{bmatrix} A_{11} & 0 \\ A_{21} & A_{22} \end{bmatrix},$$

where A_{11} and A_{22} are square submatrices (not necessarily of the same order) and 0 is the null matrix.

A square matrix that cannot be brought into this form by any process of interchanging rows and corresponding columns is said to be *irreducible* or *indecomposable*.

A square matrix is said to be *totally decomposable* if, by any process of interchanging rows and corresponding columns, it can be brought into the following block-diagonal form:

$$\begin{bmatrix} A_{11} & 0 \\ 0 & A_{22} \end{bmatrix},$$

where A_{11} and A_{22} are square submatrices, not necessarily of the same order.

I.8 *The Perron-Frobenius Theorems concerning Square, Non-Negative, Irreducible Matrices*

The following propositions have been proved, for square non-negative irreducible matrices, by Oskar Perron and Georg Frobenius, among others.[2]

Let A be a square, non-negative, irreducible matrix. Let λ_m be the eigenvalue associated with A that is maximum in modulus. In other words, for any eigenvalue of A, λ_i, $\lambda_i \leq |\lambda_m|$. Then:

(a) λ_m is associated with an all-positive eigenvector $x > 0$.

(b) λ_m is a continuous, increasing function of the elements of A. (I.e., if *any one* of the elements of A increases, λ_m increases.)

(c) The maximum eigenvalue of any square submatrix of A is smaller than λ_m.

(d) λ_m is a simple root of the characteristic equation of A.

(e) To each real eigenvalue of A different from λ_m there corresponds an eigenvector $x \neq 0$ which has at least one negative component.

(f) Given a real number $k = (1/q) > 0$, if $q < (1/\lambda_m)$ [and hence $k > \lambda_m$], then:

[i] $[kI - A]^{-1} > 0$.

[ii] $[I - qA]^{-1} > 0$.

I.e., these inverse matrices exist and all their elements are positive real numbers. Furthermore, all the elements of these inverse matrices are continuous increasing functions of q and continuous decreasing functions of k.

Section II: Formal Conventions

The following conventions are employed throughout these notes.

II.1 A technique for producing a commodity i is specified by a $(1 \times n)$-dimensional vector $A_i = [a_{i1}, a_{i2}, \ldots, a_{in}]$ together with the scalar quantity l_i giving the physical

[2] See Perron (1907), Frobenius (1908), and Debreu and Herstein (1953).

quantities of inputs of commodity 1, commodity 2,...,
commodity n and of direct labor time required for the
production of one unit of commodity i.

II.2 The total technology of an economy in which n commodities and labor are used to produce n commodities is
given by:
(a) The $(n \times n)$-dimensional technology matrix $A = [a_{ij}]$,
where a_{ij} is the quantity of the j'th commodity required for the production of one unit of commodity
i, and
(b) The $(n \times 1)$-dimensional vector $L = [l_i]'$ of direct labor
inputs l_i per unit output in industry i, $i = 1, \dots, n$.

Thus the physical coefficients of production in the i'th
industry are given by:

$$l_{i'}A_i \to 1 \text{ unit of commodity } i.$$

II.3 The levels of output at which the several industries are
run are given by the $(1 \times n)$-dimensional vector $y = [y_i]$
of activity levels, where y_i is the level of activity (i.e.,
quantity of output) in the i'th industry.

The actual structure of output in the economy is given by:

$$y_i l_i, \; y_i A_i \to y_i \text{ units of commodity } i.$$

II.4 The real wage (i.e., market basket of commodities consumed by each worker per unit of labor—assuming, thus,
that all workers earn the same money wage and spend
it in the same way) is given by the $(1 \times n)$-dimensional
vector $b = [b_i]$ where b_i is the physical quantity of
commodity i consumed by each worker per unit of labor
time worked. (It follows, among other things, that we are
assuming zero worker saving.)

II.5 The physical surplus of commodities produced over and
above what is required to run the economy at the same
activity levels for another cycle, including what is consumed by workers, is given by the $(1 \times n)$-dimensional

vector $S = [s_i]$, where s_i is the physical surplus, if any, of commodity i.

II.6 The quantities of labor directly and indirectly required for the production of unit quantities of commodities $1, 2, \ldots, n$ are given by the $(n \times 1)$-dimensional vector $\lambda = [\lambda_i]'$, $i = 1, 2, \ldots, n$.

II.7 The natural, equilibrium, or long-run prices of commodities $1, 2, \ldots, n$ are given by the $(n \times 1)$-dimensional vector $p = [p_i]'$, $i = 1, 2, \ldots, n$.

II.8 The money wage $= w$.

II.9 The rate of return on the value of capital invested $= \pi$.

II.10 The rental charge per acre of land, in those economies in which rent is earned, $= \rho$. If more than two qualities of land exist, rental charges are differentiated by subscripts.

II.11 When the physical quantities of commodities consumed by workers as their real wage are aggregated with the quantities of commodities required as inputs into production, the resulting array, called the augmented unit input coefficient matrix, is represented by $A^* = [a_{ij}^*]$, $i,j = 1,2, \ldots, n$, where A_i^* is the $(1 \times n)$-dimensional vector of physical inputs *including goods consumed by workers* per unit output of commodity i.

SECTION III: SOME ELEMENTARY RELATIONSHIPS

III.1 The vector of physical surplus, S, is equal to the vector of output, y, minus the amounts of each commodity used up in production and the amounts of each commodity consumed by the workers in one cycle. I.e.,

$$S = y - yA - yLb.$$

III.2 $A^* = A + Lb$. [Lb, note, is $(n \times n)$.] Hence

$$S = y - yA^*.$$

III.3 The fundamental labor value equations of the system are:

$$L + A\lambda = \lambda.$$

Hence

$$l_i + A_i\lambda = \lambda_i,$$

in the i'th industry.

III.4 The fundamental price equations of the system are:

$$[Lw + Ap](1 + \pi) = p.$$

Hence

$$(l_iw + A_ip)(1 + \pi) = p_i,$$

in the i'th industry.

III.5

$$w = bp.$$

Hence

$$[Lbp + Ap](1 + \pi) = p.$$

III.6 When $\pi = 0$, if we choose w as our numeraire, or standard of price, setting it equal to 1, then the price equations reduce to the labor value equations, and $p = \lambda$. More generally, when $\pi = 0$, the price vector p is proportional to the labor value vector λ, so that $\lambda = kp$, where $k = 1/w$.

SECTION IV: THE EXISTENCE OF MEANINGFUL SOLUTIONS
TO THE LABOR VALUE AND PRICE EQUATIONS

IV.1 *Lemma concerning Productive Economies*

Let us begin with a semipositive indecomposable $(n \times n)$ matrix, A, of unit input coefficients. We shall assume that there is some positive vector $y > 0$ of activity levels of the industries defined by the rows of A at which the system can reproduce itself and also generate a semipositive vector of surplus outputs, $S \geq 0$. (We assume that worker consumption is included in yA.) In short, we begin by assuming that y and S exist such that:

$$yA + S = y. \tag{IV.1.1}$$

We now wish to prove that the maximal eigenvalue of A, λ_m, is positive and less than 1. In other words, $0 < \lambda_m < 1$. Once we have established this, we will be able to make use of the Perron/Frobenius theorems listed under I.8 above, in particular I.8(f).

To Prove: The maximal eigenvalue of a semipositive indecomposable unit input coefficient matrix representing an n-sector single-product economy capable of reproducing itself with a surplus is a real number between 0 and 1.

Proof. Equations IV.1.1 can be rewritten:

$$y_1 a_{11} + y_2 a_{21} + \cdots + y_n a_{n1} + S_1 = y_1$$
$$y_1 a_{12} + y_2 a_{22} + \cdots + y_n a_{n2} + S_2 = y_2$$
$$\dots\dots\dots\dots\dots\dots\dots\dots\dots\dots\dots\dots\dots\dots\dots \tag{IV.1.2}$$
$$y_1 a_{1n} + y_2 a_{2n} + \cdots + y_n a_{nn} + S_n = y_n.$$

Let us define $R_1 = S_1/(y_1 - S_1)$, $R_2 = S_2/(y_2 - S_2), \ldots, R_n = S_n/(y_n - S_n)$. The R_i will in general not be equal to one another. With a few algebraic manipulations, we can rewrite equations IV.1.2:

$$(y_1 a_{11} + \cdots + y_n a_{n1})(1 + R_1) = y_1$$
$$(y_1 a_{12} + \cdots + y_n a_{n2})(1 + R_2) = y_2$$
$$\dots\dots\dots\dots\dots\dots\dots\dots\dots\dots\dots\dots\dots\dots \tag{IV.1.3}$$
$$(y_1 a_{1n} + \cdots + y_n a_{nn})(1 + R_n) = y_n.$$

Or:

$$y_1[a_{11} - 1/(1 + R_1)] + y_2 a_{21} + \cdots + y_n a_{n1} = 0$$
$$y_1 a_{12} + y_2[a_{22} - 1/(1 + R_2)] + \cdots + y_n a_{n2} = 0$$
$$\dots\dots\dots\dots\dots\dots\dots\dots\dots\dots\dots\dots\dots\dots \tag{IV.1.4}$$
$$y_1 a_{1n} + y_2 a_{2n} + \cdots + y_n[a_{nn} - 1/(1 + R_n)] = 0.$$

IV.1.4 is a system of linear homogeneous equations, and it has a non-trivial solution if and only if the following holds true:

$$\begin{vmatrix} a_{11} - 1/(1+R_1) & a_{12} & \cdots & a_{1n} \\ a_{21} & a_{21} - 1/(1+R_2) & \cdots & a_{2n} \\ \cdot & \cdot & \cdots & \cdot \\ \cdot & \cdot & \cdots & \cdot \\ a_{n1} & \cdot & \cdots & a_{nn} - 1/(1+R_n) \end{vmatrix} = 0.$$

(IV.1.5)

This is an equation in n unknowns (the R_i). It has $n - 1$ degrees of freedom, and we can therefore select $n - 1$ of the R_i as we wish, so long as we set them ≥ 0. Let us therefore choose R_1, $R_2, \ldots, R_{n-1}$ so that they $= R_n$. This transforms IV.1.4 into an eigenequation:

$$yA = [1/(1 + R)]y, \quad \text{where } R = R_n. \qquad \text{(IV.1.6)}$$

But $y > 0$, and A is a semipositive indecomposable matrix. Hence by I.8.(a) and I.8.(e), $1/(1 + R)$ is the maximal eigenvalue of A. Now we know that $R > 0$, so $0 < [1/(1 + R)] < 1$. Q.e.d.

IV.2 *Proof of the Existence of Meaningful Solutions*

A. MEANINGFUL SOLUTIONS FOR THE LABOR VALUE EQUATIONS

The labor value equations are given by

$$L + A\lambda = \lambda. \qquad \text{(IV.2.1)}$$

This can be rewritten as

$$L = [I - A]\lambda. \qquad \text{(IV.2.2)}$$

Equation IV.2.2 is an instance of I.8.(f), with $k = q = 1 > \lambda_m$. Hence $[I - A]$ has an inverse, and all of the elements of the inverse are positive real numbers. Assuming that at least one of the industries in our economy uses direct labor inputs, so that $L \geq 0$, we can conclude that

$$\lambda = [I - A]^{-1}L > 0. \quad \text{Q.e.d.}$$

B. MEANINGFUL SOLUTIONS FOR THE PRICE EQUATIONS

It is somewhat more complicated to analyze the conditions under which the price equations have meaningful solutions. We can best proceed by studying first the extremal cases, and then examining the general case.

The price equations for the system are

$$[Lw + Ap](1 + \pi) = p. \qquad \text{(IV.2.3)}$$

This is a system of n equations in $n + 2$ variables. We can reduce the system to a single equation in the two distributional variables, w and π. Inspection reveals that these variables bear an inverse relation to one another. Following the classical line of analysis, we suppose that the wage is fixed exogenously and that competition then equilibrates the system and determines the profit rate, π. Since a negative wage is meaningless, w may be seen to vary between 0 and some maximum value, $\bar{w}$. At this maximum value, it must be that $\pi = 0$, for if $\pi > 0$, then there is some larger $w' > \bar{w}$, while $\pi < 0$ has no economic meaning. (Obviously, the function relating w and π is continuous.) Let us consider first the extremal cases:

(a) $\qquad\qquad w = \bar{w}$ and $\pi = 0.$

At these values, if we choose the wage as numeraire, equations IV.2.3 reduce to IV.2.2, which has a strictly positive solution $\lambda = p > 0$.

(b) $\qquad\qquad w = 0$ and $\pi = \bar{\pi}.$

At these values, equations IV.2.3 reduce to

$$Ap(1 + \bar{\pi}) = p. \qquad \text{(IV.2.4)}$$

Setting $\lambda = 1/(1 + \bar{\pi})$ and rewriting, we obtain

$$[\lambda I - A]p = 0. \qquad \text{(IV.2.5)}$$

This is a homogeneous system of equations, and thus has nontrivial solutions just in case:

$$|\lambda I - A| = 0. \qquad \text{(IV.2.6)}$$

Now, we know that the maximal eigenvalue of A is associated with an all-positive vector, $p > 0$, of prices [see I.8.(a)]. Furthermore, since A is assumed to be productive, we know that $\lambda_m < 1$. But since $\lambda_m = 1/(1 + \bar{\pi})$, it follows that $\bar{\pi} > 0$, which means that when the wage is zero, the system has a positive profit rate and all positive prices.

(c) $\qquad\qquad 0 < w < \bar{w} \quad \text{and} \quad 0 < \pi < \bar{\pi}.$

Equations IV.2.3 can be rewritten:

$$Lw = [1/(1 + \pi)I - A]p. \qquad\qquad \text{(IV.2.7)}$$

Since $\pi < \bar{\pi}$, and $0 < \pi < \bar{\pi}$, and $\lambda_m = 1/(1 + \bar{\pi})$, it follows that $1/(1 + \pi) > \lambda_m$. IV.2.7 is therefore an instance of I.8.(f).[i], with $k = 1/(1 + \pi)$. Hence, the inverse $[1/(1 + \pi)I - A]^{-1}$ exists and is strictly positive. Now, $w > 0$, by hypothesis, and $L \geq 0$ (i.e., at least one industry uses some direct labor—a modest assumption). Hence

$$[1/(1 + \pi)I - A]^{-1}Lw = p > 0. \quad \text{Q.e.d.} \quad \text{(IV.2.8)}$$

SECTION V: PROOFS OF PROPOSITIONS ASSERTED IN THE TEXT

V.1 Proof that for any capitalist final demand for luxury goods and capital goods, there exists a vector of activity levels that balances supply and demand.[3]

Capitalists may choose to spend part of their profits for expansion of the level of production, and part for luxury consumption. The question arises therefore whether there exists a set of activity levels at which the economy as a whole can be run (and, in particular, at which the non-luxury goods sector can be run), so that just precisely the right mix of physical output demanded by luxury consumption and economic expansion is produced.

Let us assume that we are dealing with an n-sector single-product economy that produces a physical surplus. The first k

---

[3] This proof is due to Professor William Gibson of the Economics Department of the University of Massachusetts, Amherst.

sectors produce non-luxury goods (i.e., capital goods and wage goods), and the remaining $n - k$ sectors produce luxury goods. The unit input coefficient matrix of the economy can therefore be partitioned thus:

$$A = \begin{bmatrix} A_{11} & 0 \\ A_{21} & A_{22} \end{bmatrix}$$

$$A_{11} = [a_{ij}] \qquad i, j = 1, \ldots, k$$

$$A_{21} = [a_{ij}] \qquad i = k + 1, \ldots, n \quad j = 1, \ldots, k$$

$$A_{22} = [a_{ij}] \qquad i, j = k + 1, \ldots, n.$$

In other words, the luxury goods may play a role in their own production, but they play no role in the production of the non-luxury goods. Let $F = [F_1 \quad F_2]$, a vector of capitalist final demand, where the demand for non-luxury goods is given by

$$F_1 = [f_i] \qquad i = 1, \ldots, k$$

and the demand for luxury goods is given by

$$F_2 = [f_i] \qquad i = k + 1, \ldots, n.$$

Let $Y = [Y_1 \quad Y_2]$, a vector of activity levels for which supply and demand just balance when final demand $= F$, where

$$Y_1 = [y_i] \qquad i = 1, \ldots, k$$
and
$$Y_2 = [y_i] \qquad 1 = k + 1, \ldots, n.$$

We seek to prove that there is a semipositive Y, with $Y_1 > 0$ and $Y_2 \geqq 0$, such that

$$Y = YA + F. \qquad (V.1.1)$$

$$[Y_1 \quad Y_2] = [Y_1 \quad Y_2] \begin{bmatrix} A_{11} & 0 \\ A_{21} & A_{22} \end{bmatrix} + [F_1 \quad F_2]. \qquad (V.1.2)$$

$$Y_1 = Y_1 A_{11} + Y_2 A_{21} + F_1 \qquad [V.1.3(a)]$$
and
$$Y_2 = Y_2 A_{22} + F_2. \qquad [V.1.3(b)]$$

If capitalist final demand for luxuries, $F_2 = 0$, then $Y_2 = 0$. In that case, market-clearing investment requires balanced growth (see Chapter 6 and Section V.4 of this appendix). Let the balanced growth rate be g, and let $\gamma = 1 + g$. Then

$$F_1 = g Y_1 A_{11}, \qquad (V.1.4)$$

i.e., final demand is a scalar multiple of input. Hence

$$
\begin{aligned}
Y_1 &= Y_1 A_{11} + F_1 \\
&= Y_1 A_{11} + g Y_1 A_{11} \\
&= (1 + g) Y_1 A_{11} \\
&= \gamma Y_1 A_{11}.
\end{aligned}
\qquad (V.1.5)
$$

Or

$$(1/\gamma) Y_1 = Y_1 A_{11} \qquad (V.1.6)$$

By construction of A, A_{11} is non-negative and irreducible. (A as a whole is of course partially reducible.) We know, from Section I.8(a) and (e) that V.1.6 has a unique strictly positive solution for γ and Y_1. The maximal eigenvalue of A_{11} is $(1/\gamma)$, and Y_1 is a left eigenvector associated with $(1/\gamma)$. Hence, when capitalist final demand for luxuries = 0, V.1.1 has a unique economically meaningful solution.

If capitalist final demand for luxury goods $\neq 0$, then (from V.1.3[b])

$$Y_2 = F_2 [I - A_{22}]^{-1}. \qquad (V.1.7)$$

Substituting into V.1.3(a) the expression for Y_2, we have

$$Y_1 = Y_1 A_{11} + F_2 [I - A_{22}]^{-1} A_{21} + F_1. \qquad (V.1.8)$$

Solving V.1.8 for Y_1, we have

$$Y_1 = F_2 [I - A_{22}]^{-1} A_{21} [I - A_{11}]^{-1} + F_1 [I - A_{11}]^{-1}. \qquad (V.1.9)$$

F_2 is semipositive, by hypothesis, and F_1 is non-negative. A_{21} and $[I - A_{22}]^{-1}$ are semipositive. $1/\gamma$ is the maximal eigenvalue of A_{11}. Since $\gamma > 1$, $1/\gamma < 1$. Therefore, $[I - A_{11}]^{-1} > 0$ (see Section I.8.(f).[ii]) Hence Y_1 is strictly positive. Q.e.d.

V.2 Proof that when $\pi > 0$, labor values are proportional to prices if and only if the ratio of labor directly required to labor indirectly required is the same in all lines of production.

A: If the ratio of labor indirectly required to labor directly required is the same in all lines of production, then prices are proportional to labor values.

Lemma. If the ratio of labor indirectly required to labor directly required is the same in all lines of production, the labor values are proportional to direct labor inputs.

The labor value equations are given by

$$L + A\lambda = \lambda. \tag{V.2.1}$$

Assume

$$A_i\lambda/l_i = A_j\lambda/l_j. \tag{V.2.2}$$

($A_i\lambda$ is the labor indirectly required per unit output in sector i.) From V.2.1

$$A_i\lambda = \lambda_i - l_i$$
$$A_j\lambda = \lambda_j - l_j. \tag{V.2.3}$$

Hence

$$(\lambda_i - l_i)/l_i = (\lambda_j - l_j)/l_j \tag{V.2.4}$$

or

$$\lambda_i/l_i = \lambda_j/l_j \tag{V.2.5}$$

or

$$\lambda = kL \quad \text{for some } k > 0. \quad \text{Q.e.d.} \tag{V.2.6}$$

Proof. The labor value equations are given by

$$L + A\lambda = \lambda. \tag{V.2.7}$$

From the Lemma, it follows that

$$L + kAL = kL, \qquad k > 1 \tag{V.2.8}$$

$$AL = [(k - 1)/k]L. \tag{V.2.9}$$

$L > 0$. Hence [Section 1.8.(a)], $(k - 1)/k$ is the maximal eigenvalue of A, and L is a right eigenvector associated with the maximal eigenvalue of A. The price equations for the system are given by

$$[Lw + Ap](1 + \pi) = p. \qquad (V.2.10)$$

When $w = 0$,

$$Ap(1 + \pi) = p$$

or

$$Ap = [1/(1 + \pi)]p. \qquad (V.2.11)$$

But $p > 0$ (see IV.2.8). Hence, $1/(1 + \pi)$ is the maximal eigenvalue of A, and p is a right eigenvector associated with the maximal eigenvalue of A.

L and p are both eigenvectors associated with the maximal eigenvalue of A. Since the maximal eigenvalue is a simple root [I.8.(d)], p is proportional to L. But L is proportional to λ. Therefore, p is proportional to λ. Q.e.d.

B. With $\pi \neq 0$, if prices are proportional to labor values, then the ratio of labor directly required to labor indirectly required is the same in all sectors.

Assume

$$p = k\lambda \qquad k > 0. \qquad (V.2.12)$$

The price equations of the system are given by

$$p = [Lw + Ap](1 + \pi). \qquad (V.2.13)$$

Let the real wage be given by

$$w = bp.$$

Then

$$p = Lbp(1 + \pi) + Ap(1 + \pi) \qquad (V.2.14)$$

or

$$k\lambda = Lbk\lambda(1 + \pi) + Ak\lambda(1 + \pi), \qquad (V.2.15)$$

which gives

$$\lambda = Lb\lambda(1 + \pi) + A\lambda(1 + \pi). \qquad (V.2.16)$$

Therefore

$$\lambda_i = l_i b\lambda(1 + \pi) + A_i \lambda(1 + \pi) \qquad (V.2.17)$$

and

$$\lambda_j = l_j b\lambda(1 + \pi) + A_j \lambda(1 + \pi). \qquad (V.2.18)$$

From labor value equations

$$\lambda_i = A_i\lambda + l_i$$
$$\lambda_j = A_j\lambda + l_j.$$

So

$$A_i\lambda + l_i = A_i\lambda(1 + \pi) + l_ib\lambda(1 + \pi)$$
$$l_i = \pi A_i\lambda + l_ib\lambda + \pi l_ib\lambda$$
$$1 = \pi A_i\lambda/l_i + b\lambda + \pi b\lambda \qquad \text{(V.2.19)}$$
$$A_i\lambda/l_i = [1 - (1 + \pi)b\lambda]/\pi$$

and

$$A_j\lambda + l_j = A_j\lambda(1 + \pi) + l_jb\lambda(1 + \pi)$$
$$l_j = \pi A_j\lambda + l_jb\lambda + \pi l_jb\lambda$$
$$1 = \pi A_j\lambda/l_j + b\lambda + \pi b\lambda \qquad \text{(V.2.20)}$$
$$A_j\lambda/l_j = [1 - (1 + \pi)b\lambda]/\pi$$

or

$$A_i\lambda/l_i = A_j\lambda/l_j. \quad \text{Q.e.d.} \qquad \text{(V.2.21)}$$

The last step of V.2.19 and V.2.20 requires that $\pi \neq 0$, since we divide by π.

V.3 Proof that the ratio of labor directly required to labor indirectly required is the same in all lines of production if and only if there is equal organic composition of capital in all lines of production.

$$s_i/v_i = s_j/v_j \quad \text{for all } i, j, \qquad \text{(V.3.1)}$$

because of equal length of workday and uniform real wage. Hence,

$$(s_i + v_i)/v_i = (s_j + v_j)/v_j. \qquad \text{(V.3.2)}$$

$$c_i/v_i = c_j/v_j \quad \text{iff } (c_i/v_i)/[(s_i + v_i)/v_i]$$
$$= (c_j/v_j)/[(s_j + v_j)/v_j] \qquad \text{(V.3.3)}$$

$$\text{iff } c_i/(s_i + v_i) = c_j/(s_j + v_j). \quad \text{Q.e.d.} \quad \text{(V.3.3)}$$

V.4 Proof of the conditions under which the principle of the conservation of surplus value holds.[4]

There are three major cases, of economic interest, in which Marx's principle of the conservation of surplus value holds, namely:

(a) when the profit rate is zero,
(b) when there is equal organic composition of capital in all lines of production, and
(c) when the relative activity levels of the several industries correspond to Sraffa's "Standard Commodity" or to what I have called a quasi-one-commodity world.

(b) is the case in which the vector of direct labor inputs is a right eigenvector associated with the maximal eigenvalue of the unit input coefficient matrix. (c) is the case in which the vector of activity levels is a left eigenvector associated with the maximal eigenvalue of the augmented unit input coefficient matrix.

These three classes do not, however, exhaust the cases in which something resembling the conservation principle holds. In another rather peculiar case analyzed by Abraham-Frois and Berrebi, the value rate of profit, $S/(C + V)$, equals the money rate of profit, π, even though the ratio of total prices to total values does not equal the ratio of total profit to total surplus value.

What follows is a proof of the theorem in the first three cases, and an explanation of the peculiar fourth case.

A. THE CASE OF $\pi = 0$

When $\pi = 0$, with the wage, w, chosen as numeraire, the price equations reduce to the labor value equations, and prices equal values. Hence $y\lambda = yp$, or total prices equal total values. Furthermore, for real-wage bundle b, $1 = w = bp$, or, since $p = \lambda$, $1 = b\lambda$. Total surplus value is $yL(1 - b\lambda) = 0$, and total profit $= 0$, so in this trivial case, Marx's conservation principle holds.

---

[4] See Abraham-Frois and Berrebi (1979), pp. 218–226.

B. THE CASE OF EQUAL ORGANIC COMPOSITION OF CAPITAL

With equal organic composition of-capital, and appropriate choice of numeraire, $p = \lambda$. (See V.2 and V.3.) Hence $yp = y\lambda$. So we must prove that total profit equals total surplus value:

$$y[A + Lb]p\pi = yL(1 - b\lambda). \tag{V.4.1}$$

Proof. From the price equations,

$$y[A + Lb]p\pi = yp - y[A + Lb]p \tag{V.4.2}$$

$$= yp - yAP - yLbp. \tag{V.4.3}$$

From the labor value equations, and since $p = \lambda$,

$$L + Ap = p. \tag{V.4.4}$$

Hence

$$yL = yp - yAp. \tag{V.4.5}$$

By substitution

$$y[A + Lb]p\pi = yL - yLbp \tag{V.4.6}$$

$$= yL(1 - bp) \tag{V.4.7}$$

$$= yL(1 - b\lambda). \quad \text{Q.e.d.} \tag{V.4.8}$$

Now let us prove that equal organic composition of capital is equivalent to the vector of direct labor inputs, L, being a right eigenvector of A associated with the maximum eigenvalue. It is easiest to prove that L is a right eigenvector of A if and only if the ratio of labor indirectly required to labor directly required is the same in all lines of production. We have already shown that this latter condition is equivalent to equal organic composition.

To Prove: $AL = kL$, $k > 0$, if and only if $A\lambda_i/l_i = A\lambda_j/l_j$, for all i, j.

Proof. [i] Assume $AL = kL$ for some $k > 0$.

$$IL - AL = L - kL \tag{V.4.9}$$

or
$$L = (1 - k)[I - A]^{-1}L \qquad (V.4.10)$$

or
$$[1/(1 - k)]L = [I - A]^{-1}L. \qquad (V.4.11)$$

But the solution of the labor value equations is

Hence
$$\lambda = [I - A]^{-1}L. \qquad (V.4.12)$$

$$\lambda = [1/(1 - k)]L. \qquad (V.4.13)$$

$$A\lambda = [1/(1 - k)]AL \qquad (V.4.14)$$

$$= [k/(1 - k)]L. \qquad (V.4.15)$$

So
$$A_i\lambda = [k/(1 - k)]l_i$$

and
$$A_j\lambda = [k/(1 - k)]l_j \quad \text{for all } i, j. \qquad (V.4.16)$$

Or
$$A_i\lambda/l_i = A_j\lambda/l_j. \quad \text{Q.e.d.} \qquad (V.4.17)$$

[ii] Assume $A_i\lambda/l_i = k$, for all i. Then

$$A\lambda = kL. \qquad (V.4.18)$$

The labor value equations are given by

$$\lambda = A\lambda + L. \qquad (V.4.19)$$

Hence
$$\lambda = kL + L \qquad (V.4.20)$$

$$= (1 + k)L.$$

$$A\lambda = (1 + k)AL. \qquad (V.4.21)$$

So
$$kL = (1 + k)AL \qquad (V.4.22)$$

or
$$AL = [k/(1 + k)]L. \quad \text{Q.e.d.} \qquad (V.4.23)$$

C. THE CASE OF THE QUASI-ONE-COMMODITY WORLD

We must prove that if an n-sector single-product economy is a quasi-one-commodity world, which is to say that the gross output is a scalar multiple of the aggregate inputs, including the real wage bundle ($yA^* = ky$, for some $k > 0$), then the ratio of total prices to total values equals the ratio of total profits to total surplus value.

Assume a quasi-one-commodity world

$$ky = yA + yLb. \tag{V.4.24}$$

We wish to show that

$$yp/y\lambda = (yp - yAp - yLbp)/(yL - yLb\lambda). \tag{V.4.25}$$

From V.4.24

$$-yAp - yLbp = -kyp. \tag{V.4.26}$$

From labor value equations

$$y\lambda = yL + yA\lambda. \tag{V.4.27}$$

Hence

$$y\lambda = yL + ky\lambda - yLb\lambda. \tag{V.4.28}$$

So (substituting) we wish to show that

$$(yp - kyp)/(yL - yLb\lambda) = yp/(yL + ky\lambda - yLb\lambda) \tag{V.4.29}$$

or, dividing by yp, that

$$(1 - k)/(yL - yLb\lambda) = 1/(yL + ky\lambda - yLb\lambda) \tag{V.4.30}$$

or

$$yL - yLb\lambda = yL + ky\lambda - yLb\lambda - kyL - k^2y\lambda + kyLb\lambda \tag{V.4.31}$$

or

$$y\lambda - yL - ky\lambda + yLb\lambda = 0 \tag{V.4.32}$$

or from V.4.24

$$y\lambda - yL - yA\lambda = 0, \tag{V.4.33}$$

which follows directly from the labor value equations.   Q.e.d.

D.   A MATHEMATICAL ANOMOLY

The last case is a mathematical peculiarity which seems not to have any economically meaningful interpretation. Roughly, it turns out that if the several industries, both in their inner technical proportions and in their relative levels of activity, exhibit a measure of partial interdependence, greater than the total independence of the general case but short of the full-scale dependence of either case B or case C, then the value rate of profit, $S/(C + V)$, equals the money rate of profit, π, even though Marx's conservation principle does not hold.

The precise statement of the condition for the case of a three-sector economy is as follows. If the vector of direct labor inputs belongs to the vector space spanned by an eigenvector on the right associated with the maximal eigenvalue of the unit input coefficient matrix and an eigenvector associated with one of the other eigenvalues of that matrix, and if the vector of activity levels belongs to the space spanned by an eigenvector on the left associated with the maximal eigenvalue of the augmented unit input coefficient matrix and an eigenvector associated with one of the other eigenvalues of the matrix, then $S/(C + V) = \pi$.

The following example illustrates this theorem, whose proof can be found in Abraham-Frois and Berrebi.[5]

Consider a corn/iron/tools economy whose unit input coefficient matrix is:

$$A = \begin{bmatrix} .1 & 0 & .25 \\ 0 & .5 & .1 \\ 1 & .4 & .2 \end{bmatrix}$$

The eigenvalues of A are $\lambda_m = .748$, $.42$, and $-.375$.

Normalizing by setting the first component of each vector equal to 1, the right eigenvectors associated with these eigenvalues are:

$$p = [1, 1.0452, 2.592]'$$

$$p_2 = [1, -1.6, 1.28]'$$

$$p_3 = [1, .217, -1.9]'$$

[5] Ibid., pp. 223–225.

Choose a vector, L, of direct labor inputs that is a linear combination of p and p_2, and hence belongs to the space spanned by them:

$$L = p + .1p_2 = [1.1, .885, 2.72]'.$$

Now stipulate a real wage $b = [.01, 0, 0]$, in order to construct the augmented unit input coefficient matrix $A^* = A + Lb$:

$$A^* = \begin{bmatrix} .111 & 0 & .25 \\ .00885 & .5 & .1 \\ 1.0272 & .4 & .2 \end{bmatrix}.$$

The eigenvalues of A^* are $\lambda_m^* = .758$, $.4275$, and $-.3735$.

The left eigenvectors associated with these eigenvalues, again normalizing, are:

$$q^* = [1, .9637, .6216]$$

$$q_2^* = [1, -1.7848, .3235]$$

$$q_3^* = [1, .21685, -.4735]$$

Now choose a vector, y, of activity levels that is a linear combination of q^* and q_3^*, thus:

$$y = 3q^* + .1q_3^* = [3.1, 2.9128, 1.81745].$$

We can now form System Q, in which the vector of direct labor inputs, L, and the vector of activity levels, y, are as specified in Table 17. The real wage $= [.01, 0, 0]$/unit of labor.

TABLE 17. System Q

	Labor Input	Corn Input	Iron Input	Tools Input	Output
Corn Sector	3.41	.31	0	.775	3.1
Iron Sector	2.5778	0	1.0964	.29128	2.9128
Tools Sector	4.9435	1.81745	.727	.3635	1.81745

The labor values in System Q are:

$$\lambda_c \cong 4.1432$$

$$\lambda_i \cong 3.873$$

$$\lambda_t \cong 10.5155$$

Prices and profit rate in System Q are:

$$p_c = 1$$

$$p_i \cong 1.0422$$

$$p_t \cong 2.588$$

$$\pi \cong .31926$$

Thus, $S \cong 10.4784$, $(C + V) \cong 32.7582$, and

$$S/(C + V) \cong .31987$$

which, within the limits of accuracy of these calculations, $= \pi$.

However, a calculation of total prices, total profit, and total values shows that the ratio of total prices to total profits is 4.332 while the ratio of total values to total surplus value is 4.126, not the same within the limits of calculation. Thus the value rate of profit equals the money rate of profit, but Marx's conservation principle does not hold in the deeper sense that the mass of surplus value equals the mass of profit, for suitable choice of numeraire.

V.5 Proof that in any system of single-product industries producing a physical surplus, the labor value of the physical surplus equals the surplus labor value extracted from the direct labor inputs.[6]

---

[6] See Wolff (1981) for an alternative proof of this proposition not using linear algebra. That proof appears to be the first to be published.

The labor value equations are given by

$$yL = y\lambda - yA\lambda. \tag{V.5.1}$$

$$yL - yLb\lambda = y\lambda - yA\lambda - yLb\lambda. \tag{V.5.2}$$

$$yL(1 - b\lambda) = y[\lambda - A\lambda - Lb\lambda]. \quad \text{Q.e.d.} \tag{V.5.3}$$

V.6 Proof that every single-product economy with no luxury sector can be transformed into a quasi-one-commodity world by a set of activity multipliers unique up to a scalar multiple.

To transform an economy into a quasi-one-commodity world, it is necessary to find a vector of activity levels such that

$$yA^* = ky \tag{V.6.1}$$

Where A^* is the augmented unit input matrix.

By I.8.(a) and (e), there exists a vector y, unique up to a scalar multiple, associated with the maximal eigenvalue of A^*, which solves V.6.1. Q.e.d.

V.7 Proof that in any single-product economy producing a physical surplus, the A-value of the physical surplus equals the surplus A-value extracted from the direct A inputs, where A is any commodity required directly or indirectly in all lines of production.

Let

I_J = the input of commodity I into the J'th industry,

O_I = the gross output of the I'th industry,

V_I^a = the A-value of the I'th commodity,

and

$$I = I_A + I_B + \cdots + I_N,$$

which is the aggregate input of commodity I.

The A-value equations for the system are:

$$O_A V_A^a = A_A + B_A V_B^a + C_A V_C^a + \cdots + N_A V_N^a$$
$$O_B V_B^a = A_B + B_B V_B^a + C_B V_C^a + \cdots + N_A V_N^a$$
$$\cdots\cdots\cdots\cdots\cdots\cdots\cdots\cdots\cdots\cdots\cdots\cdots\cdots\cdots$$
$$O_N V_N^a = A_N + B_N V_B^a + C_N V_C^a + \cdots + N_N V_N^a. \tag{V.7.1}$$

Summing these equations, transferring all value terms to the left, and simplifying, we have:

$$O_A V_A^a + (O_B - B)V_B^a + (O_C - C)V_C^a + \cdots +$$
$$(O_N - N)V_N^a = A. \tag{V.7.2}$$

Subtracting AV_A^a from each side, we have:

$$(O_A - A)V_A^a + (O_B - B)V_B^a + (O_C - C)V_C^a + \cdots +$$
$$(O_N - N)V_N^a = A(1 - V_A^a). \tag{V.7.3}$$

The sum on the left is the A-value of the physical surplus produced in System C. The term on the right is the surplus A-value extracted from the direct A inputs.   Q.e.d.

V.8 Proof that in any single-product economy producing a physical surplus, and for any commodity, b, which is required directly or indirectly in the production of all commodities in the system:

[i] The vector of b-values is strictly positive.
[ii] It takes less than a unit of b, directly or indirectly, to produce a unit of b.

To calculate b-values, we must construct a system of b-value equations in which the inputs of commodity b are valued at par, and all other inputs are valued at their b-values.

Let β be the vector of b-values of the n commodities including labor but not including commodity b, and let B be the vector of direct b inputs, per unit output.

[i] The vector of b-values is strictly positive.

The b-value equations of the system are

$$B + A\beta = \beta. \tag{V.8.1}$$

Hence

$$\beta = [I - A]^{-1}B. \tag{V.8.2}$$

B is semi-positive (there is *some* direct B input somewhere in the system) and $[I - A]^{-1} > 0$ (see Section IV, with commodity b substituted for labor throughout). Therefore, $\beta > 0$.

[ii] It takes less than a unit of b, directly or indirectly, to produce a unit of b.

Making the necessary notational adjustment in V.7.3, we see that the sum on the left is positive, because the vector of b-values, β, is strictly positive, and the vector of physical output is, by hypothesis, semipositive. The aggregate input of commodity b into the economy is positive (substituting b here for A in V.7.3). Hence, the b-value of a unit of b is less than 1. Q.e.d.

*

AN ANALYTICAL
RECONSTRUCTION OF MARX'S
VALUE CATEGORIES

In his definition and use of the analytical concepts constant capital, variable capital, and surplus value, and the ratios s/v, $s/(c+v)$, and c/v, Marx falls into a number of deep confusions which permeate the thousands of pages in which he explores the anatomy of capitalism. What follows does not pretend to be an exhaustive sorting-out of the confusions—that would take more space than it would be worth. Nevertheless, it is theoretically as well as exegetically valuable to clear up the central confusions.

Let us begin where Marx begins, with the actual physical processes of production. A certain "mass of labor," as Marx frequently puts it, "sets in motion" a certain mass of means of production. Weavers run power looms and weave thread into cloth. Miners wield picks and shovels and dig ore from the ground. And so forth. A technique of production can, for purposes of economic analysis, be specified by itemizing the quantities of each input into the process that are required, in a factory, mine, or farm of average efficiency, per unit output.

Immediately, two points must be made. First, a technique of production is specified *only* if the inputs *per unit output* are given.[1] Were we simply to list the inputs without specifying

---

[1] Strictly speaking, we should specify also the period of time in which this quantity of output is produced, but throughout this work an annual production cycle is presupposed unless something is explicitly said to the contrary.

the quantity of output, the technique would quite obviously be left indeterminate. Marx knows this, but he seems not to grasp the importance of building it into the definition of his basic analytical categories. Thus c is never defined as the value of constant capital *per unit output*, nor is v so defined. Hence, it is quite unclear what analytical meaning is to be given to these terms. This problem, as we shall see, produces some very odd analytical consequences.

The second point is that in the specification of a technique of production, the means of production must be described as being set in motion by a certain mass of *labor*, as measured in time units of averagely intense and efficient laboring, *not* as being set in motion by a certain mass of labor power, as measured in units of capacity-to-labor-during-a-fixed-time.

At first, we might think that labor *power* is combined with coal and iron, not labor. After all, we speak of *coal* as an input, not of *burning*, even though burning is the use we make of coal when we use it as an input (as opposed, say, to the use we might make of a piece of coal as a deadweight to hold down a stack of papers.) But this will not do. The properties of the non-labor inputs, as they are known and used by the averagely efficient entrepreneurs and technicians of the period, are assumed to be given when one specifies a tonnage of coal or a yardage of thread. But the whole point of Marx's analysis of labor power is supposed to be that the number of hours in a day that a worker can labor is *not* assumed to be given when one posits some quantity of labor power. The number of hours extractable from a day's labor power is *variable*, a matter for determination by class struggle. Hence a technique of production is not fully specified by the stipulation that given amounts of various means of production are set in motion by a certain quantity of labor *power*. It is only fully specified by stipulating the number of hours of averagely intense and efficient labor that are required to set those means of production in motion.

Usually Marx gets this right, as when he says, in volume three of *Capital*: "It is necessary to have a certain quantity of means and materials of labour for a specific quantity of labour to materialize in commodities and thereby to produce value."[2] Sometimes he gets it wrong, as in the official definition of the "technical composition of capital," also in volume three: "A definite quantity of labour-power represented by a definite number of labourers is required to produce a definite quantity of products in, say, one day, and—what is self-evident—thereby to consume productively, i.e., to set in motion, a definite quantity of means of production, machinery, raw materials, etc."[3] And, on occasion, he gets it wrong and then adds the necessary qualifications to make it right, as in this passage from *Theories of Surplus Value*: "The technological composition of the capital remains the same; that is, the *ratio* between living labour or number of workers (since the normal working-day has been assumed to be constant) represented by the variable capital and the *quantity of the instruments of labour* required, which now, according to our assumption, consists of tons of coal or quarters of corn, remains constant for a given number of workers."[4]

Let us use Marx's phrase "technical composition of capital," to mean "the vector of non-labor inputs and of labor time required by the dominant technique of production per unit output of a specified commodity (in a single period of production)." The technical composition of capital in the steel industry will then be the physical quantities of iron, coal, cloth, corn, machine oil, and so forth, and the number of hours of (abstract homogeneous socially necessary) labor required by the dominant technique of steel production to produce one unit (pound, ton, etc.) of steel. For the sake of clarity, we can label all of the inputs into production from 1 to n, and the labor input $n + 1$. Then the technical composition of capital will be given by a $(1 \times n + 1)$-dimensional vector $\tilde{x}_i$ for industry i (assuming single product industries). The j'th element of the vector, $j = 1, 2, \ldots, n$, will be the physical quantity of input j required in the making of one unit of commodity i. The $n + 1$st element will be the number of hours of (abstract homogeneous socially

[2] Marx (1967*c*), p. 46.
[3] Ibid., p. 145.
[4] Marx (1968), p. 455.

necessary) laboring so required. (Throughout this section, I ignore the role of capital which lasts for more than one period of production.)

The technical composition of the capital employed in a given industry is a fact about the technology of production in that industry. It can be known independently of the technical composition of the capital in any other industry, and is in that sense an individual fact, not a social or systematic fact. Obviously there are historical and causal connections among the techniques used in different industries. The discovery of a new technique for making stronger and more flexible steel may open the way to a better design of machine tool, and so forth. What is more, once we allow for elements of joint production, with capitalists employing physically the same factory buildings or tools for the making of several commodities, it will obviously be the case that considerations of efficiency of production of one commodity will be influenced by considerations of efficiency in the production of other sorts of commodities. However, once the historical influences and relationships have been taken account of, and we have abstracted from joint production, it remains true that the technical composition of capital in a given line of production stands alone. A change in the technique of production in one industry *does not imply* (in the strict sense of the term) a change in the technical composition of capital in any other industry.

There is another quite distinct notion introduced by Marx which he frequently labels the "technological composition of capital" but which he also sometimes calls the "physical composition of capital." This is the ratio of accumulated labor to living labor in a particular industry or line of production. (Since this is a ratio, we need not specify that it is per unit of output.) The intuitive notion is that a mass of dead labor, embodied in the means and instruments of production, is set in motion by a mass of living labor. Consider for example the following passages:

> . . . When the *method of production*, or the *physical composition of capital*, remains the same, in other words, when

the ratio of immediate and accumulated labour remains constant.

If the method of production and the ratio between the amounts of immediate and accumulated labour used remain constant. . . .

By turning his money into commodities that serve as the material elements of a new product, and as factors in the labour-process, by incorporating living labour with their dead substance, the capitalist at the same time converts value, *i.e.*, past, materialised, and dead labour into capital, into value big with value, a live monster that is fruitful and multiplies.[5]

The ratio of immediate to accumulated labor, of living to dead labor, is exactly what we called, in discussing Ricardo, the ratio of labor directly required to labor indirectly required in a line of production. Marx frequently speaks as though he thought of this ratio as a physical fact about techniques of production, on a par with—indeed, sometimes indistinguishable from—what we have here labeled the "technical composition of capital." But this is clearly a mistake. Indeed, as we shall see, it is a mistake that results from a certain kind of fetishism, of just the sort that Marx warns us against! The quantity of labor materialized in, or accumulated in, or embodied in a certain mass of means of production is a function of the technical composition of the entire economy, not merely of the technical composition of the industry in which the mass of means of production is being worked up. The quantity of labor materialized in a mass of means of production is simply *the labor value* of that mass of means of production. Clearly, the quantity of labor materialized in a ton of coal is at least in part a function of the dominant technique for the production of the shovels used to dig the coal.

The point can be seen immediately from an algebraic perspective. In determining the labor values of the commodities in a system, we found that it is necessary to solve a system

[5] Marx (1968), p. 288; ibid., p. 279; (1967a), p. 195.

of simultaneous equations representing the techniques of production of all the (basic) industries in the system. A change in any input anywhere in the system has repercussions throughout the entire system.[6] Thus, a change in the technical composition of capital in one industry formally implies changes in the ratio of living to dead labor in other industries (assuming that the initial change is in a capital goods industry). This ratio is a social or systematic fact, not an individual or physical fact.

The third ratio to which Marx makes reference is the "value-composition of capital." Marx defines this as follows: "The composition of capital is to be understood in a two-fold sense. On the side of value, it is determined by the proportion in which it is divided into constant capital or value of the means of production, and variable capital or value of labour-power, the sum total of wages. . . . I call [this] the *value-composition . . .* of capital."[7] The use of the phrase "value of labour-power" introduces two entirely new considerations, each of which plays a role in the determination of the "value-composition of capital." The first is the length of the working day, and the second is the cost of reproduction of labor power. As we have already seen, until the length of the working day is specified, the technique of production is indeterminate. "Ten workers using five shovels and five picks to produce ten tons of coal a day" leaves the technique of production quite unspecified until we say how many hours each worker works in the day. (In particular, it leaves undetermined the quantity of value materialised by their labor in the coal.) As for "value of labor power," this clearly requires a specification of the real wage or market basket of goods consumed by one worker in a day.[8]

[6] Generally speaking, a reduction in an input coefficient of an industry whose output is required directly or indirectly in all other industries will have the effect of reducing the labor values of *all* commodities. A reduction in an input coefficient of a wage good or luxury good has no such universal effects. Under no circumstances, however, can a reduction in an input coefficient, *ceteris paribus*, lead to a rise in the labor value of any commodity. For a precise mathematical treatment, see Morishima (1973), pp. 28–35.

[7] Marx (1967a), p. 612.

[8] Marx invariably specifies wages in money terms. So long as commodities exchange at their values and all workers buy the same goods, money is

Marx knows all this, sort of, and sometimes adds qualifications that make his statements correct, albeit misleading. For example, in the key passage in volume three in which he reintroduces the concepts of technical and value composition, Marx says this: "In the case of variable capital, therefore, we assume that it is the index of a definite quantity of labour-power, or of a definite number of labourers, or a definite quantity of living labour set in motion. We have seen in the preceding part that a change in the magnitude of the value of variable capital might eventually indicate nothing but a higher or lower price of the same mass of labour. But here, where the rate of surplus-value and the working-day are taken to be constant, and the wages for a definite working period are given, this is out of the question."[9]

Finally, Marx introduces what has become the best known and most widely used of these various analytical ratios of the composition of capital, the *organic composition of capital*: "I call the former the *value-composition*, the latter the *technical composition* of capital. Between the two there is a strict correlation, To express this, I call the value-composition of capital, in so far as it is determined by its technical composition and mirrors the changes of the latter, the *organic composition* of capital."[10]

It is extremely difficult to determine what Marx has in mind here. If by the technical composition of capital he means the proportion of living to dead labor, then in fact there is *not* in general a strict correlation between the technical composition and value composition of capital. For a fixed technical composition, the value composition might vary considerably depending on the real wage, and hence on the division of the living labor into necessary labor and surplus labor. One and the same *technical* composition of capital would be compatible both with an extremely high real wage which required nearly the entire

---

as good a measure of value as labor time. As soon as prices are allowed to deviate from values, however, it becomes fatally confused to give the wage in money terms when attempting to define the value composition of capital.

[9] Marx (1967c), p. 146.
[10] Marx (1967a), p. 612.

work day for its reproduction, leaving scarcely any surplus labor time, and with a very low real wage which left most of the working day as surplus labor time.

It is possible to clarify this confused theoretical situation, but not in a way that salvages the entirety of Marx's extended analyses. At base, the analytical categories employed by Marx throughout his economic writings are imprecise or inconsistant, and must be reconstructed before they are usable. With the aid of the formalism of Appendix A, however, we can sort things out sufficiently to identify the points of confusion.

We begin with what we are calling the *technical composition of capital* in each line of production. For an economy with n non-labor production inputs, each of which is the output of a single industry, the technical composition of capital in industry i is given by an $(n + 1)$-dimensional vector identifying the amounts of each of the n inputs plus the direct labor input per unit of output of commodity i [per period of production], all measured in the appropriate physical units.

As we have already seen, once we know the technical composition of capital for each industry in the economy, we can calculate the labor values of each non-labor produced input.[11] Following Marx, let us use c for the labor value of the non-labor inputs into a production process. For a production cycle of known length (one day, one year, etc.) and for a given activity level of industry i, $c_i =$ the labor value of the total constant capital employed in industry i during one cycle of production. Thus c_i is not fully determined by the technical composition even of all the sectors in the economy, inasmuch as it depends also on the activity level of industry i (but *not* on the activity level of any other industry).

In order to calculate the labor value of labor power, we must specify the real wage, defined as a vector or market basket of

---

[11] In keeping with the practice of the classical economists, I am assuming that all inputs save land are produced. See *Capital*, volume one, p. 183: "In so far then, as its instruments and subjects are themselves products, labour consumes products in order to create products," from which Sraffa may have derived the title of his book, *Production of Commodities by Means of Commodities* (1960).

consumption goods per unit of labor power (it will not do to fix the wage in money terms unless we are assuming the proportionality of prices to labor values). Marx does not have a symbol for the labor value of labor power, and we shall therefore introduce one: Ω.

With the technical composition of capital given and the value of labor power determined, we need one more datum before we can calculate the variable capital, v_i, for industry i. We must know the length of the workday. This, taken together with the technical composition of capital, allows us to compute the number of units of labor power required per unit output. Multiplying by the activity level, or total output, gives us the total number of units of labor power required for the output of the i'th sector, and this fact, together with Ω, enables us to ascertain v_i. The surplus labor value generated in industry i by the direct labor input is then computed by substracting v_i from the total direct labor input. Thus let:

$\tilde{x}_i = [x_{i1}, x_{i2}, \dots, x_{in}, l_i]$ be the $(1 \times n + 1)$-dimensional row vector giving the technical composition of capital in industry i.

$x_i = [x_{i1}, x_{i2}, \dots, x_{in}]$ be the $(1 \times n)$-dimensional row vector of non-labor inputs per unit output of i.

$\lambda = [\lambda_1, \lambda_2, \dots, \lambda_n]'$ be the $(n \times 1)$-dimensional column vector of labor values of non-labor inputs for the system as a whole.

$y = [y_1, y_2, \dots, y_n]$ be the $(1 \times n)$-dimensional row vector of activity levels for the economy.

$d = $ the length of the workday, in hours.

Then

$c_i = y_i(x_{i1}\lambda_1 + x_{i2}\lambda_2 + \cdots + x_{in}\lambda_n) = y_i x_i \lambda.$

$v_i = (y_i l_i \Omega)/d$ i.e., the total labor hours required $(y_i l_i)$ divided by the length of the workday, d, giving the total number of units of labor power, all times the labor value of the subsistence wage, Ω, giving the labor value of the variable capital.

$s_i = y_i l_i - v_i$, i.e., total direct labor input minus the
value of variable capital equals the surplus labor
value generated in industry i in one cycle of
production;

$\quad = y_i l_i (1 - \Omega/d)$.

$(1 - \Omega/d)$ is a very important magnitude in Marx's analytical framework. It is the fraction of surplus labor time in each unit of labor, hence the quantity of surplus value extracted from each unit of direct labor input. We would expect the ratio of $(1 - \Omega/d)$ to Ω/d to be equal to what Marx calls the rate of surplus value, s_i/v_i, and so it is:

$$s_i/v_i = (y_i l_i - v_i)/(y_i l_i \Omega/d)$$
$$= [d y_i l_i - d(y_i l_i \Omega/d)]/y_i l_i \Omega$$
$$= (d - \Omega)/\Omega$$
$$= (1 - \Omega/d)/(\Omega/d).$$

One of the important consequences of the definitions and assumptions set forth here is that the rate of surplus value, or as Marx sometimes calls it, the rate of exploitation, is the same in all lines of production. To see this, consider the following:

$$s_i/v_i = [y_i l_i (1 - \Omega/d)]/(y_i l_i \Omega/d)$$
$$= (1 - \Omega/d)/(\Omega/d)$$

and this ratio is obviously independent of the choice of i. Economically, the meaning of this proposition is that Marx assumes a single quality of labor, a uniform wage, and a single economy-wide work day. These are, of course, the standard assumptions of classical political economy.

The ratio of dead to living labor, which we called the *physical composition of capital* to distinguish it from the technical composition of capital, is given by the formula:

$$c_i/(v_i + s_i) = (y_i x_i \lambda)/(v_i + y_i l_i - v_i)$$
$$= x_i \lambda/l_i,$$

which is exactly as expected. (Notice that in most of these ratios, the activity level y_i drops out, showing that we are dealing with aspects of the proportional relationships of the several elements of the economy, rather than with their absolute magnitudes.)

The organic composition of capital is given by the expression:

$$c_i/v_i = y_i x_i \lambda / (y_i l_i \Omega / d)$$
$$= x_i \lambda d / l_i \Omega,$$

where $x_i \lambda$ is the value of constant capital used up per unit of output, l_i/d is the number of units of labor power required per unit of output, and $l_i \Omega / d$ is the labor value of that number of units.

The expression for the organic composition of capital reveals that the organic composition is a function not only of the means of production per unit of output, x_i, the direct labor input per unit output, l_i, the labor values of all the inputs used in the economy as a whole, λ, and the labor value of the real wage, Ω—all of which we would expect—but also of the length of the workday, d. This is a *very* odd result, clearly not intended by Marx, and it might be worth exploring the reason for this unanticipated functional dependency.

Why should a lengthening or shortening of the workday affect the ratio c_i/v_i? The reason is that Marx has defined v_i as the value of all the labor power employed by industry i in a single cycle of production. Since the technical composition of capital is defined, necessarily, in terms of the number of hours of laboring required to set a given set of means of production in motion, it is clear that we cannot know how much labor power a technique of production calls for without knowing how long the workday lasts. This makes intuitive good sense. If you ask me how many man-days will be required to turn out one ton of steel, I shall have to know how long each worker will work each day before I can reply.

The last of the ratios Marx analyzes is the "value rate of profit," which is to say the ratio of surplus value to the value of the total capital invested:

$$\text{value rate of profit} = s_i/(c_i + v_i).$$

When commodities exchange at their labor values, this ratio is equal to the money rate of profit, π. As is well known, there is a striking relationship among the value rate of profit, the rate of surplus value, and the organic composition of capital, namely:

$$\text{Value rate of profit} = \left(\begin{array}{c}\text{rate of}\\\text{surplus value}\end{array}\right)\Big/\left(\begin{array}{c}\text{organic}\\\text{composition}\end{array} + 1\right).$$

This follows directly from the algebraic equality:

$$s_i/(c_i + v_i) = (s_i/v_i)/(c_i/v_i + 1).$$

There is no simple or perspicuous expression, in general, for the value rate of profit. It is a function of the vector of non-labor inputs, x_i, the vector of labor values, λ, the direct labor input per unit output, l_i, the value of the real wage, Ω, and the length of the workday, d. It is not a function of the activity level, y_i.

We saw in Appendix A that an economy exhibits equal ratios of accumulated to living labor in all lines of production if and only if it exhibits equal organic composition of capital in all lines of production. This may seem a surprising proposition, in light of the fact that the second of these ratios is a function both of the subsistence wage and of the length of the workday, while the first is a function of neither. The key to the proof is the invariance, from sector to sector, of the ratio Ω/d. This amounts to stipulating a single economy-wide wage and a uniform length of the workday.

To see how these various terms and ratios work out in practice, let us return briefly to System C. The technical composition of capital in System C is given by the following set of vectors:

$$\tilde{x}_1 = [1/150 \text{ bu.}, 4/75 \text{ ton}, 0 \text{ books}, 1/3 \text{ hr.}]$$

$$\tilde{x}_2 = [1/10 \text{ bu.}, 2/15 \text{ ton}, 0 \text{ books}, 1 \text{ hr.}]$$

$$\tilde{x}_3 = [1/40 \text{ bu.}, 1/20 \text{ ton}, 1/20 \text{ books}, 1/2 \text{ hr.}]$$

$$x_1 = [1/150 \text{ bu.}, 4/75 \text{ ton}, 0 \text{ books}]$$

$$x_2 = [1/10 \text{ bu.}, 2/15 \text{ ton}, 0 \text{ books}]$$

$$x_3 = [1/40 \text{ bu.}, 1/20 \text{ ton}, 1/20 \text{ books}]$$

$$\lambda = [.4 \text{ hrs./bu.}, 1.2 \text{ hrs./ton}, .6 \text{ hrs./books}]^{12}$$

$$y = [300, 90, 40]$$

$$
\begin{aligned}
c_1 = 300[&(.4 \text{ hrs./bu.})(1/150 \text{ bu.}) \\
&+ (1.2 \text{ hrs./ton})(4/75 \text{ ton}) \\
&+ (.6 \text{ hrs./books})(0 \text{ books})] \\
= 20 \text{ hrs.}
\end{aligned}
$$

$$
\begin{aligned}
c_2 = 90[&(.4 \text{ hrs./bu.})(1/10 \text{ bu.}) \\
&+ (1.2 \text{ hrs./ton})(2/15 \text{ ton}) \\
&+ (.6 \text{ hrs./books})(0 \text{ books})] \\
= 18 \text{ hrs.}
\end{aligned}
$$

$$
\begin{aligned}
c_3 = 40[&(.4 \text{ hrs./bu.})(1/40 \text{ bu.}) \\
&+ (1.2 \text{ hrs./ton})(1/20 \text{ ton}) \\
&+ (.6 \text{ hrs./books})(1/20 \text{ books})] \\
= 4 \text{ hrs.}
\end{aligned}
$$

$$s_1 + v_1 = y_1 l_1 = 300(1/3 \text{ hr.}) = 100 \text{ hrs.}$$

$$s_2 + v_2 = y_2 l_2 = 90(1 \text{ hr.}) = 90 \text{ hrs.}$$

$$s_3 + v_3 = y_3 l_3 = 40(1/2 \text{ hr.}) = 20 \text{ hrs.}$$

$$c_1/(s_1 + v_1) = 20 \text{ hrs.}/100 \text{ hrs.} = 1/5.$$

$$c_2/(s_2 + v_2) = 18 \text{ hrs.}/90 \text{ hrs.} = 1/5.$$

$$c_3/(s_3 + v_3) = 4 \text{ hrs.}/20 \text{ hrs.} = 1/5.$$

[12] It is useful to include the units in which such magnitudes as labor values are measured, in order to make sure that the various algebraic manipulations are meaningful.

There is no way of knowing the value of d from the characterization given of System C. However, the hourly real wage has been specified as (.2 corn, .1 iron)/hour of labor. We can therefore calculate the quantity Ω/d, which is the labor value of labor power per hour (i.e., the fraction of each hour devoted to what Marx calls "necessary labor"):

$$\Omega/d = [(.2 \text{ bu.})(.4 \text{ hrs./bu.})$$
$$+ (.1 \text{ ton})(1.2 \text{ hrs./ton})]/\text{hr.}$$
$$= .2 \text{ hrs./hr.}$$
$$= .2.$$

Note that Ω/d is a pure number. Ω is the labor value of labor power. Labor power is measured in workdays (= the capacity to work for one day). Hence the dimension of Ω is hours/workday. The length of the workday in hours is d. The dimension of d is therefore also hours/workday. Thus, Ω/d has the dimensions (hours/workday)/(hours/workday), and hence is a pure number.

Now we can calculate the v_i and s_i:

$$v_1 = y_1 l_1 \Omega/d = (100 \text{ hrs.})(.2) = 20 \text{ hrs.}$$

$$v_2 = y_2 l_2 \Omega/d = (90 \text{ hrs.})(.2) = 18 \text{ hrs.}$$

$$v_3 = y_3 l_3 \Omega/d = (20 \text{ hrs.})(.2) = 4 \text{ hrs.}^{[13]}$$

$$s_1 = y_1 l_1 - v_1 = 100 \text{ hrs.} - 20 \text{ hrs.}$$
$$= 80 \text{ hrs.}$$

$$s_2 = y_2 l_2 - v_2 = 90 \text{ hrs.} - 18 \text{ hrs.}$$
$$= 72 \text{ hrs.}$$

$$s_3 = y_3 l_3 - v_3 = 20 \text{ hrs.} - 4 \text{ hrs.}$$
$$= 16 \text{ hrs.}$$

[13] It is purely accidental that $c_i = v_i$ in System C.

$$s_1/v_1 = s_2/v_2 = s_3/v_3$$
$$= (1 - \Omega/d)/(\Omega/d)$$
$$= .8/.2 = 4/1.$$
$$c_1/v_1 = c_2/v_2 = c_3/v_3 = 1.$$
$$s_1/(c_1 + v_1) = (s_1/v_1)/(c_1/v_1 + 1).$$

BIBLIOGRAPHY

✳

I. Works by Marx and Engels

Marx, Karl. 1963. *Theories of Surplus Value.* Part I. Moscow: Progress Publishers.

_____. 1967a. *Capital.* Vol. 1. Trans. Samuel Moore and Edward Aveling. New York: International Publishers.

_____. 1967b. *Capital.* Vol. 2. New York: International Publishers.

_____. 1967c. *Capital.* Vol. 3. New York: International Publishers.

_____. 1968. *Theories of Surplus Value.* Part II. Moscow: Progress Publishers.

_____. 1971. *Theories of Surplus Value.* Part III. Moscow: Progress Publishers.

Marx, Karl, and Friedrich Engels. 1958–66. *Karl Marx-Friedrich Engels Werke.* 39 Bände mit Ergänzungsbände. Berlin: Dietz Verlag. Cited as MEW.

II. Other Works Cited

Abraham-Frois, Gilbert, and Edmond Berrebi. 1979. *Theory of Value, Prices and Accumulation.* Trans. M. P. Kregel-Javaux. Cambridge: Cambridge University Press. (First published 1976.)

Althusser, Louis, and Etienne Balibar. 1970. *Reading Capital.* London: New Left Books.

Böhm-Bawerk, Eugen. 1974. *Karl Marx and the Close of His System.* London: Merlin Press.

Bowles, Samuel. 1983. The production process in a competitive economy: Walrasian, neo-Hobbesian, and Marxian models. Department of Economics. University of Massachusetts. Mimeo.

Bródy, András. 1970. *Proportions, Prices and Planning*. New York: American Elsevier.

Cameron, Burgess. 1952. The labour theory of value in Leontief models. *The Economic Journal* 62:191–197.

Debreu, Gerard, and I. N. Herstein. 1953. Non-negative square matrices. *Econometrica*. 21:597–607.

Dobb, Maurice. 1973. *Theories of Value and Distribution Since Adam Smith*. Cambridge: Cambridge University Press.

Folbre, Nancy. 1982. Exploitation comes home: A critique of the Marxian theory of family labour. *Cambridge Journal of Economics* 6:317–329.

Frobenius, G. 1908. Über matrizen aus positiven elemente. *Sitzungsberichte der königlich preussischen Akademie der Wissenschaften* 1: 471–476.

———. 1909. Über matrizen aus positiven elemente II. *Sitzungsberichte der königlich preussischen Akademie der Wissenschaften* 1: 514–518.

———. 1912. Über matrizen aus nicht negativen elemente. *Sitzungsberichte der königlich preussischen Akademie der Wissenschaften* 1: 456–477.

Garegnani, Pierangelo. 1983. Ricardo's early theory of profits and its "rational foundation": A reply to Professor Hollander. *Cambridge Journal of Economics* 7: 175–178.

Hollander, Samuel. 1983. Professor Garegnani's defence of Sraffa on the material rate of profit. *Cambridge Journal of Economics* 7: 167–274.

Hume, David. 1888. *A Treatise of Human Nature*. Ed. L. A. Selby-Bigge. Oxford: Clarendon Press.

Hunt, E. K., and Jesse G. Schwartz, eds. 1972. *A Critique of Economic Theory*. Harmondsworth: Penguin Book.

Leontief, Wassily W. 1937. Interpretation of prices, output, savings, and investment. *Review of Economic Statistics* 19 (August).

———. 1941 (1951). *The Structure of American Economy 1919–1929*. 1st ed. Cambridge, Mass.: Harvard University Press. (Second edition, *The Structure of American Economy 1919–1939*. New York: Oxford University Press.)

May, Kenneth. 1949–50. The Structure of Classical Value Theories. *Review of Economic Studies* 17:60–69.

Medio, Alfredo. 1972. Profits and surplus-value: Appearance and reality in capitalist production. In *A Critique of Economic Theory*, ed. E. K. Hunt and J. G. Schwartz. Harmondsworth: Penguin Books.

Mill, John Stuart. 1897. *Principles of Political Economy*. 5th ed. New York: D. Appleton and Co.

Morishima, Michio. 1973. *Marx's Economics*. Cambridge: Cambridge University Press.

Morishima, Michio, and F. Seton. 1961. Aggregation in Leontief matrices and the labour theory of value. *Econometrica* 29:203–220.

Nell, Edward. 1982. Understanding the Marxian notion of exploitation: The "Number one issue." In *Samuelson and Neoclassical Economics*, ed. George R. Feiwell. Hingham, Mass.: Kluwer-Nijhoff.

Newton, Isaac. 1953. *Newton's Philosophy of Nature*. Edited and arranged with notes by H. S. Thayer, New York: Hafner Publishing Company.

Pasinetti, Luigi L. 1977. *Lectures on the Theory of Production*. New York: Columbia University Press.

Perron, Oskar. 1907. Ueber matrizen. *Mathematische Annalen* 64:248–263.

Ricardo, David. 1951–73. *Works and Correspondence of David Ricardo*. 11 vols. Ed. Piero Sraffa. Cambridge: Cambridge University Press.

Roemer, John. 1982. *A General Theory of Exploitation and Class*. Cambridge: Harvard University Press.

Rosdolsky, Roman. 1977. *The Making of Marx's "Capital."* London: Pluto Press.

Samuelson, Paul A. 1957. Wages and interest: A modern dissection of Marxian economic models. *American Economic Review* 47:884–912.

Smith Adam. 1897. *The Theory of Moral Sentiments*. Reprinted in *British Moralists*, ed. L. A. Selby-Brigge. Oxford: Clarendon Press.

————. 1937. *The Wealth of Nations*. Edited with introduction and notes by Edwin Cannan. New York: Modern Library.

Sraffa, Piero. 1960. *Production of Commodities by Means of Commodities.* Cambridge: Cambridge University Press.

Vegara I Carrio, Josep Ma. 1979. *Economía política y modelos multisectoriales.* Madrid: Editorial Tecnos.

Von Neumann, John. 1945. Über ein ökonomisches gleichungssystem und eine verallgemeinerung des brouwerschen fixpunktsatzes. In *Ergebnisse eines mathematischen Kolloquiums*, vol. 8, (Vienna, 1937), pp. 73–83; translated as "A model of general economic equilibrium," *The Review of Economic Studies* 12:1–9.

Wolff, Robert Paul. A critique and reinterpretation of Marx's labor theory of value. *Philosophy & Public Affairs* 10 (2):89–120.

————. 1983. The rehabilitation of Karl Marx. *The Journal of Philosophy* 80 (11):713–719.

INDEX

✳

Abraham-Frois, Gilbert, 146n
accumulation of stock: Ricardo
and, 42, 75; Smith and, 29, 37
agriculture, 177; labor intensity
of, 74, 124; material reproduction model and, 8-16; rents
and, 130; Ricardo's theories
and, 39-42; technical change
and, 81n. *See also* one-sector
economy; three-sector economy
(corn/iron/theology books);
three-sector economy (corn/
iron/tools); two-sector economy
(corn/iron)
appropriation of land: Ricardo
and, 42, 75; Smith and, 29, 37.
See also land
Aveling, Edward, 110n

Bacon, Francis, 26n
Bailey, Samuel, 28n
bargaining (labor/management),
86
beaver-deer example, *see* natural
price, beaver-deer labor example and
Berrebi, Edmond, 146n
Böhm-Bawerk, Eugen, 109n
Bowles, Samuel, 163n, 178n
Bródy, András, 10n

Cameron, Burgess, 49n
capital: accumulation of, 122, 139,
163; conversion of money into,
92-93; equal organic composition of, 74, 93, 123, 124, 125,
126, 129, 135n, 147-48, 152, 154,

155, 170, 171, 213-14, 217; fixed
and durable, 65; industry and,
74; Marx and origin of profit
and, 99; production and physical composition of, 216-17; production and technical composition of, 209-212, 213, 214-16,
217; production and value composition of, 212-13; return on
invested, 53. *See also* constant
capital; variable capital
capital goods, 83, 191-93
capitalism, 82; confusion and
anatomy of (Marx), 207; English
Protestant, 14; equilibrium and,
5; labor and labor power and,
177-78; Marx and mystification
of, 122-37; natural price deviation from labor values and, 147;
natural price theory and understanding, 21; reality of, 98; Ricardo's assumptions and, 52;
separation of working class
from means of production and,
81; study's aims and, 6; surplus
labor and exploitation and, 135-
36
capitalists, 84, 173; investment
and, 124; Marx and profit and,
98-102, 103-106; natural wage
and, 86; profits and, 92; Ricardo
and profit and, 61, 69, 70; Ricardo's assumptions and consequences and, 53; workday
length and, 122
class conflict, 5, 80
classification, 175-76

labor (*cont.*)
quired," 49; retroactive, 112; Ricardo's theories and, 45-48, 49, 50, 53-56, 61-64, 137; skill levels and, 87, 175-76; Smith's theories and, 27, 29-37, 174; as substance of value, 107-110; surplus labor time and, 122; in terms of hours or money, 91-92, 103, 111, 122, 123, 128, 208, 220; value categories and, 207-210; wages (Ricardo) and, 81-88
labor/management bargaining, 86
labor power: creation of new value and, 89-90, 93; distinction between labor and, 110, 122, 139; exploitability of, 164; production and, 208-209, 212; production and calculating labor value of, 214-16; Ricardo and, 105; socially necessary labor and, 111, 112; wage earners and, 103-106
labor services, 52
labor value: calculating labor power and, 214-16; calculations of, 141; commodities exchanged at, 91-97, 102n, 106n, 111, 174; of a commodity, 144-45; corn-value fantasy and, 163-78; derivation of natural prices from, 93, 95, 100-101, 147; derivation of price from (problem of), 133, 134-35; determination of surplus value and, 119-22; directly required and indirectly required labor and, 164; labor and, 177-78; mystification of capitalism and commodities and, 124-28; natural prices proportional to, 73; prices and, 171, 172, 173; production and determination of, 211-12; profit selling at, 98; proportional to labor inputs, 194-96; Ricardo's theories and, 55-61, 62, 64, 65-72; surplus value and, 124
labor value equations (solutions), 189

Lafargue, Paul, 136
land, 83; Ricardo and rent and, 74-81; Ricardo and wage labor and, 87; Ricardo's assumptions and, 52. *See also* appropriation of land
landlords, 37, 75, 81, 130, 147
last in first out (LIFO), 45
Leibniz, Gottfried, 98
Leontief, Wassily, 5, 48, 49n
Locke, John, 75
luxury sector, 14, 156, 161-62, 191-93, 204

machinery, 65
Malthus, Thomas Robert, 41, 42, 82, 83
marginalism, 4, 5
market system, 136; extraction of surplus value from workers and, 127-28; labor value calculations and, 116; Ricardo's assumptions and, 52; Smith and, 18, 20, 23, 24, 38
Marx, Karl, 21, 32, 37, 82; abstract homogeneous socially necessary labor and, 111-16; analysis of work of, 6; conservation of surplus value and, 146-57; conservation of surplus value numerical example and, 158-62; defining value and, 20, 28n; doubts concerning theory of value and exploitation and, 163-78; examination of position on natural price and, 137-40; labor as substance of value and, 107-110; Leontief's ideas and, 49n; mystification of capitalism and, 122-37; natural price and, 43, 117-40; profit and, 61; rent and, 75; Ricardo, theories of, and, 95, 97, 98; Smith and, 24n; spending of wages and, 59; subsistence and, 86; surplus value and critique of exploitation and, 97-107; surplus value determination (quantitative) and, 117-22; theoretical eco-

LIBRARY OF CONGRESS CATALOGING IN PUBLICATION DATA
Wolff, Robert Paul.
Understanding Marx.

(Studies in moral, political, and legal philosophy)
Bibliography: p.
Includes index.
1. Marx, Karl, 1818-1883. Kapital. I. Title. ·
II. Series.
HB501.M37W65   1985   335.4'1   84-42908
ISBN 0-691-07678-2 (alk. paper)
ISBN 0-691-02231-3 (pbk.)

ROBERT PAUL WOLFF is Professor of Philosophy at the University of Massachusetts, Amherst. Among his many works are *Understanding Rawls* (Princeton), *In Defense of Anarchism* (Harper & Row), and *The Poverty of Liberalism* (Beacon).